Mystics, Mavericks, and Merrymakers

STEPHANIE WELLEN LEVINE

MYSTICS, MAVERICKS, AND MERRYMAKERS

An Intimate Journey among Hasidic Girls

Foreword by Carol Gilligan

New York University Press • *New York and London*

NEW YORK UNIVERSITY PRESS
New York and London
www.nyupress.org

© 2003 by Stephanie Wellen Levine

Please note that all names and many details
have been changed to protect confidentiality.

Library of Congress Cataloging-in-Publication Data
Levine, Stephanie Wellen.
Mystics, mavericks, and merrymakers :
an intimate journey among hasidic girls / Stephanie Wellen Levine.
p. cm.
Includes bibliographical references and index.
ISBN 0–8147–5192–X (cloth : alk. paper)
1. Teenage girls—New York (State)—New York—Religious life.
2. Jewish teenagers—New York (State)—New York—Religious life.
3. Habad—New York (State)—New York—Religious life.
4. Crown Heights—(New York, N.Y.)—Religious life.
5. Teenage girls—New York (State)—New York—Social life and customs.
6. Jewish teenagers—New York (State)—New York—Social life and customs.
7. Habad—New York (State)—New York—Social life and customs.
8. Crown Heights—(New York, N.Y.)—Social life and customs.   I. Title.
HQ798.L49   2003
305.235'2'09747—dc22   2003014983

New York University Press books are printed on acid-free paper,
and their binding materials are chosen for strength and durability.

Manufactured in the United States of America

10 9 8 7 6 5 4 3 2 1

For my parents
   and in memory of my grandparents

Contents

Acknowledgments

I am deeply grateful to many people who have nurtured and guided me throughout this project. My parents, Carol and Arthur Levine, offered emotional support during this book's countless challenges. I could never sufficiently thank them for everything they have done. When thorny issues arose, I counted on Sheila Tarabour's expertise. My cousin Louise Guy is the best listener around. And my brother, Larry— my first pal—has championed this project from the beginning.

This book never would have materialized without the support of my graduate school advisers. Carol Gilligan's interviewing technique strongly influenced my own methods; I owe much of my project's success to her example. Her suggestions and encouragement have profoundly enriched my work. Laurel Thatcher Ulrich's rigorous, insightful input has led me to crucial improvements, and I deeply appreciate her encouragement as well.

Jennifer Hammer has been a superb editor: enthusiastic, thorough, patient, and always friendly. Her support and insights have been invaluable. Special thanks to Heather McMaster, Melissa Scheld, and Despina Gimbel for their hard work.

Several other people read parts of this manuscript or offered critical advice, including Elena Paolini (who helped me in countless ways as I worked on this project), Sherrie Inness, Lis Harris, Emily Levine (the book's subtitle reflects her wise advice), Sharon Lamb, Meryl Zegarek, Susan Zeckendorf, Bill Madden, Rabbi Shmuel Posner, and Sam Brown. Sherrie deserves particular mention; she read nearly every chapter of this manuscript with a careful, discerning eye. Though they hadn't yet read the book, my incredible students at Tufts showed genuine enthusiasm for this project.

Friends provided fabulous conversation, laughs, and moral support: Elena Paolini, Laurie Pearson, Andrew Pearson, Michael Richter, Bill Madden, Rachel Noel, Dan Noel, Linda Prince, and my wonderful Leverett House lunch buddies, Diamond Cephus, Kate Holbrook, Sam Brown, Leeanna Varga, John Matthew, Geoffrey Shamu, and Chip Robinson. And I must not forget Christine McFadden, who always knew my adventures with Hasidic girls would become a book.

Privacy concerns do not allow me to name the most crucial contributors of all—the many Lubavitch girls and community people who made this project possible. To everyone who offered me the hospitality and warmth that made my Crown Heights stay so rewarding, thank you. In particular, I must thank my Crown Heights landlords; they made Brooklyn feel like home.

Finally, I thank several remarkable family members who died while I was writing this book. My Aunt Selma and Uncle Nat Guy encouraged me to succeed since early childhood. My grandmother Miriam Levine was an inspiring role model. She was a fighter, stubborn and determined, who nearly always managed to achieve her goals. Abraham Wellen, my grandfather, was confident that I would achieve all my dreams, and I will always remember his constant encouragement, generosity, and love. And my grandmother Helen Wellen was my unwavering fan from the day I entered this weird world. She gave me enough love, confidence, fabulous memories, and optimism about my future to last a lifetime.

Foreword

Carol Gilligan

As a graduate student in American studies at Harvard, Stephanie Levine spent a year living as a participant observer in the Lubavitcher Hasidic community in Crown Heights, Brooklyn. Drawn to a world infused with spirituality, she was impelled by the question, Do adolescent girls raised in a strict religious orthodoxy have what could be called a "free voice"? *Mystics, Mavericks, and Merrymakers* provides a resounding answer to this question, dispelling stereotypes of meek and blindly submissive girls and bringing a hidden and seemingly cloistered world to life. We hear the distinct voices of pious girls, errant girls, and good-time girls who wear high-topped sneakers under their long skirts, finding individuality within lives driven by stark expectations and bound by an iron framework. But as the focus on girls highlights the tension within Hasidism between mysticism and the dictates of a patriarchal order, the inquiry opens into a series of powerful insights into the human psyche and the interplay between psychology and culture.

I remember a conversation with Stephanie at the time when she was completing her research. She had drawn fresh and engaging portraits of the girls she interviewed, rendering their inner lives and daily worlds in vivid detail. With a writer's eye and ear, she captured the spiritedness that impressed her, depicting a liveliness and freedom of expression commonly associated with younger girls. I asked her how she accounted for the evidence of strong personal voice, given what would seem on the face of it a most unlikely setting, and I found her answer riveting. She spoke of the convergence of the method she used in her research—the Listening Guide that directed her attention to inner voices—and the Lubavitch philosophy that emphasizes the importance of cultivating an inner voice, the voice of the individual soul or psyche.

Her discovery of a voice apart from the voice of the orthodoxy alerted her to an aspect of orthodoxy that is frequently overlooked. The *Tanya*—the central book of Lubavitch philosophy which the girls carefully study—teaches them to attend to and cultivate their *neshama,* or soul, conceived as the divine spark within them.

Given this emphasis on self-awareness and self-exploration, everyone is encouraged to develop a relationship with a *mashpiah,* a confidante who will serve as a spiritual guide. Ideally, each girl will have as a confidante an older woman with whom she can share her deepest fears, her most disturbing thoughts, her wishes and dreams, with the ultimate goal of personal and spiritual growth. This psychological wisdom—the encouragement of voice and the recognition that voice depends on resonance, on a relationship that encourages and enlarges its expression—can explain the seemingly paradoxical finding of psychological strength in a context that otherwise seems daunting. The development of a personal voice is further encouraged by the mystical belief of the Lubavitchers that each individual harbors a spark of the divine and is thereby crucial and worthy of intense scrutiny. Alongside a religious order that is strictly patriarchal, girls see themselves as central to the unfolding of divinity within the world.

Erik Erikson observed that ideology is the flip side of identity, that in order to answer the question "Who am I?" the adolescent also needs to address the question of belief, a worldview that gives the self meaning. He observed in adolescents what he called a "rock bottom" attitude, a search for a firm ground on which they could plant their feet. Levine finds such a ground in the Lubavitch worldview. It is not a ground on which she personally could stand, but the power of her book lies in part in her ability to adopt a non-judgmental attitude—not a dispassionate stance, but that of an affectionate outsider, viewing with loving attention customs to which she herself could never adhere and finding beauty in beliefs that diverge sharply from her own. In a world where religious convictions threaten to tear people apart, she models an openness to taking in the experiences of others that illustrates the true meaning of appreciating diversity. Her writing voice—inviting, shrewd, lively, and at times lyrical—challenges us to follow her path.

In the Lubavitch philosophy of life, Levine thus finds a way to account for the voice and the confidence that impress her in girls. By providing us with a candid account of her own adolescence, she gives us a context in which to understand her own responses to the Lubavitchers.

We can see why the single-sex social life of the girls and the deferral of sexuality draw her so powerfully, given her own high school encounters with boys and the suffering she observed in girls whom boys judged undesirable or not sexually attractive, as well as the meanness experienced from other girls. As her study focuses on adolescents, she raises but cannot fully answer the question of what happens to these girls, their lives and free voices, once they become wives and mothers.

One doesn't necessarily have to agree with the comparisons she draws between Lubavitch girls and girls in secular schools and settings to appreciate the wisdom of the insights she comes to regarding the importance and the fragility of the human psyche. In a cogent statement, Levine argues against the framing of many current discussions about identity: "We are more than our genetics, more than our life histories, more than our cultural baggage. These are all important, but the human psyche . . . contains an independent power we must respect and master if we want any real hope for a vital life."

Whether conceived as a divine spark or as part of the natural wonder of the human being, the psyche is the wellspring of our minds and our hearts, our voice and our capacity for resistance. Thus a study of adolescent girls living within a rigid orthodox framework comes in the end to discover, aided by the insights of Lubavitch philosophy although not bound to its specific formulation or language, the importance of cherishing and cultivating the human psyche. When every act has meaning that reverberates mysteriously throughout the universe, hastening or delaying the coming of the Messiah, "to savage the confidence of a classmate would carry profound implications, for every human being is a fragile balance of drives, desires, and a potential for goodness struggling to triumph." Freed from its cultural or theological baggage, it is "an insight so simple it aches: the human spirit is a delicate instrument that needs care to flourish."

This is, in the end, the profound truth in this book. A gifted writer, a Harvard student clad in blue jeans and raised in a secular environment, dons a long skirt and spends a year living among Lubavitcher girls and comes back with a sense of awe and wonder about the human psyche. It is not the outcome the Lubavitchers wished for. When she left in tears, one of the mothers handed her a box of Shabbos candles, encouraging her to light them as a beginning. She tells us they rest unburned on her mantel. But what she has brought back to us is an invaluable caution against ignoring or neglecting the psyche. Americans place a high value on individuality and independence but these values quickly become hollow in the absence of practices that cultivate an inner voice and relationships that encourage its expression. In their study of the *Tanya*, adolescent girls in a Hasidic community are given a rich language for exploring their inner worlds, a plethora of descriptive words for the nuances of our souls.

Levine ends her book by translating an exclusive faith into common psychological wisdom: "The Lubavitch version goes something like this: At Mount Sinai, Israel accepted the laws of the Torah, and with the yoke came a gift from God—a piece of the Divine Soul, the cherished birthright of all future Jews." Levine's version is that we all are born with a psyche—with a voice, I would say. However mystical this belief is in its religious incarnation, it converges with the insights of novelists as well as the findings of psychologists and neuroscientists who have explored human consciousness. A study of adolescent girls growing up in orthodoxy thus becomes a powerful reminder to attend to and listen for the voice of the psyche.

Introduction

What I Sought, What I Found

"IF YA WANNA SEE, YA GOTTA *PUSH*." I tried, lamely, stunned to be getting a lesson in assertiveness from a middle-aged Hasidic woman. *"Harder,"* she admonished, and I fell into the rhythm of the women and girls surrounding me. Clawing my way to the front, I carved a tiny niche for myself by the window offering a view, far below, of the men's section of this Hasidic synagogue. I glimpsed the group's religious leader, the Rebbe: the goal of this shoving game. An instant later my victory collapsed, and I found myself far from the window amid a sea of jabbing hands. This may sound dangerous, but I never worried. The atmosphere was benevolent, the pokes hard yet somehow affectionate.

Satisfied with my short Rebbe sighting, I relaxed near the back of the women's section. It was Shabbos, the weekly Jewish Sabbath, and people were saying the appropriate prayers, swaying and bowing in accordance with Orthodox Jewish custom. I noticed a girl, about seventeen, who prayed with particular passion. Her eyes teared slightly as she spoke. I was enthralled. Shabbos is the centerpiece of Orthodox Jewish life, a weekly island of holiness infusing the workaday world with regular intervals of awe; on that day Jews are free from work-related tension and can concentrate on holy thoughts. Members of this Hasidic group feel the holiday offers a taste of a future Messianic period that will banish all concerns beyond the universal goal of knowing God. I thought, "This girl really believes that," and I watched her in fascination.

She finished, closed her prayer book, and kissed it. I imagined she was having a mystical experience. Then she turned to her friend and asked, "Which skirt do you think I look fatter in, this one or the one I was wearing last Shabbos?" To me, she looked slender and graceful in her elegant blue sweater and long, straight woolen skirt. I stared,

1

amazed, and she stared back, amazed at my amazement. This question should not have surprised me at all; it was just the sort of thing I myself might have asked someone when I was seventeen. It clashed only with my own musings on Shabbos, the Messianic age, and mystical experiences, as if people who lived steeped in such notions should be beyond the usual worries.

That weekend with Hasidim was a whim, one of many I indulged after graduating from college. I never forgot it. The aggressiveness I saw bludgeoned my stereotype of the mousy Hasidic female. The weight-conscious young woman particularly intrigued me, and I found myself wondering about Hasidic teenage girls in general: How do they think? What are their dreams? Do they ever rebel? How do they perceive themselves? Several years later, I returned to this community, hoping to find out.

For over a year, I lived in Crown Heights, Brooklyn, headquarters of the Lubavitchers, a sect of Hasidim famous for their efforts to inspire secular Jews to become more observant and for their Messianic fervor: their sincere belief that every act of kindness a Jew performs, each Judaic ritual she completes, brings the Messiah that much closer to earthly revelation. The two traits are mystically entwined; each new practicing Jew performs hundreds of rituals and holy acts that might usher in the Messianic age. I spent my time among Lubavitchers exploring the daily lives and inner worlds of their adolescent girls—their thoughts, habits, dreams, struggles, and triumphs. I aimed to know them as individuals, in all their complexity and mystery, to cut through the shroud of secrecy so many Americans associate with Hasidim.

Immediately, I sensed how timeless it all was, and yet how changed since my last Crown Heights stint. I saw the same sights: men braving the heat in black coats and long beards, long-skirted young women joshing each other on their way home from the pizza shop, college-aged mothers with shopping bags hanging from strollers. But when my first Shabbos rolled around, I waltzed right up to the front and landed a seat, which I retained effortlessly throughout the service. The Rebbe had died. There was no longer a reason to gaze at the men's section; the rest of those bearded characters were boring old brothers, fathers, uncles, and neighbors whom you could see any time, and most women were content reciting the service quietly to themselves without seeing the public rituals down below. A nearly unanimous reverence for the Rebbe had given way to bitter debate about how Lubavitch should be run without him and whether he would return as the Messiah. This incendiary issue pits the *meshichists,* those convinced the Rebbe will reenter this world and lead us into a blissful state of holy perfection, against the anti-*meshichists,* who tend to believe the Messiah must come from the ranks of the living, that Rabbi Schneerson's death disqualified him.

Numbers are impossible to draw in the Messiah controversy; it's not as if formal polls have been taken. As in most ideological disputes, there are gradations. Some Lubavitchers believe in their hearts that the Rebbe is the Messiah ("Moshiach" is the commonly used term) but oppose their peers who want to spread the word throughout the non-Lubavitch world. The public relations risk, they say, is simply too great. Indeed, ire is brewing among some in non-Lubavitch Jewish circles who bristle at the notion that the Rebbe will revive as Moshiach.[1]

Most Lubavitchers I met did believe that the Rebbe is the Messiah, but I encountered some wavering and plenty of opposition. Some families, I've been told, have endured painful rifts because of the dispute. I saw few signs of this tension among the girls, though. I knew one young woman who believed but whose parents did not, and she would listen good-naturedly to her father's impassioned arguments on the subject. One afternoon, he railed against a Moshiach Day Parade—"those people have another thing coming if they think a bunch of flags is going to bring Moshiach"—and she kept looking from him to me, smiling. He was, in his own way, teasing her. In school, at social gatherings, on trips, girls of all persuasions got along; the controversy rarely surfaced for them.

Most girls paid little attention to Crown Heights politics, and the crux of their lives—the patterns, rules, and philosophies of Hasidism—remained solid. Hasidim are among the strictest followers of Orthodox Judaism, which touches every imaginable facet of human behavior. They must circumscribe their diet, dress, life goals, and, of course, beliefs and religious rituals within a narrow band of acceptability. Gender distinctions are sharp. Outside the immediate family, males and females inhabit separate worlds. Girls learn in early childhood that the woman's domain is the home, and that women must be modest in dress and behavior in the company of men. Within their own single-sex universe, though, the young women I met often exuded vibrancy and true chutzpah. I spent many hours with them, and their energy and spirit were the first qualities I noticed—contrary to popular belief, they seemed every bit as expressive as their peers in mainstream America.

Of course, the term "mainstream" is fraught with ambiguity in a country boasting an astonishing range of cultures, classes, colors, and creeds. Each group has its own tendencies in terms of insecurities, difficulties, and sources of pride. Eating disorders are most common among affluent white girls;[2] poor girls of color struggle disproportionately with teenage pregnancy.[3]

But for all this diversity, an underlying common culture pervades America. A middle-class suburban kid, a dairy farmer's daughter, a Brooklyn-born child of Thai immigrants, a girl from an inner-city ghetto, and a film producer's daughter in Beverly Hills could all probably get together and debate about television, movies, McDonald's versus Burger King, tight versus baggy jeans, their opinions of the boys in their lives. Their particular experiences and biases would range widely, but American popular culture would have insinuated itself into all of their minds and provided common ground.

Lubavitch girls fall outside this conversation, though, as you will see, not as far as some may think. They are not cloistered—the billboards and newsstands of New York City are everywhere visible, and many have at least some familiarity with television and movies. Still, their exposure to mainstream American culture is limited. Their dress code prohibits pants, shorts, short skirts, and short-sleeved shirts: all standard American goods. Their dietary rules accept only the most stringently kosher restaurants and foods; a snack at Dunkin' Donuts or McDonald's is verboten. Most know few boys beyond their families.

Usually, media exposure is meager. A typical Lubavitch girl might sneak in an hour of TV every few weeks when she visits a friend whose parents work after school, freeing her to explore other uses for the monitor they use to watch videos of the Rebbe. She may catch an occasional secular movie—nearly always with minimal sexuality and violence—on a VCR, far from the soul-corrupting cinema, with its entwined couples and vulgar conversations. Likewise, she may inch her radio dial to a local rock station periodically when her parents are out of earshot. But guilt and anxiety often plague these activities; awareness of the media's ability to tarnish spiritual purity is strong. This is far from the typical American's placid enjoyment of the diverse visual and musical goodies our entertainment world offers. Many Lubavitch girls do not have even this level of contact with the outside cultural universe; the stricter contingent allows only Jewish videos and songs. In all these senses—dress, food, social life, cultural diet—Lubavitch girls are beyond the vast

United States "mainstream," despite their undeniable awareness of typical American habits.

"Secular" is another potentially confusing term that crops up often throughout this book. I refer periodically to "secular culture" and the "secular world." This word in no way implies a lack of spirituality among non-Hasidim; most Americans have some faith in a higher power, and the majority identify at least somewhat with a particular religious heritage.

The issue is degree. Hasidism teaches that mystical notions and the pursuit of holiness should underlie every action. When a Hasidic girl dresses in the morning, she is fulfilling her religious obligation to keep her body modest; before eating even a tiny snack, she says a prayer thanking God for her food. The typical Lubavitch young woman's classmates and friends are other Hasidim. Her community's social events nearly always have spiritual underpinnings and include none of her non-Jewish neighbors. Intricate religious injunctions make close relationships with people who are not Orthodox Jews difficult to maintain.

This situation distinguishes Hasidim from passionately spiritual groups like Mormons and fundamentalist Protestants, whose children commonly attend public school, and devout Roman Catholics, whose kids can easily make friends with non-Catholics, even if they go to parochial school. The relationships young Lubavitchers do have with other people usually center on the drive to bring all Jews around to Orthodoxy—say, a young woman's chats with the college student who visits her home sometimes to learn more about her Jewish roots. Ideally, Hasidism is all-encompassing spirituality; its adherents view the world outside its purview as starkly Other—in a word, secular. My task, as a lifelong member of this secular sphere, was to commune with a new world and its young inhabitants.

Participant observation, knowing the girls by joining in their lives, drove this project. Most days, I observed classes at Bais Rivka, the lively educational home for about five hundred high school students, one hundred post–high school seminary students ("seminary" for Lubavitch girls is post–high school religious education; the word does not imply rabbinical training, which is open only to men), and twenty diehard learners continuing their studies at night for a year after completing the two-year seminary program. I attended their school trips, class gatherings, community service events, parties, and dramatic productions. Many girls invited me to their homes, both for holiday meals and for relaxed conversation. By plunging myself into their world, I imbibed the texture of their lives.

People often ask how I managed to ease my way into this community. Moving into Crown Heights was possibly the bravest thing I've ever done, for I had no assurance that I would reach such intimacy with these girls. But I was determined. I contacted the high school principal about my desire to attend classes; she wrote back explaining that my presence would exacerbate the overcrowding that already plagued the high school. Then I met with the seminary principal, who allowed me free rein to attend as many classes as I wished. Slowly, I got to know the girls, who began including me in their holiday celebrations and social activities. Since the high school was in the same building, I became known there as well; before long a few of the teachers had invited me to their classes, and I spent time with the girls in the cafeteria and after school. Eventually, I was granted the privilege of observing these young women in a vast array of settings; I became an eager and grateful participant in the rhythms of Hasidic girlhood.

My genuine respect for Hasidism was fertile ground for the well-honed Lubavitch flair for proselytizing among secular Jews. We engaged in a sort of unspoken trade: by spending time with me, the girls helped with my research *and* got the chance to share the beauty of Lubavitch. And despite Hasidism's mistrust of secular universities, everyone was impressed when I told them my work was part of Harvard University's Ph.D. program in American studies. That detail gave my project importance in their eyes, which spurred interest in me and my work. This was certainly a break from the usual reactions: "American studies? But what can you do with that?" or even better: "Leave it to you to avoid the workforce for all those years."

As I alternated between the Hasidic universe and my usual identity as a lax Jew with no particular spiritual allegiance, I felt an intense mixture of tension and joy. I led a strange, liminal life in Brooklyn, maneuvering between cultures, ideologies, and frames of reference. I emulated Lubavitch customs, but I was always a foreign observer, struggling endlessly to keep up and understand.

Impulsive and clumsy, I made glaring mistakes despite my best intentions, asking pointed questions in the midst of holy silences, eating before the appropriate prayers were said, arriving at Shabbos lunch with wet hair despite the injunctions against showering on the Sabbath. One Friday evening I miscalculated the time and arrived in Crown

Heights after Shabbos had begun, bulky knapsack hanging like a bull's-eye on my back. Carrying is not permitted on Shabbos. I dashed, head down, toward my apartment, but the Fates were not on my side. A group of little boys spotted me; they chased me down the street, yelling, "Shah, shah, shah," a scampering battalion with large black yarmulkes on their heads and white ritual fringes swinging from their waists. Of course, they were used to seeing non-Jews who don't observe Shabbos, but, for better or for worse, I had become familiar to them as a member of their community.

On the whole, the girls and their families extended incredible tolerance and allowed me to become a true participant in their lives. I befriended a delightfully heterogeneous group of girls, and I tried to empathize as much as possible with each young woman's ideas, difficulties, victories, and discoveries, to partake in her mind and heart as well as her deeds. My days were active and diverse: I often spent the morning at school; the afternoon chatting with a bunch of girls at Crown Heights's kosher pizza shop; the evening studying Hasidic philosophy with a sensitive young woman who yearned to catapult me into Orthodoxy; the wee hours at a hidden hangout for the rare Lubavitch questioners, sniffing the pot-scented air and listening to the poignant poetry a talented young dissident had decided to share with her friends.

Daily observation offered wonderful insight into the adolescents' lives, concerns, and values. But I wanted more: access to the elusive realm of their inner worlds. Thus, intensive interviews with thirty-two girls aged thirteen to twenty-three (in this community all single females are girls, since they have not yet begun their second major stage of life) formed the crux of my project. Unless deep friendship emerges, this is a writer's best hope of gaining a pipeline into people's self-conceptions, beliefs, goals, and desires.

In conducting these discussions, I followed the wisdom of Carol Gilligan and her colleagues at the Harvard Project on Women's Psychology and Girls' Development. In their studies of adolescent girls, they have adapted the clinical interviewing method pioneered by Sigmund Freud in his clinical case studies. Rather than sticking to an unyielding interview protocol, they use their initial questions as pathways to discover the young women's own concerns. Lyn Mikel Brown and Gilligan explain this technique in *Meeting at the Crossroads*, a book based on interviews with students at a secular private girls' school: "We would follow the associative logic of girls' psyches, we would move where the girls led us."[4] I did likewise. Although I had prepared questions, I encouraged interviewees to veer from them and share the ideas and memories they found crucial. I was traveling in a foreign world, and I wanted the girls' thoughts, not my preconceptions, to guide my exploration. Often, these conversations took hours; many young women were eager to share their ideas and experiences with a non-judgmental outsider who respected thoughts that might have scared parents or provoked ridicule from peers.

The Harvard Project is deeply concerned with "voice," a person's idiosyncratic mode of expression that shares her feelings and ideas with others.[5] After transcribing an interview, I followed the Harvard Project's "Listener's Guide" and read the interview several times, first focusing on the actual stories told, then analyzing the interviewee's self-conceptions, and finally moving on to the girl's descriptions of her relationships—the way she perceives herself within her social world.[6] It is a stunning exercise in empathy, in exploring the contours of another person's mind; this method perfectly suited my goal of capturing the girls' inner complexity.

The combination of observing and interviewing allowed me to dramatize both outward behavior and interior grappling. Every girl I got to know well ushered me into a life filled with drama and intensity. I soon came to a fabulous realization: this material was downright juicy. I found an adventurer who checked out a strip club but later reembraced the Orthodox way, brilliant young rebels who spent their evenings debating Jewish philosophy and agonizing over their loss of faith, a girl whose parents banned her from the house when she began flouting Jewish law, an intensely religious young woman who longed to be a boy, a fervently Messianic girl with a lineup of intense male phone friends, and many other rich stories. I decided to transform my experiences into a book because my young Hasidic friends provided such provocative surprises. They would intrigue anyone who loves exploring people—their quirks, their quandaries, their cultural influences.

Of course, yet another complicated character infuses every word of this book: me. Those who know me well often wonder whether I became Hasidic, or at least more ritually observant, because of my stay in Crown Heights. After all, my attraction to Hasidim stems from a long-standing fascination with religious conviction. My parents are secular Jews. Their decision to enroll my brother and me in a Reform temple's biweekly afternoon Hebrew classes had no supernatural undertones; they simply wanted us to explore our cultural heritage. I never linked the depressing ritual of reciting Hebrew prayers in a stuffy classroom with spirituality. Still, passionately religious people have drawn me since early childhood, from the smiling cult members I would see during trips to Manhattan to the nuns who lived in the convent near my suburban New Jersey home. As a kid, I spent countless afternoons in front of that convent's windows, spying on the unsuspecting sisters as they chatted or ate lunch, trying to soak in some understanding of a life devoted to God.

Years later, I wrote my undergraduate thesis about an evangelical Christian group; I adored the weekly meetings filled with impassioned prayer, lively song, and exhortations to spread Christ's message of eternal life. Lubavitch, too, promises immortality. And yet I continue in my miserable, death-fearing ways, never taking the friendly hand of faith my religious travels have offered in so many different forms.

You could consider me a reformable relativist. Eventually, I might choose a particular faith or philosophy. It's unlikely but possible. I approach every ideology I encounter with a balance of fresh openness and underlying doubt. Lubavitch was no exception. I went into Crown Heights an outsider. I left with a heartfelt appreciation for this community and a deep-seated disbelief that the traditional Hasidic woman's lifestyle—marriage, followed by caring for as many children as God will provide—was best for me or for many of the Jewish women I know. In other words, you're reading the impressions of an extremely sympathetic skeptic.

But why do I resist embracing a religious system despite my spiritual yearning? The answer seems locked within my quirkiness, my deeply embedded nonconformity. The girl who collected insects at recess while her female peers jumped rope matured into the woman who spent a year exploring a Hasidic community while her relatives worked as accountants and lawyers. My brother tells me I dress like a seventh-grade boy; I have been known to order dessert first in restaurants; I frequently walk miles out of my way because I get lost whenever I leave my immediate neighborhood.

In short, I fit no mold. Hasidism's stringent regulations concerning dress, diet, gender roles, behavior, beliefs, goals, and lifestyle seemed unendurable to me. For a year, it was fascinating. Much more than that would have taxed me beyond my capacity. But, of course, I grew up with much more freedom along all these dimensions. My difficulty stemmed at least partially from unfamiliarity.

The supreme role individuality has played in my life filtered into my concerns as I explored Lubavitch girlhood. Do Lubavitch young women develop independent thoughts, desires, and personal styles within the context of a seemingly all-encompassing Orthodox Judaism? Is there room within Lubavitch for eccentricity? Is personal oddness tolerated? How far can these young women go in thought and behavior before they are considered rebellious? How do Hasidic girls perceive themselves: their idiosyncratic characters, difficulties, and gifts? These questions tantalized me and guided my exploration.

Recently, a host of writers have chronicled mainstream American girls' sometimes grueling attempts to conform to our own culture's ideals for young women's bodies and behavior. Clinical psychologist Mary Pipher's *Reviving Ophelia* describes young women diverse in personality and family background, lobbying painful evidence that all too many lose confidence as they approach adolescence, developing deep-seated insecurity that radiates out into their body image, their academic performance, their sexual development, and their relationships. They often shed the assertiveness, rambunctiousness, and playfulness that had carried them through childhood. Books and articles focusing on eating disorders and body image obsession have proliferated. I think of Joan Jacobs Brumberg's acclaimed book *The Body Project: An Intimate History of American Girls,* whose jarring central argument is captured within the title: many girls lavish their most intimate, life-defining energy and thoughts on perfecting their bodies.

Sensitive renditions of American teenage girlhood often describe a profound tension. Pressure on many young women to shape themselves into the pretty, nice, amenable, friendly but not overly boisterous specimens our society adores can breed inner turmoil and obsession with physical appearance. But resistance to these expectations crops up everywhere. Harvard Project research places particular emphasis on girls' struggles against cultural norms. Conscious, overt rebels find ways to express themselves: A working-class girl featured in *Meeting at the Crossroads* continually shares her unusual opinions and life experiences, often to the dismay of her prep school teachers and wealthy classmates. A Korean contributor to an anthology that explores girls' resistance to mainstream mores bitterly remembers her white peers' refusal to accept her heritage; at fourteen, she renounced her school's social life and worked to improve her Korean language skills.[7]

Others assert subtle but heartfelt efforts to retain a sense of inner strength. Psychological jockeying often accompanies outward conformity. For one *Crossroads* interviewee whose behavior epitomizes the norms of feminine goodness, remaining aware of emotions that feel unseemly, like anger or hatred, seems like a last-ditch attempt to hold on to the person who simmers beneath the veil of perfection. In other words, there are expectations that appear unshakable. And then there are the adolescents, whose personal characteristics rub up against cultural norms with infinite variety.

Not long ago, yet another media frenzy focused on adolescent girls, this time on the nastiness that can poison their friendships with one another. The surface buzz about the "alpha girls," the popular teens who rule their cliques with iron hands and venomous tongues, suggests a breed of young woman who is confident, secure, and powerful—if not kind. But the actual research illuminates the underlying ambivalence and self-doubt that typically propel this meanness.

In *Odd Girl Out*, Rachel Simmons argues that our culture's expectation that young women conform to the feminine ideal of "nice and kind" can cause rage to fester beneath the surface. Believing that open confrontation with friends or peers who make them angry would be unseemly, girls release their fury in covert but deeply harmful ways: gossiping; spreading out at the lunch table when an unwanted girl comes by; ignoring people; taunting a girl as a group, so no one person bears responsibility. Usually, they target their own friends, picking one person from within their clique to tease and ostracize, making her the "odd girl out." Rosalind Wiseman's *Queen Bees and Wannabes* reports similar problems of subtle but devastating cruelty among girls. And the victims are not the only sufferers. Far from bastions of confidence, many perpetrators endure loss of self-esteem, obsession with reputation, and inability to express their feelings. These girls are living a terrible irony: an illusion of niceness with an undercurrent of fury.

So what does all this have to do with the Lubavitch girls? Cliques are certainly a part of their social landscape, as is catty, underhanded meanness. I picked up loud whispers meant to be overheard by a third-party target (e.g., "Look at Fruma's shoes!" whispers Gittel to Malka, within earshot of Fruma). I also saw cruelty to girls who lacked social skills. One young woman, who suffered with illness and a severe learning disability that hampered her ability to read social cues, was continually ignored by her classmates—she'd say something odd yet inoffensive and receive silent scowls in return. "Out-of-towners," whose parents lived outside of Crown Heights but who boarded with neighborhood families to attend Bais Rivka, often complained that the locals were snobs, that they were not as friendly and accepting as they could have been.

From my observations, though, Lubavitch young women didn't tend to have as much trouble within their actual friendship groups; mainstream girls' most serious problems often come from their "good friends." Lubavitch girls tend to be boisterous and direct, and passive-aggressive subterfuge carries less allure when people share their emotions directly.

On a Bais Rivka trip, Shira stormed into the dining area, crying. Someone asked what was wrong, and she bellowed: "Feigie said I'm fat and ugly!"

Then Feigie herself ran in, yelling, "I didn't mean it like that!" Soon about ten girls were involved in moderating the dispute. The discussion was very open, and eventually Shira realized that she had misunderstood Feigie's comment. Sobbing, Shira apologized to Feigie for accusing her of meanness. If a similar dispute had developed in a suburban middle-class high school, Shira might have been mortified to confront Feigie directly, let alone shout about her gripe in a room filled with her classmates. Shira's anger would have rankled beneath the surface, and she might have begun spreading noxious gossip, hoping that all her friends would turn against Feigie. The short blowup I witnessed might have averted unbearable long-term tension. Shira's honesty and openness startled me, but the girls found this scene unremarkable, a typical spat that played itself out like hundreds before it.

My gut expectation was that Lubavitch would narrow the window of self-expression, that strict regulation would stunt girls' personal voices with much more force than in America at large. Others shared my preconceptions. When I told a Harvard Divinity School professor I wanted to explore how Lubavitch girls' individual personalities developed within their stringent religious system, he admonished, "Back up. The first question is whether this happens in the first place. You're dealing with a very strict group, with very rigid expectations for women." My grandmother, who emigrated from Poland in 1908, yanked me into her living room to impart a dire observation drawn from early memories among Polish Hasidim: "Personality? Hasidic girls? Naahh. Those people, they're dirty, they're stupid, and they treat the girls like *shmattes* [Yiddish for 'rags']."

The possibility that these girls' lives could be anything other than the Platonic essence of feminine subjugation seemed as unlikely as a suckling pig on a Shabbos table. Yet there they were—long skirts and remote synagogue seats notwithstanding—teasing, running, playing, and downright enjoying; their personal styles shone through to any aware observer. An impressive depth undergirded the zest. Lubavitch girls' self-understanding and ability to express their thoughts and feelings were often stunning.

Like their mainstream American counterparts, their reactions to their culture's expectations for young women ranged widely, from the full-blown rebellion of apostasy and employment at a strip club, to subtle limit-pushing like too-short skirts, to studied embrace of their society's vision for them. The issue is complex, though, for Lubavitch does rein in many outward expressions of individuality to promote the kind of conformity this community's survival demands. Future goals, so diverse and personal among most American teenagers, fall within a narrow realm among practicing Lubavitch girls—they all plan to marry, have children, and devote their lives to Judaism. The biggest question for most is whether to settle in Crown Heights or to support a Lubavitch outpost elsewhere. Sexuality, a wide arena for self-expression among secular adolescents, is strictly forbidden before marriage in Lubavitch. Mainstream teenagers examine song lyrics, films, friends' convictions, family traditions, and books to help them develop their own values and life-defining philosophies. Typical Lubavitchers look only at Jewish sources for inspiration, since they have been taught never to consider any idea that contradicts Hasidic teachings.

Tension emerges: Lubavitch culture lovingly nurtures each girl's developing persona but keeps many domains under careful surveillance. This conflict is the centerpiece of my project; every one of the girls I profile offers a variation on the theme of selfhood in the context of tight conformity.

From the beginning, I was impressed by the Lubavitch girls' command and power—qualities that, within their all-girl domain, were not only tolerated but encouraged. I asked many young women what sort of person was well liked at Bais Rivka. By far the most popular answer was the loud girls, an unlikely response in the high schools I attended, where outwardly aggressive young women often struck people as obnoxious and grating.

Writers frequently suggest that girls tend to lose something as they shift from childhood to adolescence—a certain energy, honesty, or unselfconsciousness. Mary Pipher remembers her cousin Polly as a daring, argumentative, zestful child. As Polly's teen years approached, both the boys and the girls excluded her because she didn't conform to the restrained, feminine ideal. Eventually, she calmed down and learned the new rules for social success. But Pipher sensed a tragedy here, that she had witnessed "the loss of our town's most dynamic citizen."[8] Pipher uses this anecdote to introduce *Reviving Ophelia*; Polly serves as an exemplar of the many girls who seem to lose some of their spirit as adolescence hits.

Lyn Mikel Brown and Carol Gilligan frame this sense of loss more theoretically, viewing the problem as a submersion of "voice." In their words: "Over the years of our study, even as they became more sophisticated cognitively and emotionally, young girls who had been outspoken and courageous in both an ordinary and a heroic sense became increasingly reluctant to say what they were feeling and thinking or to speak from their own experience about what they knew."[9] Brown and Gilligan write about girls who learn to hide their strong feelings, to paper over their disagreements with others in order to maintain outward civility. The meanness Rachel Simmons describes results directly from this process; eventually, squelched emotion can spur passive-aggressive conniving.

The Lubavitch girls fell outside these trends; they typically cultivated strong, clear personal voices in their relationships, engaging their conflicts with stunning clarity. Shira and Feigie's argument, an everyday event to the girls who witnessed it, underscores the open honesty that often drives Lubavitch friendships. And, as you will see throughout this book, Lubavitch girls often maintain the childlike playfulness that Pipher mourns in so many of the girls she describes. Their impishness struck me as remarkable; I haven't seen anything quite like it among other young women I have known.

Of course, in many ways the Lubavitch girls are granted much less tether than most American young women. I will always remember the pain one girl felt when her parents ousted her from their home for violating Jewish law and the sense of rebellion she attached to studying

Judaic texts with men. But within the confines of Orthodox regulations, an unusual license often reigned.

A question looms: Why? Why would Lubavitch girls tend to hold on to the childhood voice and spirit that many in America at large seem to lose? Why would they cultivate a much richer self-awareness than one might expect from a sect that appears to downplay the power of the individual in deference to the glory of God? I can offer many possible explanations—the camaraderie and safety of their single-sex social world, their tight-knit community, the power of their religious faith, their unusually close families, values within Hasidism, the Lubavitch zeal for nurturing every Jew's unique and vibrant soul. Most likely, all these factors play a complex and interrelated role.

On one level, the Lubavitch girls' liveliness and openness should come as no surprise. The research unveiling inhibited young women who channel their pent-up emotions into covert anger focuses on middle-class or affluent, largely white communities. But the world of American girlhood encompasses much more. Young women from backgrounds that don't fit this mold often imbibe quite different messages about ideal behavior. Lubavitch Crown Heights is, on the whole, white and financially secure (with a large minority of poor Hasidim), but its core habits and values diverge radically from mainstream middle-class American mores.

In a study of young women identified as being at risk for early pregnancy and/or school dropout, Jill McLean Taylor, Carol Gilligan, and Amy M. Sullivan found that "there is little evidence that the majority of these girls experience pressure to conform to the idealized standards of femininity so prominent in the dominant culture."[10] These girls were all poor or working-class, from a range of backgrounds: African American, Caribbean, Latina, Portuguese, Irish, and Italian. Research among both African American and working-class white girls suggests that the stereotypical white middle-class ideal of the nice, kind, quiet woman is alien to them. Often, black girls are pushed to develop inner strength and independence so they can successfully juggle the roles of breadwinner and nurturer; they will likely have vital, if not total, responsibility in both of these domains. Black girls must also learn to defend themselves against the racism they will endure.[11] Fascinatingly, research suggests that black girls on the whole maintain higher levels of self-esteem throughout adolescence than their white and Latina peers despite disproportionate poverty, broken homes, and exposure to violent crime.[12] Their characteristic psychic strength and ability to assert their needs and opinions overtly seem to boost self-confidence. Lyn Mikel Brown, who studied white girls from the working-class town of Mansfield, Maine, found that the young women developed a certain toughness, a willingness to express both anger and love with stark openness, an attraction to fighting and debate, and an admiration for people who defend themselves.[13]

Economic stress and ethnic bigotry may foster scrappiness and open aggression, the sense that one must fight to reap any reward in this world. And perhaps cohesive social groups help young women develop confidence and ease of self-expression—whether the bond stems from racial discrimination, cultural tradition, religious passion, or small-town ties unbroken by middle-class rites like residential college. A study of black and Latina girls found that the young women with the strongest sense of ethnic identity tended to enjoy the highest self-esteem;[14] defined social networks of all kinds might buoy girls (and all human beings) as they struggle through life. Lubavitch youth take enormous pride in their background. Even the staunchest rebels often relished their status (as one girl bragged while enjoying her third glass of beer at a club, "I'm Lubavitch, so my tolerance for alcohol is impressive").

Today's Lubavitchers have inherited community coziness from their forebears; in some ways, Crown Heights, Brooklyn feels like a tight-knit nineteenth-century eastern European Jewish village, where townspeople developed very particular roles: the patient fish store man who offered advice on countless domestic squabbles, the dressmaker whose beautiful clothes were legendary, if only within her tiny neighborhood. Several girls did long for an even closer community bond, complaining that a school grade of over one hundred students is too large, that they've never gotten past surface friendliness with their neighbors, and that cliques divide Bais Rivka. But their benchmarks differ from mine. Shared beliefs, ultimate life goals, and intricate social networks bind people in ways I never imagined when I was growing up in a tiny New Jersey suburb. Everyone seems to know most of Lubavitch Crown Heights, and girls develop distinct and memorable reputations—the brilliant rebel, the charismatic leader, the thoughtful mystic.

This community tightness contributes critically to the Lubavitch girls' emotional strength. Their cohesive all-girl social world (schools and all socializing are single-sex) seems to minimize some of their tension by allowing a refreshing openness about their concerns. These young women speak forthrightly, at school and social events, about their insecurities, without fear that their peers will seize on their vulnerabilities and mock them. One very heavy girl at Bais Rivka told me in a loud voice during a crowded lunch break, "My weight gives me pain, always." At my high schools, someone would almost surely have jumped in here, thrilled at the opportunity to savage an easy victim, but the surrounding girls just smiled sympathetically. Another plump young woman told me, right in the midst of a social gathering for the tenth grade, "If I could change one thing about myself, it would be my size." She laughed, embarrassed, and several girls chimed in with various remarks to assuage her discomfort: "She likes to joke about herself"; "She's such a great girl to talk to about these things." The social atmosphere can be catty and cliquish, and many girls are dismayed to find themselves on the margins, but a certain underlying comradeship pervades these young women's lives. While it doesn't banish typical concerns, it makes them less fearful.

The girls' bonds are continually reinforced. Mothers host regular gradewide gatherings, where young women come together to play games, eat home-baked goodies, sing Hasidic songs, and chat together in an informal setting. The host often knows her guests' mothers, and she'll ask about them as she weaves around the living room and talks to the girls. Occasionally, parents or community recruits give talks on Jewish themes. Seminary girls organize these events for the high school grades, and two or three seminary students will show up at a typical high school gathering and try to inspire enthusiasm for the planned activities; these parties can foster friendships between girls of varying ages. Not surprisingly, the more rebellious types are the least likely to attend, but most girls come at least a few times throughout the year. Even the most disaffected young women often reminisce wistfully about recent class trips—yearly events that can inspire nonstop pranks and laughter.

Perhaps for many girls the very boundaries of acceptable belief and behavior that can seem so limiting to secular minds actually maintain and nourish their independent voices. Cross-gender friendships are strictly banned, so young women do not have the opportunity to lapse into mainstream America's familiar routine of girls subverting their brash, bold sides to impress the boys. Since exploration of social universes beyond Orthodox Judaism is forbidden, the community becomes extremely tight-knit, and people feel known and appreciated, a powerful motivation to develop their talents and personalities. The gifted young singer can share her talent with all of female Crown Heights during the high school's yearly musical production; the jokester becomes famous throughout school for her pranks.

Of course, this intense closeness carries dangers as well. The airtight consensus and warmth of the majority can make the few infidels feel like strangers in the promised land. Rampant gossip affects nearly everyone, blemishing reputations and breeding casual discussion about acquaintances' intimate pains. A rebellious student at the post–high school seminary thought she enjoyed a pristine name, when in fact several of her classmates whispered of her exploits with neighborhood boys. A Bais Rivka teacher who clashed with the girls inspired a continuous stream of speculation based on choice tidbits from her life: perhaps she's bitter because of her disabled son; maybe she never got over her father's early death. . . . The atmosphere was rather like one huge extended family—everyone is known, but everyone is exposed.

Crown Heights's aura of community begins with the family. The family is the fundamental unit in Orthodox Judaism, the place where past, present, and future merge: holidays commemorating ancient events passed from parent to child. A Hasidic girl's family life is fascinating for yet another reason; it is the one place where the genders converge. As I began to spend time at girls' homes, I wondered whether this was the true source of all the horror stories about Orthodox girlhood, whether the power the young women enjoy at school must in fact be traded in at the end of each day for domination by fathers and brothers. Maybe the males in their lives were downright cruel, or, more likely, perhaps they sweetly, subtly, and unconsciously squelched girls' initiative and drive, all in the name of spirituality.

I discovered many families that exuded warmth, and a few with overwhelmed, distraught, or emotionally distant parents. During my countless hours spent among Crown Heights families, for both holiday celebrations and informal visits, the majority of homes struck me as caring, safe places. The few questioners often deeply resented girls' backseat functions during religious rituals and disproportionate household chores, but most young women enjoyed their families and their roles within them. Typical girls expressed their opinions with passion during family discussions, and the playful spirit I saw at school was nearly as strong at home.

Profound disturbances like physical abuse or verbal berating by parents certainly exist here; one young woman shared nightmarish tales of being thrown down the stairs by her perpetually agitated mother. I have spent several afternoons in her home, and the family's conversations often hinge on put-downs—

DAUGHTER: "I put the fruit salad out on the table."
MOTHER: "You idiot! That was supposed to be for tomorrow. You're always ruining something."

I have no doubt that this sort of behavior was more common than I was able to observe. Getting a sense of a family's darker side as a guest, particularly one with the well-known goal of writing about her impressions, can be like trying to appreciate a rainbow in a black-and-white photograph. People can always modulate their actions and stamp out their most embarrassing impulses. When I was growing up, my mother used to lament that she couldn't be a fly on the wall, observing my non-family life. She knew that her actual presence would distort everything; instead, she yearned to be an invisible camera, taking everything in on the sly. Throughout this project, I was very visible, and my presence certainly affected the behavior of the people I was watching.

Even so, I spent so much time in Crown Heights and immersed myself in so many dimensions of this community that I truly believe I soaked in the texture of Lubavitch life. In many cases, I may have received a somewhat packaged vision of the truth, a movie version as opposed to messy, haphazard life. I will never know for sure the subtleties and gradations of my effect on the people I observed. Yet I realize from my own family that acting only goes so far. Much as we may want a certain guest to think everything is well among us, tensions and disputes somehow crop up, regardless of the company.

Thankfully for my blood pressure, I will never experience the raw emotion of any family other than my own, but the combination of widespread snooping and in-depth interviews gave me a strong sense that most girls enjoy their family lives. With a few stark exceptions, families received enthusiastic praise, even from girls who unthinkingly exposed their dissatisfactions with school, community, and social life. A girl venting about her peers' snobbishness or her teachers' unfairness would grin and visibly calm down when I turned the questioning to her parents.

Lubavitch youngsters' single-sex social life seems to enhance their communal spirit beyond their families. The girls never see young men in their schools, camps, or activities, which may help them develop assured, powerful personalities. In mainstream America, boys can dominate the social scene, pulling the most striking pranks in school, graphically sharing their impressions of girls' looks, imposing their preferences when discord arises.

Certainly, not all young women fall into these trends; if you know several teenage girls, you can most likely picture some who steal the show in mixed-gender settings. I speak of tendencies, not inevitabilities. In my own memory, boys *tended* to be the ones who caused the zany scenes in class, made the most raucous jokes, and shared aloud the desires and revulsions certain girls sparked within them. Myra Sadker and David Sadker, whose book *Failing at Fairness* reports on their intensive observations within America's schools, corroborate these memories. Even confident, socially adept young women sometimes look back and lament that the coeducational social scene silenced their ideas and squelched their physical energy. Take Naomi Wolf, now a well-known writer and speaker. As a girl she was popular, bright, and ambitious, but her desire to please the boys made her meek and submissive to her male peers, stopping her from running down the school hall with her friends and sharing her wit.[15]

For Lubavitch girls, these problems are alien. In their all-female world, they shout, run, and vigorously express their opinions. They are blissfully unacquainted with the day-to-day drubbing boys struggling to overcome their own insecurities can dish out. I recently joined two Lubavitch girls, Brocha and Malkie, on a coeducational ski trip for modern Orthodox high school and college students. Modern Orthodox Jews follow Jewish law but are more lenient than Hasidim; many of their social activities include both boys and girls. Hasidism bans mixed-gender socializing, but these girls were a bit rebellious (though they were passionate believers, with a fervent pride in Lubavitch). They had heard about the trip through a friend at the Orthodox but not Lubavitch Touro College and, being prone to adventure, decided to go along, try out a new sport, and meet some Jewish young people from a somewhat different background.

The boys dominated the bus; they shouted and nudged each other while the young women chatted quietly. A diminutive young man announced that the girls would sit in the back (the trip was coed, but each gender needed to sit separately). The modern Orthodox young women began trooping off to the back, but the Lubavitch girls complained: "Hey! What do you mean? What is this?" Malkie moved up a few rows, beckoning impishly to Brocha to join her.

"Move *back*!" the boys yelled, but the Lubavitchers were intransigent, and eventually the young men managed to arrange their seating so that the errant duo did not interfere with religious injunctions.

A few last stragglers, all girls, ran toward the bus, and a chunky boy offered his expert assessment as each approached: "Ugly, ugly, ugly, so-so." The modern Orthodox young women fidgeted and glanced at each other nervously, each probably wondering how he would have judged her. The Hasidic girls looked uncomfortable as well; Lubavitchers are hardly immune to common concerns about physical appearance. But they were also shocked, unlike their modern Orthodox peers, who accepted a familiar event with quiet resignation. Such comments certainly plagued both of my high schools, where the girls were just as apt to shrink back and take their lumps.

Brocha, normally a shy young woman who kept her rebellious leanings under careful wraps, yelled out, "Excuse me, but I know which bus never to take again!" For a long minute, the entire bus was silent. The boys' right to hurt the young women had been questioned by someone new to girl-bashing. The quiet was particularly noticeable in the front half of the bus, where the boys had been yelping, whooping, and singing Adam Sandler's pop hit about Hanukkah while their female peers chatted softly in the back. Lubavitch girls are used to taking control; on *their* trips, they are the ones who shout and play, all over the bus—front, back, and center. The situation seems to have given some of them more confidence than many mainstream and modern Orthodox girls, who must contend not only with their own anxieties but with the fallout from the boys' as well.

Beyond the single-sex lifestyle, historical and cultural trends within Hasidism encourage strength among women. While modern feminists would cringe at Hasidism's demarcation of gender roles, the movement has encouraged women to be aggressive within the boundaries of their wifely and motherly responsibilities. Since Hasidism's beginnings in eighteenth-century eastern Europe, Hasidic women have developed qualities that far transcend stereotypes of retiring, impotent females: verbal sparring, sarcasm, economic expertise, multilingual knowledge, an understanding of politics.[16] Jewish theology has supported women's power in certain key arenas. Eastern European Jewish women often worked to support their families—and learned the necessary information about the wider world—while the men spent their days analyzing Judaic law in accordance with their religious obligations.

Many eastern European Jewish mothers developed into do-it-all superwomen, supporting their households financially, emotionally, and physically while their husbands studied; self-assertion and a sense of power were logical outgrowths of their omnibus role. The rampant Jewish mother jokes that poke fun at domineering moms hint at very real historical tendencies among eastern European Jewish women, many of whom had Hasidic ties. Jewish immigration brought these traits to America. This legacy has enormous influence on contemporary Lubavitch girls.

Here in the United States, Lubavitch is no bulwark against common adolescent concerns: these young women worried that they were unattractive, overweight, and unpopular. Many lavished impressive energy on their looks. The girls would glance nervously at the mirrors in their homes. At school there were no mirrors, but people were constantly fixing their hair or arranging their clothes. Many Bais Rivka students hated the high school rule that shirts had to be tucked in because they feared that everyone would notice their large stomachs. On Shabbos, most girls were impeccably dressed—one young woman described the female section of the synagogue as a "fashion show."

By the second year of seminary, when the girls were beginning the marriage search, they had often developed a heightened interest in designer clothes and makeup. Some of the heavier girls began losing weight. After all, impressing the right young man would mean landing the perfect husband, the most heavenly gift they could attain, and everyone knew that Crown Heights boys place beauty high on their list of priorities for a wife.

When I asked girls if they wanted to change anything about themselves, the overwhelming majority conjured wish lists about their appearance, longing for slim, tall bodies; clear complexions; exquisite facial features. Eating disorders have certainly touched this community; people whispered about the young woman who starved herself to death and the girls who hovered suspiciously near the toilet after fear-some feats of consumption. For a few girls, every snack inspired an internal maelstrom of debate: Should I have the orange drink? Even with the pizza? Does that mean I can only have one slice? Or maybe I can still have two if I take off the cheese. . . .

Indeed, both spiritual and earthly concerns tug at these girls, sometimes colliding and often fusing in fascinating ways. They are real people with human desires, growing up in media-saturated New York City; of course they want to look good. This sect is not completely cloistered—Lubavitcher Hasidim do have some contact with the mainstream media. Typical young Lubavitchers have seen clothing advertisements and magazine covers with willowy, air-brushed models. As I've mentioned, many girls have had at least some exposure to television and movies. Hollywood notions of beauty, femininity, and sexuality can easily creep into their minds; even G-rated films often carry all sorts of messages about these issues.

However, the backdrop of the girls' lives offers the far more profound values of spiritual grappling and community, inextricably intermeshed. The goals of shedding fifteen pounds or wheedling the money for high-top sneakers from conservatively dressed parents press, but so does the drive to follow the commandments and cultivate kindness in order to spur the coming of the Messiah. Lubavitch philosophy teaches that everything has mystical significance, that there are no accidents, that every last particle on earth mirrors a divine counterpart in heaven. You may hate your thighs or your nose, but you have them for a very particular reason; they serve some purpose in helping you fulfill your godly mission. This message, constantly reinforced by home, school, and community, competes mightily with material concerns and insecurities and helps these girls maintain their vibrancy while they struggle with ideals like beauty and social popularity. It is no panacea, as the eating disorders and distress about body image attest, but it can place worries in a larger context and stop them from enveloping the girls' personalities.

Hasidic thought influences these young women with such depth because it merges completely with their lives. The rituals, philosophy, and lifestyle of Lubavitch pervade their existence from the moment of birth, undergirding their families, their school, and their interactions within the Crown Heights community.

The *Tanya*'s paramount importance among Lubavitchers is part of what distinguishes them from other strictly Orthodox Jews. Its author, first Lubavitcher Rebbe Schneur Zalman, published his masterwork back in 1796. Today's Lubavitchers still study this work intensively throughout their lives. Rabbi Zalman envisioned a lifelong process of spiritual growth, drawing on intellect, emotion, and self-discipline. Within Lubavitch, the *Tanya* is living, God-infused philosophy, an indisputable guide to our world.

In school, girls explore the *Tanya* (translation: it has been taught), along with more standard Orthodox Jewish subjects like Bible and Jewish law. Their studies reflect the rules, behavior codes, and theology that steer their lives. When they examine the minutiae of the dietary laws or the regulations governing Shabbos, they need the information not just for the test but for their daily existence. When they read the *Tanya*'s views on the Jewish psyche, they are not merely analyzing ideas; they are exploring their souls. They may joke through some classes, but they understand that, fundamentally, the messages are profoundly relevant to their lives and thoughts.

Religious occasions fill the lives of Orthodox Jews. Shabbos comes every week, offering a daylong respite from mundane duties and an elaborate family meal each Friday night and Saturday afternoon. Other holidays arrive regularly, pulling at the full spectrum of human emotion. They range from the somber Yom Kippur, when fasting Jews atone for their sins, believing that their sincerity and observance level on this day will directly influence their lives throughout the coming year, to the joyous Purim, which commemorates ancient Persian Jews' miraculous salvation from the designs of an evil man intent on exterminating them and features costume parties, baskets of food delivered to friends, a festive family meal, and drunken revelry.

In Crown Heights, everything revolves around the Jewish calendar. As each religious event approaches, school classes teach the relevant observance codes, history, scholarly commentary, and mystical notions—each year in slightly more depth. Ambitious mothers often organize all-grade parties at special times for the girls so people can celebrate with friends as well as families. During major holidays, the hundreds of Jews on the streets seem to form a single body: one mass of black hats, long dresses, and pattering children's feet heading toward the main synagogue. It's a complex life, rife with rules and never-ending rituals. But it adds order, predictability, and comfort to the girls' struggles and insecurities; no matter how fickle the social life at school, Shabbos arrives once a week, with its glowing candles and its family meals.

Make no mistake: this is far from an ideal community. The pain and alienation at the margins, the pure torture endured by the few who dare to take their minds and actions beyond Lubavitch boundaries, stop me far short of endorsing universal Hasidism. This book will introduce several young Lubavitchers—bright, vibrant questioners—who simply cannot conform to the stringent expectations that rule Lubavitch lives. Their hurt is unnerving and unforgettable.

In a sense, it's pointless even to ask whether Lubavitch would in some absolute sense be "better" than mainstream America for the typical young woman; Hasidism is not a viable path for most Americans, including myself. I will escort you through the girls' lives and minds more for the pure delight of knowing them than for any lessons you might glean.

Indeed, I observed a sampling of Lubavitch girls, in one place and at one time; I do not present my impressions as representative of anything larger—of Orthodoxy as a whole or of life in all religious enclaves. I view these young women simply as individuals who expanded my notion of what it means to come of age in our world. And yet I had certain reactions to the girls I knew, which I do not hesitate to share. I was entering a new culture that disturbed me at times, charmed me at others. These young women are not archetypes, but they do serve as a window into a universe few outsiders have glimpsed.

My portrayal of the girls has inspired strong reactions among some early readers. Lubavitchers themselves are often stunned that my year among them has not drawn me into the fold. Lubavitch regulations alienated me early on; this system would hurt anyone, male or female, who feels a fundamental kinship with the other gender's prescribed path, or whose creativity clashes with Lubavitch strictures. I ache for Rochel, who longed to study Judaic texts with the same intensity as her brothers, and for Chaya, who struggled for the right to express her musical vision. Still, I do feel that Lubavitch has insights that could benefit the world at large, which I explore in my concluding chapter, unsettling people who worry that I seem to promote the Orthodox way. It's a sticky conundrum, for I may offend both "liberal" and "Orthodox" worldviews.

I love spending time with people driven by ardent belief, whether religious, political, or moral. Throughout my life, I have explored various groups, thinking that one might offer me an understanding I could embrace as my own. But truth does not necessarily come in neat packages. Truth is a slippery, ever-evolving notion; I cannot expect to corner it in one place, ideology, or frame of reference. Gems of insight exist nearly everywhere—and within philosophies that seem to conflict.

I want nothing more than to expand options for women and girls, to help them nurture their talents and their psychic strength. After a year among Lubavitch girls, I wonder whether certain aspects of their traditionalism—their single-sex lives, their passion for meaning, their respect for the human soul—might help some young women who now suffer. In other words, Orthodoxy may have something to add to the feminist project, if "feminist" implies the desire to help as many girls as possible grow into confident, secure adults.

We live in a world defined by black-and-white dichotomies: modern versus traditional, West versus East, liberal versus Orthodox. Complexities and nuances are bleached out in our zeal to codify others and pinpoint our own beliefs. It's a dangerous view of human diversity that at best constricts our ability to learn from other visions, and at worst stokes mutual ignorance and untamed animosity. I want to transcend that notion, to view Lubavitch girls with the hope that their great, flawed culture can enrich the conversation in our own.

1

The Community

A Cultural and Psychological Tour

BENEATH THE CHUTZPAH, Lubavitch girls are deeply enmeshed in their religious roots; some sense of their rich Hasidic heritage is crucial to understanding their lives and thoughts. Lubavitch is one contemporary sect among several spawned by the eastern European Hasidic tradition. The originator of modern Hasidism, Rabbi Israel ben Eliezer (born in 1698 near the Carpathian Mountains in what is now part of southern Russia), had spiritually invigorated much of the eastern European Jewish community by the mid–eighteenth century. He began life humbly. In his early years ben Eliezer was poor and academically undistinguished, with no hint that he would one day galvanize Jewish history.

According to tradition, he first revealed his spiritual gifts at age thirty-six.[1] He had become an itinerant healer and preacher, and word spread of his vast powers. Hence, he acquired the title Besht, an acronym of Baal Shem Tov, or "Master of the Good Name." The appellation stems from his practice of "name magic"; he fell within a Jewish tradition of healers, magicians, and miracle workers who would invoke secret mystical names of God believed to control the forces undergirding our world.[2]

The Besht was a gifted speaker who could express central Jewish mystical notions of the human condition and its relationship to God in the form of simple, engaging stories accessible to the uneducated masses.[3] His core message was that pure faith, passion, and ardent prayer are as important as Talmudic scholarship in achieving godliness. Wholly unlearned Jews could pray lovingly and attain spirituality on a par with the greatest scholars. This notion was revolutionary in a culture that revered study of the Talmud, a collection of ancient rabbinical writings that define Jewish religious and civil law, as the truest path to holiness. Contemporary Lubavitchers' fervent efforts to persuade all Jews to perform religious rituals hark back to this egalitarianism; Lubavitchers believe that even Jews with no religious knowledge release sparks of holiness that reverberate throughout the world whenever they complete a Judaic rite.

The Besht stressed God's mystical presence in all of creation and wanted to infuse holiness and joy into every aspect of life. By the end of the eighteenth century, about half of eastern European Jewry had become followers of the Besht's ideas. These people were called Hasidim, or "pious ones." And while the Baal Shem Tov drew his initial base of followers mainly from the poor and uneducated, he eventually attracted some leading Talmudic scholars.[4]

Some of the Besht's followers became leaders in their own right and spread their particular interpretations of Hasidism. They became known as Rebbes. Distinct sects sprang up around these men. Each Hasidic group centered its existence around a Rebbe, who was seen as a *tzaddick,* a perfectly righteous man with extraordinary spiritual powers. The Rebbe's centrality was key to Hasidism. Hasidim looked to their Rebbe to guide them through life decisions, and members of a given Rebbe's court would become intensely intimate. Through the generations, the Rebbes have passed their leadership on to successors, usually sons or other male family members.

Revolutions inspire angry detractors, and Hasidism attracted its share of bitter foes within the European Jewish power structure. Many adversaries of the movement were of Lithuanian origin; Lithuania was known for rigorous Talmudists deeply invested in the notion of scholarship as the most direct path to God. These *misnagdim* (opponents) bristled at what they perceived as Hasidism's excessive valorization of the Rebbe, overemphasis on mysticism, and disrespect for Talmudic scholarship. Eventually, though, the groups reconciled somewhat. Spiritual descendants of both *misnagdim* and Hasidim are numerous in Israel and America, and despite differences in philosophy, they follow the same laws and feel united in their unwillingness to assimilate into mainstream culture.

Certainly, the early enemies did not stem Hasidism's growth. The various sects grew in strength and influence, with their revered Rebbes at the helm. Rabbi Schneur Zalman (born in 1745) was the first Rebbe of Lubavitch, named after the Byelorussian town that hosted the group's leaders from 1813 to 1915. Rabbi Zalman's philosophical system, still the foundation of Lubavitch wisdom, was called Chabad, an acronym representing the Hebrew terms for wisdom (*chochma*), understanding (*binah*), and knowledge (*daath*). Lubavitchers are also known as Chabad Hasidim, and the Lubavitch outposts around the world, where the sect's emissaries try to inspire nonreligious Jews to become more observant, are called Chabad Houses. The spiritual foundation that Rabbi Zalman built continued to define Lubavitch through a succession of several beloved Rebbes.

The sixth Lubavitcher Rebbe, Rabbi Yosef Y. Schneersohn (the most recent Rebbe's father-in-law), escaped to the United States in 1940 after the Nazis invaded Poland, his home at the time, and organized Lubavitch's current world headquarters in Crown Heights, Brooklyn. Schneersohn's story is typical of Hasidim, many of whom first left Europe when World War II demolished their world. The Jewish refugees and survivors of World War II who came to America included a much higher proportion of people with an entrenched, spiritually inspired Judaism than did earlier groups of Jewish immigrants. They had grasped their European way of Jewish practice until the war destroyed their communities. Unlike their predecessors from the previous wave of Jewish immigration in the late nineteenth and early twentieth centuries, these Jews tended not to enter America with the primary goal of achieving financial security and the often attendant willingness to relinquish religious observance. Dire emergency, not economic ambition, compelled their exodus. They often arrived in America with a sense of mission: here they would carry on the Torah way, a final victory over their prior tormentors.

The Hasidim among them set up new roots in the United States, with the largest concentrations in the New York City area. Today Hasidim number about 250,000 in North America and 650,000 worldwide, with about 150,000 in Brooklyn alone.[5] Williamsburg, Brooklyn is home to the Satmar Hasidim, the most cloistered of all the American Hasidic groups, and Borough Park, Brooklyn has an eclectic mix of various sects; insiders can spot the distinctive hats, coats, and beards sported by different types of Hasidic men. The overwhelming majority of the approximately 15,000 Crown Heights Hasidim are Lubavitchers, and the neighborhood's few members of other Hasidic sects typically have an affinity for Lubavitch. New York City is a radically different setting from pre–World War II eastern Europe, but the Hasidim have done a remarkable job of replanting their cultures here, complete with Rebbes who center their lives in the New World.

Modern-day Lubavitch is a clear heir to the Rebbe-centered roots of Hasidism. Until he became ill in the early 1990s, the seventh Lubavitcher Rebbe, Rabbi Menachem Mendel Schneerson, galvanized his followers. He was the nearly unanimous choice for Rebbe when the previous Rebbe, his father-in-law, passed away. At first the brilliant Sorbonne-educated engineer shied away from the position and the enormous responsibility it entailed. But his fellow Lubavitchers were so insistent that in 1950 he took his sect's helm.

His post did indeed require unfathomable energy, wisdom, and strength. Every major decision in a Lubavitcher's life inspired a letter to Rabbi Schneerson, and each word of his response was seen as a divine gem. The Rebbe regularly held community-wide celebrations filled with song, dance, and spiritual bliss. During his later years he gave out dollars, along with brief prayers, to all who appeared at a special weekly gathering. Stories of his miracles—advice that shrank tumors, unclogged arteries, filled long-barren wombs and long-empty pocketbooks—proliferated. He was like a sun powering and centering the Crown Heights Lubavitch community, and his light radiated out into Lubavitch outposts around the world.

Rabbi Schneerson guided Lubavitch from a small group nearly extinguished by the Holocaust to a thriving international network. Actual population figures are elusive. Lubavitch does not keep official membership lists, and outreach work creates a large gray area: people who, perhaps, aren't observant by Hasidic standards but who have become more or less faithful to Jewish law because of Lubavitch mentors. Still, Simon Jacobson, author of a popular book on Rabbi Schneerson's wisdom, writes that there are "hundreds of thousands" of full-fledged Lubavitchers.[6] The Rebbe worked passionately toward spreading the Lubavitch message throughout the globe, establishing a corps of emissaries known as *shluchim* who have built Lubavitch centers—Chabad Houses—in over fifty countries.

Chabad Houses have nurtured Lubavitch's outreach success through classes, holiday celebrations, and cultural events geared toward secular Jews. The *shluchim* who run them base their lives on a few central goals: to teach Jews throughout the globe about their religious heritage and to convince as many Jews as possible to follow Judaic law.

Their lives are radically different from the Crown Heights Lubavitchers' world. They are often the lone Hasidim in the area, with no surrounding religious community. Their children typically travel far for school or attend places with no Lubavitch affiliation. Kosher food can be scarce, and some families must have supplies flown in from Jewish centers. They usually operate their own programs but occasionally team up with other Orthodox Jewish institutions, say, in cosponsoring a public menorah lighting ceremony during Hanukkah. This outreach work, or *shlichus*, is difficult but enthralling. Chabad Houses attract a lively assortment of curious souls. Many come just for kicks, but some gradually take on Hasidic beliefs and rituals. These outposts are surely among the Rebbe's proudest legacies.

Rabbi Schneerson's death in 1994 spurred anguish and impassioned theological debate. There is no new Rebbe. The Schneersons had no children, and there is no heir. Rabbi Schneerson's influence was too profound and too vital to allow for a replacement. The scene I described in the book's opening paragraph can now occur only in memory; the atmosphere at the main synagogue is much more subdued these days.

The Rebbe still undergirds this community. Lubavitchers regularly pray at his grave, and advice seekers examine letters he had written in the past to help his followers negotiate their lives. Videos and portraits in homes and community shops capture his kind, piercing eyes. While the community bustles as always, the Rebbe's absence is omnipresent. Many of the girls I interviewed offered poignant reminiscences of Rabbi Schneerson. Most feel a profound emptiness, but a few sense his presence just as strongly now. A complex emotional world has emerged. Typical Lubavitch girls are content, energetic, even joyful; Bais Rivka is hardly a center of grieving. Mention the Rebbe, though, and tears may well form. It's rather like the distant loss of a parent. Years have elapsed; life progresses; the death does not engulf existence. But a permanent sadness hums inaudibly.

The Rebbe's influence is one of many qualities that distinguish Lubavitchers from other Hasidic groups. Rebbes are crucial within Hasidism, but Rabbi Schneerson's centrality is unparalleled even among Hasidic sects. Hasidism is one movement among many in the Orthodox world. "Orthodox" is an umbrella term encompassing all Jewish groups that adhere strictly to traditional Jewish law. Contemporary American Hasidim differ from the more assimilated "modern Orthodox" Jews, who interpret religious law less stringently and embrace a much broader spectrum of secular culture, and from certain fellow "ultra-Orthodox" Jews (spiritual descendants of the *misnagdim,* the original opponents of Hasidism) who are nearly as strict in observance but do not follow a Rebbe. Ultra-Orthodox Jews (both Hasidim and *misnagdim*) constitute about one-quarter of the approximately 9 percent of American Jews who are Orthodox.[7] The Hasidic sects themselves are hardly uniform. Each group reveres a different Rebbe, and customs and philosophies vary somewhat.

Hasidic beliefs and culture have even influenced certain brands of non-Orthodox Jewish expression. The *havurah* movement attempted to merge the communal and spiritual aspects of Hasidism with the countercultural politics of the late 1960s and 1970s; it offered a general openness to Jews with varying beliefs and levels of observance. Jewish prayer groups sprang up around the country, emphasizing family-like intimacy among members, typically young adults. *Havurah* members sometimes viewed themselves as neo-Hasidim; they identified with Hasidism's communal spirit, mysticism, and unabashedly Jewish character.[8] Most, but not all, of these original groups have fizzled out. Today more mainstream synagogues around the country offer their own brand of *havurah*: small-group fellowship for people who would like to study Jewish issues together, socialize around Jewish themes, celebrate holidays with other members, or pool their efforts in community service.

The *havurah* movement strongly influenced the development of Jewish Renewal, still active today. Inspired by ex-Lubavitch rabbis Zalman Schachter-Shalomi and Shlomo Carlebach, this intriguing brand of Judaism fuses Prophetic, Cabalistic, and Hasidic traditions with gender equality, feminist spirituality, ecological consciousness, political activism, openness to homosexuality and single life paths, desire to learn from other faith traditions, and individual power to decide which aspects of Jewish tradition to follow and which to overlook.[9] Because Jewish Renewal emphasizes direct spiritual experience and mysticism, some refer to it as neo-Hasidic Judaism.[10]

Despite these offshoots, though, traditional Hasidism is staunchly Orthodox, and much of the ritual and lifestyle that defines Lubavitch lives is common to all Orthodox Jews. The basic dietary laws, the daily prayer schedule, the holidays, the sense that one's actions must conform to a higher purpose—these qualities are not Hasidic per se; they are intrinsic to all Orthodox Judaism, whether the modern variety that allows Americanized dress and enjoyment of secular culture within certain bounds of decorum, or the ultra-Orthodox branches. Indeed, many of the conflicts and issues that surface among Lubavitchers could crop up in any stringently Orthodox Jewish group or, for that matter, in any religious community with strict expectations for behavior and belief.

The Lubavitchers' most distinctive traits—their reverence for their Rebbe, their focus on the Messianic era (which many believe is imminent), and their zest for outreach among secular Jews—define their unique niche in the Jewish universe. All truly Orthodox Jews believe the Messiah will come one day; it is a central article of their faith. But Lubavitch places unusual focus on this conviction. For many religious Jews, the Messiah's coming is an ethereal, seemingly remote event that may take generations. And most Hasidic groups avoid outreach. They fear spiritual contamination from their secular counterparts and harbor skepticism that Jews raised outside the Orthodox world can ever embrace Hasidic doctrines and rituals with the proper spirit.

Desire to influence secular Jews profoundly affects the entire Lubavitch community, including the adolescent girls. I chose to study the Lubavitchers among all the Hasidic groups because their friendliness to outsiders makes them accessible and because the combination of religious intensity and worldliness spawns intriguing dichotomies: street smarts and Messianism rolled into one. Many people around the globe have experienced the Lubavitch touch. These Hasidim love to work the streets, exhorting their lax coreligionists to observe upcoming holidays or say their daily prayers. The sect's emphasis on worldwide outreach allows some people to travel extensively, which gives them international exposure that is rare in America at large. Older girls attend summer camps and post–high school seminaries throughout the country and the world, where they help spread Orthodox ideals and Lubavitch philosophy to less observant Jews.

Lubavitchers' gift for proselytizing has shaped their demographic makeup. Most members of other Hasidic sects hail from ancestral lines of Hasidim. The Lubavitchers' outreach success has created a different sort of Hasid—the *baal teshuvah,* or returnee to Judaism (plural: *baalei teshuvah*). *Baalei teshuvah* (often known as BTs) have become so numerous that a term has arisen for the old-line Hasidim, to distinguish them from their newly religious counterparts; they are known as the *frum* (religious) from birth, shortened by insiders to simply "FFB."

Often from thoroughly secular backgrounds, Hasidim-in-the-making slough off their past and embrace the Lubavitch way. They feel they are reclaiming their true heritage, since non-Orthodox brands of Judaism have only emerged in the past few generations. These people's children have extended family members who are not religious and parents who have a broad familiarity with the secular world.

The 1960s began a fruitful time for producing *baalei teshuvah*. Hasidism may seem a strange place for ex-hippies to land, but for some, Lubavitch mysticism and desire to transform the world through Jewish ritual was a natural way to channel their idealism once they became ready to marry and settle into family life. The momentum has continued through the ensuing decades; for Jews searching for ultimate values, Lubavitch outreach attempts can be alluring.

As the *baalei teshuvah*'s children grow older, they may begin to outnumber their classmates with pure ultra-Orthodox lineage. Two young women who grew up in the Crown Heights community perused yearbooks and estimated that 10 percent of the high school graduating class of 1990 had *baal teshuvah* parents (they are generally matched together when it comes to marriage, for reasons of both compatibility and residual snobbery on the part of the old-line Hasidim). About half of the class of 1994 hailed from *baal teshuvah* homes, and by the class of 2000, the number rose to 70 percent.

These figures may well be inflated; most current students offered lower estimates. Teachers requested that I not do full-scale surveys because they didn't want to emphasize their students' differences. This was probably wise, for most girls are refreshingly unconcerned with their classmates' family backgrounds. At any rate, exact numbers miss the point of this community. From the woman who accepts whatever guests come her way on Shabbos—no counting or planning—to the school administrators who say they genuinely do not think in terms of determining numbers from various backgrounds among their students, this is a community of heart, not precision. Suffice it to say that *baalei teshuvah* and their children are numerous and influential.

Beyond producing full-fledged Hasidim who move to the community and start families, Lubavitchers' openness brings to Crown Heights a motley assortment of seekers, misfits, and plain old mainstream Americans who happen to be Jewish and feel like having a cultural experience. Guests at a family's holiday meal might include a curious college undergraduate; a young surgeon with a newfound interest in spiritual concerns; a recently divorced middle-aged woman who has moved to Crown Heights to study Judaism at the local school for *baalei teshuvah*; an unemployed man in his thirties living with a Lubavitch family because he has nowhere else to go; and even a writer, awkward in her newly donned skirt and tights, trying to develop a sense for the lives of the community's girls.

Typical Lubavitch children know how to engage all these people in conversation; they have constant training in handling diverse crowds. The more separatist Hasidic groups communicate primarily in Yiddish, but American Lubavitchers tend to speak English. The heavy influence of *baalei teshuvah* may be at work here, for when Lis Harris first published *Holy Days: The World of a Hasidic Family* in 1985, she suggested that Yiddish was the primary language of most Lubavitchers.[11] Now a large percentage of Crown Heights youth grow up with secularly raised parents whose command of Yiddish is limited to choice phrases from their immigrant forebears. Girls tend to sprinkle their English with Yiddish and Hebrew words ("I ate Shabbos lunch *by* the Rothsteins, and I *mamash* couldn't believe how *chutzpadick* those kids are" loosely translates as: "I ate Shabbos lunch at the Rothsteins' house, and I really couldn't believe how obnoxious those kids are"). Those from old-line Hasidic families usually speak Yiddish fluently. But while Lubavitch Crown Heights is an international, multilingual hub where Yiddish, Russian, Hebrew, French, and many other languages fill the air, English is the tongue of choice for most young people. There is no linguistic barrier between Lubavitchers and secular culture.

Even if a girl never left Crown Heights (a highly unlikely scenario; Lubavitch's international scope and emphasis on outreach make travel, both near and far, a popular pastime), a stroll around her local streets would offer her quite a range of sights and exposure to a tremendous variety of people. The majority of Crown Heights Lubavitchers—some two thousand families, plus a sprinkling of students and single *baalei teshuvah*—live on about seven square blocks, with a fair scattering on the immediate outskirts of this main hub. In general, the closer you are to the main street of Kingston, a cross street running through the residential blocks, the more desirable the real estate. The outer streets tend to have fewer Jews and are perceived as carrying more danger. Which side of Kingston you're on also makes a difference. The homes between Kingston and New York Avenues tend to have more elite, old-line Lubavitchers than those on the other side between Kingston and Troy, which are heavily peopled with *baalei teshuvah*. This is a simple matter of timing; old-time Crown Heights Lubavitchers often clustered in certain areas, so by the time the *baalei teshuvah* began looking for homes, they typically had the best luck in less heavily staked territory. The Hasidim who live in the apartment buildings scattered throughout the area are generally either young couples just starting out or families with insufficient funds for a house.

The rough similarity in social class usually found in mainstream communities does not exist here; followers of the Rebbe, regardless of economic circumstance, have moved to Crown Heights from all over the world to be close to their revered leader. Living quarters range from a few stately mansions to solid attached brownstones to tiny apartments.

Walks spanning diverse worlds are common in this neighborhood. Suppose Chani, a young woman living in the most affluent corner of Crown Heights, decides to join a friend and shop for clothes on Manhattan's Upper East Side. She begins her walk on her own tree-lined, mansion-covered block on President Street between Brooklyn and Kingston Avenues. Quickly she comes to Kingston, the main thoroughfare, lined with convenience stores, clothing stores, and religious bookstores, as well as small restaurants and food shops specializing in a wide range of fare: delicatessens, a fish market, an ice cream shop, bakeries, a grimy storefront with some of the airiest, freshest bagels around. Chani spends much of her free time on this block, hanging out with friends at the kosher pizza shop, browsing through stores, talking and laughing with friends as she passes them on the street.

A middle-aged woman in threadbare clothes and beet red lipstick, probably a homeless person who has gravitated to Crown Heights out of some sort of attachment to the Rebbe, asks her for money. Her round face, red lips, and fraying bright yellow skirt give her the appearance of a hapless clown. "It's a *mitzvah* [good deed]," the woman reminds Chani, who hands over a dollar. Chani looks around and sees mostly fellow Hasidim but also several black people and a white family in jeans. It's a Sunday, so families in spiffy suits and dresses pass her on their way to church. A teenager with a vacant expression lolls by, and Chani figures he's probably on drugs. She continues on President Street and finds roomy attached brownstones—pleasant houses, though nothing like her family's stately brick home. There is also an apartment complex, cheerless but clean, with a mixed clientele of Hasidim and non-Jews.

At one of the brownstones, Chani picks up her friend, and the two girls walk on, away from Kingston. The proportion of Jewish-owned homes dwindles as they move farther from Kingston. Pictures of the Rebbe and posters proclaiming the imminent coming of the Messiah are interspersed with wreathes and sparkling Christmas lights. Finally the girls reach Utica Avenue, where they catch the subway. The train to Manhattan's East Side does not stop at the station in the heart of Jewish Crown Heights on Kingston Avenue, so, ironically, their desire to shop in Manhattan's most exclusive area has brought them to a gritty street far from the center of Lubavitch activity. They pass a nonkosher pizza shop, teeming convenience stores, a Jamaican bakery, and sidewalk vendors toting designer watches. They walk quickly and purposefully through the crowd, as if to say, "Don't mess with us; we know just where we're headed." Their company waiting for the subway is mostly black; the yarmulkes of Kingston Avenue have given way to the dread-locks of Utica.

As this duo's travels illustrate, the racial diversity and strife that have made Crown Heights famous broaden denizens' perspectives far beyond the confines of traditional Judaism. The gentiles in this neigh-borhood are primarily middle-class blacks, often West Indian immi-grants. Usually, race relations are strained but contained. At times the tension erupts, most infamously during August 1991, when a Lubavitch driver accidentally killed a black neighborhood child and gravely in-jured another. A rumor spread that the Lubavitch ambulance that ar-rived on the scene ignored the children and cared only for the Hasidim. Riots against the Hasidim powered by agitators from outside Crown Heights racked this community for several days, exacerbating the ten-sions that always fester here. The violence is not entirely one-sided. Bands of Lubavitch male vigilantes have been known to attack black people they connected to various crimes, some of whom turned out to be innocent.

Usually, things are quiet but tense. Crown Heights houses parallel universes that meet in space but almost never in mind. The different groups looked right through one another, rarely making eye contact, let alone smiling; this division was an entrenched part of the social land-scape. Occasionally, glimmers of friendliness emerged: a black young man behind the kosher pizza shop's counter would tease his customers, who enjoyed his openness and humor. But even this sort of nod toward relationship was rare.

A wary détente prevails. People walk the streets at all times with no repercussion. Nonetheless, through the years, many girls have faced

crime. Some have amicable (but rarely warm) relations with their gentile neighbors, who on the whole are middle-class people who present
no threat. Others associate them with bitter memories of robberies and
violence. Crown Heights kids are children of the streets of New York,
and many have cultivated a certain savvy, knowing where not to walk,
whose eyes not to meet, how not to carry themselves.

Still, traditional Hasidic beliefs, values, and expectations define
Lubavitchers' lives. The center of Lubavitch Crown Heights is the synagogue, a converted old apartment house known as "770" for its street
address. It represents a religious passion that permeates this community. Listening to the radio on Shabbos is as unthinkable to most Lubavitchers as jumping off a twenty-story building; switching electricity on
or off is one of hundreds of activities forbidden on the Sabbath.
Throughout the neighborhood (in store windows, in front of homes, on
cars) pictures of the Rebbe proclaim the imminent coming of the Messiah. Even the current debate raging through Crown Heights—whether
the recently deceased Rebbe was the Messiah, and, if so, whether to emphasize that fact in outreach work to secular Jews—shows that, while
not monolithic, this community is driven by spiritual concerns.

The sacred and the profane mix constantly in these girls' lives;
every few minutes bring a new fusion of urban grit, daily rounds, and
holiness. For a concrete sense of what this means on a typical day, let's
rejoin Chani and follow her path once again, this time during the summer, between the end of camp and the start of school. It is late morning,
and she is about to make herself a salami sandwich for lunch. She
makes sure to take her silverware from the meat side of the kitchen; Orthodox Judaism forbids eating meat and milk at the same time, and the
prohibition extends to cooking and eating utensils, which may contain
trace elements of food even after washing. One set of cabinets contains
the milk items; on the other side of the kitchen are the meat cabinets. As
Chani arranges salami slices on rye bread, she frowns at the noise outside—it sounds like two non-Jewish teenage boys are arguing right in
front of her house, a common event on these Brooklyn streets. "Asshole,
it's your fault!" one screeches.

A reply comes swiftly: "Oh, go to hell."

The interchange continues in this vein for a while, but Chani blocks
it out as she performs her before-meal rituals. She pours water three
times over each hand with a cup and then says the appropriate blessing:

"Baruch ata adonai elohainu melech ha-aolam asher kidishanu bamitz-vatov vitzivanu al nitilat yadaim" (Blessed art thou, Lord our God, King of the universe, who has sanctified us with his commandments, and commanded us concerning the washing of the hands). Before eating, she intones yet another blessing to thank God for her food: "Baruch ata adonai elohainu melech ha-olam hamotzi lehem min ha-aretz" (Blessed art thou, Lord our God, King of the universe, who brings forth bread from the earth).

Chani eats slowly, mulling over possible afternoon adventures in her head; she would love to see a few of her friends. When she's done, she says the after-meal grace and contacts her pals. They can't all get together for over an hour, but Chani doesn't mind the wait, which gives her time for her afternoon prayers. Unlike men, women are not strictly required to complete formal prayers three times a day, but *minha*, the afternoon service, is an entrenched custom among Hasidic women. Chani is a bit distracted; visions of possible afternoon activities compete with her words. But she does try to feel what she says, for the Sages warn against rote speech to express such serious sentiments: she is praising God, asking that he meet her most essential needs, and thanking him.

When she's done praying, it is about time to leave. Chani loves Manhattan, so it's not surprising that she has planned another subway ride. Soon after the girls board the train, Chani's friend Hindy begins saying her psalms. Many Lubavitchers recite a group of psalms every day according to a monthly cycle. This is in no way required, but it's considered a powerful good deed. It is also known to pave the way for divine assistance in troubled times, and Hindy's grandfather was just diagnosed with lung cancer. Her mouth moves with incredible speed; she has said these psalms many times throughout her eighteen years. As she speaks, two Hispanic friends about her age nudge each other, pointing at her and laughing. Hindy looks up and sees them doubled over in hysterics as they whisper about "motor-mouthed Jews." She takes a deep breath and returns to her psalms, trying to erase her mind's vision of the cackling young man's nose ring.

When the girls arrive at their stop, Chani's friend Sheina suggests that they all go to Jerusalem 2, a popular kosher pizza place, for a snack. Unfortunately, Chani can't have any pizza, since it has only been about three hours since she finished her salami sandwich, and after eating meat, she must wait six hours before she can have dairy again. So she settles for a Coke and the entertaining view. All sorts of people have stopped in for pizza on this hot day, including one girl with the skimpiest outfit Chani has ever seen: a scanty blue bikini top with skintight shorts that leave most of her thighs bare. Chani is a bit jealous of the girl—she looks much more comfortable in the heat than Chani feels in her required long skirt and long-sleeved shirt—but also disgusted; that kid looks one small step away from being naked, and she's out in public!

Next the girls hit the Gap, one of their favorite hangouts, but the store doesn't have much for them in the summer. At the moment it's featuring khaki shorts and short-sleeved T-shirts in a rainbow of colors. Shopping is much more fruitful in the cooler months, when the stores are loaded with long-sleeved tops and calf-length skirts are easily found. The girls browse for a bit and then realize they should get back— Chani needs to make it home on time to attend a marriage class for young women who are engaged. Chani buys a beaded necklace, and a teenage salesman jokes with her at the cash register: "Hey, great choice. I love that one. You win the good taste prize. Congratulations." He sticks out his hand for Chani to shake. She cringes; Hasidic girls follow the laws of *negiah,* so she is not supposed to touch men or boys, even to shake their hands, unless they're members of her immediate family. If a situation becomes extremely awkward, her family has told her she should shake hands quickly to avoid embarrassment, but Chani always feels a bit impure when this happens. Thankfully, the guy takes the hint and retracts his hand.

Back on the subway, two middle-aged Jewish women sit next to the girls; one starts talking about her daughter, the president of Hillel at a college in Maine. Chani's friend Bluma loves doing outreach work and senses that these women might be amenable. "Excuse me, but I overheard you say your daughter is active with Jewish issues up at school. That's great."

"Oh, yes. I'm very proud of her. She's made a lot of great Jewish friends up there." The woman looks at these youngsters and chuckles. She has lived in New York for years and can certainly pick out an Orthodox girl, especially when it's hot and nobody else is wearing long skirts and long-sleeved shirts. "But, you know, our families are nothing like you girls. You must be pretty Orthodox."

Bluma makes her move. "Yeah, you guessed it. We're Hasidim, Lubavitchers. But you're obviously involved with Judaism. Like, do you light Shabbos candles?" Jewish women are supposed to light candles before Shabbos every week. In Lubavitch life, the scene is as predictable as day becoming night: every Friday, shortly before sundown, the woman of the house lights candles and says a blessing. Often her children and husband watch. The husband then goes off to synagogue; typically the wife stays behind and prepares the dining room for the upcoming feast, though many women do attend the service.

Like most American Jews, Bluma's new subway pals do not follow these traditions. Both women laugh. "No, no. We're not too involved with the rituals," the Hillel president's mother says, and her friend nods in agreement.

"Believe me," Bluma tells them, "the rituals are amazing when you understand the significance behind them. I have the feeling you've never learned about that stuff; most Jews never have. I certainly understand that you wouldn't want to take everything on at once, but how about if you just lit Shabbos candles one time, just this week? Who knows, maybe you'd like it and want to keep doing it. I'll give you both pamphlets explaining how it's done, and the spiritual meaning behind it." Bluma whips out two brochures featuring a cheery woman lighting candles, which her new acquaintances accept graciously. She carries several extras in case the opportunity to distribute them should arise. Lubavitch prints pamphlets about virtually every major Judaic ritual; they are indispensable tools for teaching secular Jews about their religion. Chani often feels awkward about doing outreach, but she loves seeing Bluma in action and silently hopes the women make the right choice and start lighting candles. One more woman lighting candles could be just the thing that launches the Messianic era.

Chani tries to keep her mind focused on the Messiah when a menacing, wild-haired homeless man lurches onto the subway. He does not sit near the girls, to Chani's great relief, but he makes strange gurgling sounds that she can hear clearly from her vantage point. Before long, everyone realizes the man is harmless, and people relax again.

They get home a bit later than Chani had hoped, so she must eat dinner quickly and rush off to her marriage preparation class. When she says her required after-meal blessings, she speaks as quickly as possible and doesn't concentrate on the words. It is not an ideal way to pray, but Chani forgives herself; she can't always be flawlessly holy. She apologizes to her mother for not doing the dishes—this is usually Chani's job—but her excuse is unimpeachable. To make up for it, she promises to prepare dinner *and* do the dishes the next night. Her class covers the laws of family purity—the central rules and rituals governing married life—so she does not want to miss any of it. She is engaged, and she will need this material to function as a married woman.

Tonight there's a guest lecturer, a gangly *baal teshuvah* in her fifties who worked as a marriage counselor before she became Lubavitch; she spices her talks with real-world examples from both secular and religious life. Her audience, fifteen young women in their late teens and early twenties, is captive. These rules will have tremendous influence over their lives before long.

Of course, Chani knows the basics: A husband and wife cannot touch, not even to pass a plate from one to the other, while the wife is menstruating, and for one week after that. During this time, sex is verboten. Every month, at the end of this period, married Orthodox women go to the *mikvah,* a ritual bath, to purify themselves in preparation for the rest of the month, when touching, including sexual contact, is allowed. Orthodox thought stresses that this ritual in no way implies that the menstruating woman is unclean. Rather, the *mikvah* immersion spiritually refines wives to honor the sacred act of sex. Women elevate themselves to a higher spiritual level through their monthly ablution. Some men use the *mikvah* every day, and most do before the Sabbath, contrary to the popular notion that this is a purely feminine ritual. Not surprisingly, the men have a separate *mikvah* for their rituals, but the goal is the same: spiritual cleansing, though men's use of the *mikvah* has no bearing on sexual activity or physical contact with their wives.

Today Chani learns some intriguing information that bolsters her respect for this system. The guest lecturer describes several cases from her previous life as a marriage therapist in the secular world. She believes most of her clients, who hailed from a wide range of backgrounds, would have benefited from the family purity laws:

One woman—not Jewish—came to me in a tumult. She and her husband just weren't connecting on a personal level any more; they hadn't had a real conversation in over a year. I told her to try limiting physical contact—to make an agreement that, once a week, they wouldn't touch at all. She thought I was completely *meshugeh* [crazy]. But they did try it. After a few weeks of this, they had rekindled their old conversational spark. By limiting physical contact, they were forced to develop other ways of connecting. I guarantee this will happen to you, too.

The girls all nod knowingly; there are questions galore, but everyone agrees that the basic laws work well.

After class, one of Chani's neighbors, a gregarious redhead, suggests they catch the tail end of another neighbor's wedding festivities. By this time, Chani is exhausted and longs for her bed. But Mushkie is a great girl, and Chani would feel guilty later on if she skipped out on her wedding. Since her house is on the way, she can stop off quickly and change into her blue dress. Most of the other neighbors will be there; she'll probably see her own parents. So the two young women head over, and though she has walked to countless late weddings in this town, the night Brooklyn streets jar Chani; the stray street people seem to clash with the purity she feels after discussing the *mikvah.*

But she is thrilled to see Mushkie on her big day, and once she starts dancing, she's glad she came. The dreary catering hall with its cavernous rooms feels somehow rejuvenated when it houses a wedding. Crown Heights weddings are open affairs, attended by a wide range of friends, family members, and little-known acquaintances; invitations apply only to the sit-down meal, not the informal chatting and dancing that follow. The dancing can last for hours, blasting any notion that Hasidim suffer from a constitutional lack of physical fitness. Men and women are separate, divided by a partition. Even the bride and groom do not see each other at the celebration. Despite the single-sex atmosphere, guests can meet a remarkable diversity of people: nonreligious tourists, vagrants, and the secular relatives of *baalei teshuvah* mingle with the Lubavitchers. When the dancing begins, differences evaporate; the suburban seeker and the Hasidic girl twirl side by side. Chani joins the spinning circle of girls in the center and grins.

Finally she takes a break and watches from the sidelines. Chani has always loved weddings, but now that she herself is engaged, she feels a special connection to the bride. Like most Lubavitch girls, she needed to date a few boys before she found the right person. She does not regret the experience; she actually enjoyed trying out different date settings: a homey eatery in Borough Park, another Orthodox Brooklyn neighborhood; a hotel lobby; an upscale Manhattan kosher restaurant.

Manis was just too holy for her; he planned to become a *shliach,* an emissary of the Rebbe who devotes his life to Rabbi Schneerson's goal of bringing as many Jews as possible to the laws of Torah. He told Chani he would go anywhere he was needed to do the Rebbe's work. Chani, very frankly, wants to stay in Crown Heights. She admires people like Manis but craves the security of New York, with friends and family nearby and a wide range of Orthodox food stores and social activities. To be perfectly honest, she also wants more money than a life of outreach could provide. She envisions sharing her life with someone like her father, a kind man who runs a successful jewelry business. Her mother called the matchmaker and told her so, and Chani stopped dating this young man.

Chani rather liked the second boy, but his family was turned off by the fact that one of her sisters is divorced. In their minds the red flag was impossible to ignore; Chani, after all, had been brought up in the same house as the divorcée. If Chani had truly managed to charm the young man, his family would have supported the marriage, but he did not feel that anything about her sufficiently compensated for the sister. His mother told the matchmaker her son was not interested. That was that.

And then there was Simon. He was bright, witty, pleasant-looking if not ravishing. Like Chani, he descends from a long line of Lubavitchers. His family is quite wealthy, and Chani thinks this energetic young man will do a wonderful job helping his father run his large appliance store. Though she was nervous on their first date, they had an enjoyable conversation, laughing a bit about the social lives at their schools. They met four more times and began to feel comfortable with each other. Both mothers notified the matchmaker that the pair was compatible, and so, plans were made. In a few short months, Chani will be a wife. On a day-to-day basis, Chani does not think much about Simon, but she is sure her love for him will grow over time. This was a central message of all the dating discussions from her seminary classes: Immediate infatuation is worth little. Live with him. Get to know him. The rest will come.

Anyhow, she is certainly grateful she dated within the Lubavitch scheme. She imagines secular dating often involves baring your body in ultrarevealing clothes like that girl in Manhattan with the skintight shorts. Chani looks at the bride, gorgeous in her long white gown, and then at the other young women in their long-sleeved, high-neck blouses despite the heat outside. Many of them are beautiful, but in a way that acknowledges the *neshama*, the Jewish soul. They look good, but they also look holy. She smiles to herself, thankful for the laws of *tznius*, the Jewish modesty codes.

The notion of *tznius* drives this sect's expectations for girls and women; the word incorporates the ideas of modesty, sanctity, and purity.[12] As in so many spheres, Lubavitch imbues *tznius* with complex mystical ramifications. Women who achieve a high level of *tznius* can expect abundant blessings, including wealth, children, and grandchildren.[13] Beyond personal gain, behaving with proper *tznius* unleashes sparks of holiness throughout the world and encourages the coming of the Messiah.

The most obvious implications of *tznius* involve dress. Females must wear dresses or skirts, not pants, for a few reasons: Neither gender may wear the clothing of the other, and pants are considered male apparel. Women are also prohibited from wearing clothes that reveal the shape of their legs. Dresses and skirts must be long enough to conceal the knees at all times; shirts must cover the elbows and collarbone. Stockings are imperative. After marriage, women cover their hair with wigs. The driving idea is that, even though women can and should look good (many Lubavitch women and girls love few things more than a day of clothes shopping), they should save their sexual attractiveness for their husbands. At the high school, girls wear uniforms. In seminary, they select their own clothes, but their choices must be in strict accordance with Jewish modesty codes.

Beyond physical appearance, *tznius* encompasses expectations for general behavior. Females must not call attention to themselves in public or in the company of men. They must exalt their private natures and resist enchantment with the possibility of widespread glory.

The idea of *tznius* derives from this verse from the Psalms: "The entire glory of the daughter of the king lies on the inside."[14] Within an Orthodox Jewish scheme, this concept is not at all pejorative; true holiness is by nature private. Moshe Meiselman, author of *Jewish Woman in Jewish Law*, explains: "This verse, which underlies much of the Jewish attitude towards the female role, has been used in rabbinical literature in two ways. First, it has been viewed as a statement on the private nature of the female role, and second, as a panegyric on the private nature of the religious experience in general."[15]

The Hasidic social structure helps to solidify different norms for men and women. Outside the family, Lubavitch maintains separate universes for males and females from preschool through adulthood.

Schools and friendship networks are completely single-sex. The laws of *negiah,* which prohibit any form of touching between males and females other than spouses or some family members, preclude boy-girl closeness. Most of the girls I met praised their all-female lifestyle and were horrified by the idea of dating boys before they were ready to marry. On the other hand, a few suffered guiltily with crushes on the forbidden young men.

Historically, the boys' and girls' schools have differed in curriculum and goals. Boys stay at school far into the evening, and they concentrate most, if not all, of the time on Jewish studies. Young men have several educational options. Some boys never study English subjects formally; others learn basic English and math through eighth grade; a handful cover a full program of secular subjects through high school. A Bais Rivka education is more well-rounded. Judaic studies is the centerpiece. Young women spend their mornings, presumably when they are most intellectually alert, on these subjects, which range from typical Orthodox fare like Bible study and Jewish law to Hasidic philosophy and the history of Lubavitch. But they all cover a full program of secular classes in the afternoon through high school. School ends about 4:00 P.M.

Various factors contribute to these differences. Males are required to study Torah at every possible moment. Girls are not, so they are free to spend substantial time on other subjects and to end the school day earlier. Several young women also mentioned the notion that females are innately on a higher spiritual plane than males, so they are better able to withstand the potential dangers of secular subjects—say, the non-Jewish values implicit in secular history or literature. The girls' curriculum is carefully chosen to avoid sexuality or contradictions with Lubavitch ideals. But once students move from the domain of Orthodox Judaism, even the most seemingly innocuous books can open their minds to banned possibilities, like cross-gender friendships or nonkosher food. Many feel that someone in the family should be familiar with basic aspects of secular acedemics; the girls are given this task. Complete ignorance of the world at large could foster legal or financial vulnerability and undermine efforts at outreach to secular Jews.

As usual in Lubavitch, variations have emerged. The past few years have welcomed two new girls' schools to Crown Heights. Bais Chaya Mushka infuses a special brand of religious passion into its small, intimate student body (the principal was leery of offering exact figures, since the school is still growing). Some families wanted their girls to spend more time on Judaic learning, and this school's curriculum offers only limited secular studies. Even secular classes try to maintain a Jewish slant; gym activities, for example, are set to Hasidic music, and English courses cover books like *Chassidic Portraits*[16] rather than the mainstream novels Bais Rivka often favors. Students spend much of their time doing outreach to less religious Jews, and *tznius* is strongly emphasized both in and out of school. The belief that the Rebbe is Moshiach is strong, and according to the high school principal, Bais Chaya Mushka offers a "very close, live connection to the Rebbe."

B'nos Menachem offers similar strengths; it is also small but growing, with a close-knit student body. Modesty is key here as well, as is a close relationship with the Rebbe (the school supports the belief that the Rebbe is Moshiach, though it welcomes children from non-*meshichist* families). B'nos Menachem offers a full range of secular subjects in addition to Judaic studies; the school's distinguishing educational philosophy is that students should be able to learn according to their unique intellectual styles. Some children learn better verbally, some visually. Some may need extra enrichment to make full use of their gifts, others a modified test that will compensate for their difficulties. Students cultivate warm, friendly relations with teachers, though discipline is never compromised.

As I write, these schools are just beginning high school programs—they started in elementary school and are growing along with their students (when the oldest grades reach senior year, the schools will have their first high school graduating classes). My observations focused purely on Bais Rivka, but it will be fascinating to see how these new schools influence life for Crown Heights girls. Still, while Crown Heights is beginning to offer a surprising level of variety for girls' education, one feature is universal and unbending—total gender separation.

How does marriage happen in this gender-split world? Chani's story is typical. Dates are arranged by community adults, often professional matchmakers. Teachers, neighbors, and parents' friends also get involved; setting up a date that leads to marriage is a revered and holy deed. Prospective spouses make the ultimate decision. Young women (generally aged nineteen to twenty-one) are introduced to young men (typically twenty-one to twenty-four). If either party is dissatisfied, no further dates ensue, and new matches are organized.

Similarity in personality, interests, and religious orientation is an impetus to suggest a match. Now, with politics raging, compatible beliefs about the Rebbe are crucial; a young woman who fervently hopes to spread the word that the Rebbe will soon spearhead the Messianic era could never marry a young man who cringes at the thought of a deceased man as the Messiah. Preference in terms of physical makeup is also important; young Lubavitchers are well aware that their spouses will be their sole sexual partners and critical influences on their children's genetic endowment. "Yes, she is on the short side. You're absolutely right—that is a family tendency. But it may make you feel better to know that they're a strong bunch; I don't know of many health problems over there," the seminary principal informed a young man's anxious mother over the phone while I waited in her office.

Marriage partners usually come from similar backgrounds. One important criterion is *yichus,* or religious lineage. A girl who can trace her roots back to Lubavitch Rebbes on both sides of her family has sterling *yichus;* a girl whose parents are *baalei teshuvah* hailing from nonreligious homes has none. Even among people with strong *yichus,* issues like divorce in the family or religious level of extended family members can affect desirability. As in virtually all communities, wealth is a factor as well. Matchmakers often do background checks on marriageable young people that would impress the FBI, asking everyone from teachers to second cousins about their impressions.

At their first meeting, prospective couples go to some public place, like a hotel lobby or a restaurant, where they can talk. If both parties agree, a second date follows. People generally see each other four to eight times over a period of two weeks to two months before getting engaged. Engagements rarely last longer than six months. The rules of *negiah* apply until marriage; even a quick tap is forbidden before the big day. Young Lubavitchers do not date until they are ready to marry; until then, they remain in their single-sex worlds.

Segregated social life amid a two-gender universe creates a fascinating dualism for Lubavitch girls. In the larger society, modesty and decorum must prevail. Hasidic girls should not draw attention to themselves in mixed-gender settings. Prohibitions abound. Among men, young women mustn't sing, speak publicly, or dress provocatively. But in their own all-female world, they are refreshingly uninhibited.

On buses during class trips, girls ranging from thirteen to twenty sing, shout, and jump. Often, they retain a childlike wonder. During a seminary trip to Montreal, some Lubavitch young women skied for the first time. Clumsy in their long skirts, most spent more time on the ground than on their skis. They rolled around in the snow and marveled at the long, smooth blades on their feet. Some picked up the basics and whizzed down the small beginners' slope. They laughed, mushed snow in each others' hair, and said, over and over, "This is *so* fun!" I felt like I was watching five-year-olds who could still revel in simple pleasures with no self-consciousness.

In school, the gender of the teacher strongly influences the girls' behavior. Bais Rivka hires a few men to teach religious subjects; with them, in accordance with the expectations of *tznius,* the students are quiet and unassuming. With the female teachers who lead most of their classes, they speak their minds with gusto. The building itself is drab, drafty, and a bit run-down. Lubavitch is a relatively poor Hasidic group, and girls' education hardly dominates the list of financial priorities. Yet the girls' energy livened up this dingy building. At times, it seemed almost cheerful, particularly between classes or at the end of the day, when screaming, giggling young women tore through the halls.

The first class I observed at the high school was tenth-grade biology. The teacher was reviewing material from the previous day, and the students complained, "Do we *have* to learn this? We did this yesterday!" They demanded, quite rightfully, to know who I was and why I was there. A young woman announced that it would be much more interesting to hear from me than from the biology teacher and earned resounding applause. This behavior may seem cruel, and many in the community complain that the girls lack respect for their teachers. One intriguing explanation I've heard is that the only true authority is the Rebbe; everyone else is roughly equal. Even so, I sensed no ill will. Through it all, the teacher smiled, shrugged, and tacitly egged the girls on. The students clearly did not mean to hurt this woman. In a way it was all a joke, like in a big family with children who are always teasing the parents. I saw none of the stiffness and formality I remember from high school. These students acted as if they were home.

When the girls feel attacked by a teacher, they balk. During an education class at the seminary—the post–high school seminary includes a continuation of Jewish subjects and some educational methods courses to prepare students to teach—the instructor gave the girls a connect-the-dots exercise. In the upper-left-hand corner of the paper was a model. One young woman asked if she had to follow the model; she thought she would learn more from forming her own designs. The teacher was appalled: "How do you think you're going to teach others? You can't wait, and direction means nothing to you."

The girls, winking and laughing, pounced. They wanted to know: Why can't imagination be a tool? Were they being taught how to teach, or how to connect the dots? Why wasn't this teacher giving them the "positive reinforcement" she had been claiming was so important? The teacher finally gave the example of Torah. There, she said, you have to follow the rules. "This isn't Torah," was the immediate rejoinder.

This incident exemplifies the mood at Bais Rivka. All that questioning and playfulness take place in the same school where the principal measures skirt slits to make sure they don't reveal too much skin, and students are given detention for being caught with long socks instead of stockings. The overwhelming majority of these girls would never consider rebelling against the basic dictates of Jewish law. Reach beyond Judaism, and you had better be convincing if you want their respect and attention. God's demands range widely and demand impressive discipline, but where he leaves off, energy explodes. The goals of religious modesty and spiritual refinement join a clear encouragement of liveliness and force of personality.

Multifaceted and sometimes conflicting expectations for Lubavitch girls complicate the question of individuality and expression of independent voice. The spiritual model of excellence is the *chassidishe* girl, who strives to become an ideal Hasid of the Rebbe, someone who completely and unhesitatingly follows his wishes. The overarching idea is spiritual passion and discipline that transcend personal desires, interests, or gain. The truly *chassidishe* person goes beyond the letter of Jewish law and enters into the spirit of the commandments.

For girls, the concept encompasses several dimensions. A *chassidishe* girl's dress conforms completely to the standards of *tznius*. She eschews trendy or overly fashionable clothes, even if they technically meet the standards of Jewish law, since a *chassidishe* girl does not call undue attention to her body. These young women avoid TV, movies, and secular reading material other than school assignments. They focus the time they might have spent with these things on studying Torah and Hasidic philosophy and helping out in the Lubavitch community. In school they are obedient and show respect for their teachers (some do giggle as the real troublemakers perform). They are extremely unlikely to attend college, though Touro College, a school catering to the most stringently Orthodox Jews, has recently become popular among a sub-stantial minority of Lubavitch girls. The Rebbe had said that, ideally, Lubavitchers should not receive any higher education outside Lubav-itch auspices; the *chassidishe* girl dedicates her life to the Rebbe's ideals. Her future goals focus on bettering the Jewish community. Typically, she wants to become an emissary of the Rebbe and help run one of the Chabad Houses that have been set up all over the world to teach nonob-servant Jews about Judaism.

A quite different ideal is the "normal" girl. The majority of Lubav-itch girls fall roughly into this category; they themselves have coined the term. They create the lively, impish atmosphere at school and tend to be the most well liked by their peers. They would never question the fundamentals of Judaism, but they push the limits of Lubavitch stringencies along certain dimensions. They often try to get away with wearing socks, not full-length stockings, at school. Most have seen TV and secular movies, and some watch regularly. Many listen at least oc-casionally to popular music. They usually love to shop for clothes. Within the limits of *tznius,* they enjoy experimenting with fashion. One of these girls might wear a Gap sweater, high-top sneakers, and a long denim skirt after school. On rare occasions, those among the more experimental cadre may find themselves in places that would horrify their parents, like a kosher pizza parlor in Manhattan that often serves as a mixed-gender hangout for modern Orthodox youth. Fundamental ambivalence plagues many of these girls. They worship the Rebbe and would love to meet his expectations, but fun beckons everywhere, temptations overwhelm, and the thrill of social popular-ity is more immediate and tangible than the subtle rewards of spiritual refinement.

Ostensibly, the adults of the community strive to create *chassidishe* girls. Many of them are dismayed by the encroachment of modern cul-ture and values on the "normal" girls. Some speculate that the Rebbe's death has spurred a slackening of standards among Crown Heights youth. Lubavitchers often sensed that the Rebbe knew all. A young woman who had sneaked in some rock music would stare into Rabbi Schneerson's mesmerizing blue eyes and feel the pain of rebuke. How-ever powerful the Rebbe may remain in spirit, his charismatic physical presence is gone. Whatever the reason, many young people have veered from the stringent avoidance of secular culture Rabbi Schneer-son had upheld.

An emergency meeting was recently called for all Lubavitch women. The theme of the evening was that too many Lubavitch young people were straying from *chassidishe* values and behavior. Speakers highlighted the psychological dangers of compromises in *tznius* and exposure to secular culture. One woman discussed a mainstream movie she had seen as a child; its disturbing scenes still replayed through her mind and tormented her. Presenters, ranging from community women to rabbinical authorities, stressed the mystical implications of seemingly small deviations. The underlying message was: The Messiah is still not here. Maybe our children's behavior is somehow responsible.

On one level, the Lubavitch young women's culture contains a hint of a conflict I clearly remember from my own high school days: the ideals of the most powerful and popular adolescents often diverge from those of the people in authority. But the tension is not merely generational. The adults themselves seem a bit ambivalent about their goals for girls. When I mentioned to a high school teacher the name of an intensely religious, *chassidishe* girl whom I had interviewed, her response was to frown and say, "She is not at all typical. Most of our girls are not like her." When I brought up an interviewee who was more of a "normal" type, she smiled and praised her: "Oh, great. She's a great girl. I'm so glad she talked to you." Mention of another *chassidishe* young woman to the mother of a "normal" girl elicited the laughing response: "Oh, she's *so* holy."

Among these two types of girls, the issue of questioning and independent voice is difficult to pinpoint. On the surface, the girls who strive to be *chassidishe* are the ultimate conformists. They attempt to follow all dictates of Judaism as closely as they can. Lubavitchers are taught from early childhood that they should mold their lives according to the Rebbe's teachings, and these young women live accordingly.

Of all the Lubavitch girls, the most staunchly *chassidishe* ones best fit stereotypical notions of femininity: they are unassuming; they hesitate to express anger; their goal of devoting their lives to the world's spiritual growth is profoundly unselfish. Their overarching life purpose, to transform their will and energy to fulfill God's demands, seems to quash the budding of individual voice. As one young woman explained to me, "There's nothing personal. The only thing is to serve *Hashem* [God]." But a paradox often emerges, for the spiritual passion that sparks willingness to merge the psyche with God's master plan can push these girls into intensive contemplation of their own ideas and feelings and create the courage to buck their peers' expectations.

One young woman melds a love for drawing and crafts; a delight-fully whimsical appreciation of the smallest pleasures (the way a pair of earrings sparkles in the sun, the sound of her voice when she prays); and a fierce adherence to her stringent interpretation of Jewish law, re-gardless of her peers' habits. Another quietly blazes a path for herself as a female Judaic scholar and mystic, never compromising Jewish law's expectations for women, but allowing her intellectual bent to flourish within this context. The *chassidishe* girls at times combine an intriguing imperviousness to peer pressure with their devotion to spiritual life.

The "normal" girls may have more difficulty shaping their individ-ual desires to fit Lubavitch ideals, but they conform more strictly to so-cial convention. Like most secular schools, Bais Rivka has its cliques, and the cliques of "normal" girls tend to have the power to decide what's cool and what's *nebby,* a popular term among the girls that means "geeky" or "nerdy." The term grew out of the common Yiddish word *nebbish* (a pathetic person or loser) and displays this community's intriguing penchant for anglicizing Yiddish and Hebrew words. Lubav-itch young women have created their own nominative form of the word, which they bestow on some of the *chassidishe* girls: *neb,* a person who may not be a loser but who lacks even the faintest glimmer of chic. With their less fashionable clothes, minimal knowledge of secular cul-ture, and quieter demeanor, many *chassidishe* girls never achieve social prestige.

Of course, the issue is more complex. Many passionately spiritual girls with real charisma are extremely well liked. Some people are so charming that they can win popularity despite seemingly *nebby* ways; others manage to combine style and *chassidishe* ideals. And not all *nebs* are overly religious. Nevertheless, there seems to be a certain acceptable level of compliance with Lubavitch law and custom on the whole. De-viation in either direction can create stigma. Both the least and the most observant young women are often willing to place personal beliefs and tendencies above peer approval.

The fear many community members harbor that the "normal" girls' craving for popularity and secular culture saps their spiritual drive de-rives from a very particular yardstick. For all their shenanigans and cool clothes, even the most chic "normal" girls are unflaggingly Lubavitch.

At the frequent class gatherings held at schoolmates' homes, they belt out tunes of longing for the Messianic age and the Rebbe's return to the world.

Take Sara, the queen bee of her eleventh-grade clique. Striking and fashion savvy, she spends her weekends in chunky boots, long skirts, and sweaters that could line the Urban Outfitters display window. Unbeknownst to her highly traditional parents, she catches an occasional mainstream movie on a friend's VCR. She walked me home one Shabbos after services and began explaining why she knows the Rebbe is the Messiah: "He's just so perfect. He is such an amazing, amazing man, beyond words even. And he is still with us. I can feel it. He'll be coming back any day now as Moshiach [the Messiah]. I just know it." Her bright eyes, so often used as subtle tools to goad her friends into joining her pranks, sparkled with spiritual energy. In the secular world, her lucky combination of brains, personality, and looks may well have yielded her a dazzlingly successful career, but her future goals are clear: to raise a Jewish family and to help out in the Lubavitch community.

I did discover a few girls, perhaps 1 percent, who juggle a strong commitment to Lubavitch observance with an unusual interest in high-powered professions. One young woman plans to be a doctor. She attended the modern Orthodox Stern College—a highly atypical move, since Stern upholds a different, more modern form of Orthodoxy—because it outstrips the ultra-Orthodox Touro in resources and reputation. During my year in Crown Heights, she got married; she is now a medical student who zestfully balances domestic duties and intense study.

This young woman's emphasis on career goals is atypical for both men and women in this culture. For most Lubavitchers, jobs are only a necessary means to provide for a family. The vast majority of men and a substantial number of women work, since the average Lubavitch family has eight children who need financial support. Teaching in the community's schools and secretarial work are typical jobs for Lubavitch women. Many Lubavitch men teach as well; education is central to this group. Business is also common among the men, particularly the diamond and computer industries. The *baalei teshuvah* often have college degrees and add a heavy sprinkling of professionals to the community. But career identification is not an important source of prestige or self-esteem here. The old-line Lubavitchers, who rarely attended college and sometimes have blue-collar jobs, often have more status than the newly religious professionals in Crown Heights.

As in nearly any community, money does bestow a certain power. Deep pocketbooks can tip the balance in seminary admissions, placement in the choice spots for outreach work, teaching jobs right in Crown Heights, enrollment in the most desirable camps, marriage decisions; the list is nearly infinite.

Even so, a reputation for true holiness will yield a Lubavitcher far greater respect than a large bank account or job success, and girls who emphasize professional goals often hail from exceptional situations. Some have *baal teshuvah* parents who retain a secular emphasis on high-powered careers. Others come from families of *shluchim*—emissaries of the Rebbe who run the worldwide Chabad Houses, exposing secular Jews across the globe to Orthodoxy. Most *shluchim*'s children take little from their surrounding neighborhoods, but in a few cases the prevailing attitudes of the non-Lubavitch Jews from the area influence them. When they reach high school, they often come to Crown Heights, where they board with families, but their prior associations from their hometowns can indelibly shape them.

The most career-oriented young women are typically outstanding students who are well liked by their peers. Their independent goals are tolerated and even respected; they are frequently praised for their intelligence and diligence. Of course, they are seen as being a bit unusual, but people attribute these girls' differences to their backgrounds and do not consider them rebellious.

About 10 percent (an average impression; some estimated far fewer) of Lubavitch young women are branded as rebels or, as some referred to them, often while wrinkling their noses in disgust, "bummy girls." They tend to push the limits of acceptable dress much farther than the "normal" girls do. Often their skirts are quite tight or a bit too short, perhaps just above the knee. Dress in itself doesn't define them, though—"normal" girls sometimes make similar clothing choices. The key is their behavior. These girls tend to be heavily involved with secular music, television, and movies. Many rebels flirt with neighborhood boys; some develop phone friendships with them; a few see their male friends in person. In very rare cases, these relationships can become physical. Hard-core rebels may sneak off regularly to Manhattan, where they explore clubs, cafés, and movie theaters. Some smoke cigarettes, and a few smoke pot. The wildest rebels have formed a small ganglike clique that features drugs, heavy-duty partying, and violent escapades. The majority of these young women have complete faith in the tenets of

Judaism, and most follow the basic aspects of Jewish law. Some say they wish they lived in a more modern Orthodox neighborhood; others hope someday to calm their impulses and become upstanding Lubavitchers.

Unlike the "rebels," the "questioners" doubt the core of Orthodox Judaism and Lubavitch thought. In time, they often shed the essentials of Orthodox Jewish law. Most are exceedingly bright. This group is tiny, about ten girls in the entire community. When these girls begin losing their faith and breaking Jewish law, they suffer. A complex interplay of fear that Orthodoxy might after all be "the truth," guilt at leaving behind a centuries-old tradition that their ancestors fought to preserve, and love for their parents whose values they are defying can torture the questioners. Their sanity seems to depend on finding like-minded friends.

Questioners and rebels come disproportionately, but by no means exclusively, from atypical Lubavitch families. Perhaps to compensate for their less religious backgrounds, some *baal teshuvah* parents are unusually strict, expecting extramodest dress or avoidance of social activities that typical Hasidim from birth might allow, like an outing to a public roller-skating rink. Their kids can buckle under the demands. Others maintain ties with secular culture and influence their families accordingly. If a father is still addicted to televised sports, his children may rationalize that late-night romance movies aren't much worse. Most Lubavitch proselytes find a comfortable middle ground and skillfully navigate the intricate terrain of Hasidic family life as new but savvy travelers. The vast majority raise children with a loving, unshakable faith in Hasidic doctrines and rituals. But the balance is tricky, and some falter.

The Lubavitchers' openness to all Jews produces *baalei teshuvah* from diverse backgrounds. There is a small but growing number of newly religious single or divorced mothers, and their children are much more likely to traverse basic boundaries than their peers from traditional homes. Their rebellion can range from subtle deviations from the dress code to full-scale renouncement of faith.

For some people, Lubavitch offers a seeming solution to psychological problems that linger long after they settle into Hasidic life, and their emotional difficulties are certain to plague their children, even if their families are technically intact. Typical new Lubavitchers are well-adjusted, likable people whose success out in the "real world" makes their choice incomprehensible to their nonreligious friends. The *baal teshuvah* crowd includes many accomplished doctors, lawyers, teachers, journalists, artists, and academics. In some cases, though, Hasidism fills gaping needs—the depressed woman who escapes her misery by exulting in the Rebbe's powers, the socially awkward man who lands in Crown Heights because of all the ready-made friends there who love him because he is Jewish. Sensing their parents' underlying turmoil, these people's children can feel unsettled and dissatisfied with Lubavitch.

Among the old-line Hasidim as well, divorce and severe family tension are rare but certainly exist and can predispose children to rebellion. Still, background is hardly all-determining. Some young women from nontraditional homes are unswervingly *chassidishe*, and some from elite old-line Lubavitch families with no unusual problems resist basic expectations, running to Manhattan clubs with friends, throwing wild parties, even losing faith in Judaism. A complex of factors may compel young Lubavitchers to rebel. For some, family dynamics are key; for others, an inborn inclination toward independent thinking or thrill seeking seems to provoke nonconformity.

The most contemplative girls—those who have wrestled with the fundamental issues of Lubavitch theology—often fall into one of two categories: Some embody the *chassidishe* ideal. The power and splendor of Lubavitch philosophy awe them, and spirituality drives their behavior, thoughts, and dreams. Others doubt. Troubled by perceived conflicts and inequities, a few lose faith. Lubavitch philosophy is exquisitely refined and poetically sensitive. It also propounds unyielding conceptualizations of holiness and appropriate human behavior. Incisive, concerned exploration in this realm cultivates passion. Spiritual ecstasy can result, as can anger, bitterness, and resentment.

The *chassidishe* girls and the questioners were the easiest for me to get to know. Both groups attracted unusually bright young women who were fascinated by the idea of a secular writer studying their lives. Since they were often less immersed in the social life of Crown Heights, they were more open to the friendship of an outsider. The *chassidishe* girls hoped to persuade me to become more religious, and the questioners relished the chance to hear about growing up in a secular community. I did interview several "normal" girls, and many of them were quite friendly. But I had to work to ingratiate myself with them; they were too busy enjoying their active lives to gravitate to me spontaneously.

The girls at both extremes of the spiritual divide tended to be less satisfied with the status quo of Crown Heights than their more average peers. "Normal" girls' dissatisfactions often revolved around surface rules. Most complained about aspects of the school dress code. They were annoyed that they had to wear full-length stockings when their teachers often wore socks; they did not understand why their shirts had to be tucked in; some wished they could wear nail polish or longer earrings to school. A few noted that girls have shorter tethers than boys in the reputation arena. A night out with friends at, say, a mixed-gender pool hall can tarnish a girl's name but will probably leave a boy's honor unscathed.

Despite their minor complaints, most of the "normal" girls are fundamentally content. They praised the warmth of their community and the social life of their school. The "normal" girls are the mainstay of the strong network of organized social activities for high school and seminary students. Shabbos and weeknight gatherings at classmates' homes, dramatic productions, and other events are infused with their energy and liveliness. On the whole, they are thankful that they are girls, not boys, because the boys spend much more time at school and have fewer outlets for nonacademic interests. When I asked one of these young women to consider what her life would be like if she were a boy, her response was unequivocal: "*Baruch Hashem* [thank God] I'm a girl. I don't know how the boys stand being in school for so long."

Many of the most spiritually passionate *chassidishe* girls longed for a holier community. One girl shared her anger at the pettiness of many of her peers; she wished for classmates who focused less on shopping, causing trouble at school, and impressing their friends and more on honing their spirituality. This young woman felt alienated from Bais Rivka's social atmosphere: "Half the time I don't know what to say to most of the girls," she complained. Others hinted at similar feelings. They said little outright in deference to the belief that a true Hasid loves all fellow Jews and realizes that it is impossible to judge others' behavior; one human being can never truly understand the challenges of another. In keeping with her thirst for a holy life, an ardent *chassidishe* girl yearned to be a boy, since the boys' education is more intellectually rigorous and spiritually charged. Her desire had been much more intense a few years before our interview, but she still felt a dissonance between her scholarly bent and the Lubavitch expectation that she focus her energies on the home.

This young woman's dissatisfaction combined with most "normal" girls' distaste for the boys' lives underscores a crucial point: Stereotypes notwithstanding, the boys don't have it better than the girls in any absolute sense. They may appear to have more power in certain spheres, but they do not on the whole seem more content or more optimistic about their futures than the girls. The potential difficulty with Lubavitch gender roles lies in their rigidity. The few people, male or female, who feel they fall outside the boundaries of their defined gender role can endure pain and confusion.

People who dislike Judaic studies or who have varied interests would prefer the girls' lives because girls have much more latitude than boys to pursue the arts and academic subjects beyond Judaism. On the other hand, the boys' schools are better funded. For those who enjoy Judaic studies, the boys' classes in this area are more extensive and more profound. Girls' household chores are considerably more copious, and their reputations are more easily tarnished by infractions large and small. Of course, in the religious sphere, men are given the public roles in the synagogue and community. Most girls were unconcerned with the men's preeminence in public religious life; they accepted the notion that privacy is the epitome of holiness.

Each situation has its advantages and its limitations. A studious sort with a theological bent would relish the boys' long hours of Talmudic study. An artistic type would love the yearly theatrical production written and performed by the girls and might feel lost and unappreciated in the boys' schools, which offer few diversions from traditional academics. Most people simply accept their roles, but a few bristle.

Not surprisingly, the most impassioned questioners are the most embittered against Crown Heights society. They rail against beliefs they find irrational and expectations they find absurd. Many particularly deplore the role of women in Hasidic culture: they want improved academics and more overt power both in public life and in the family. Through friendship and intensive interviews, I developed an intimate sense of the alienation young women at the margins of Hasidic culture can feel; anyone who senses complete dissonance between her central beliefs and her community's expectations will endure deep psychic strife. These people form a minuscule proportion of the Crown Heights Hasidim, but they gave me a fascinating perspective on the issues of independent voice, individuality, and the boundaries of acceptable behavior in Lubavitch.

The group that would gather on Montgomery Street at the edge of the Hasidic neighborhood was exemplary. Most Crown Heights Lubavitchers knew nothing about the apartment at 888 Montgomery Street, but rumors were spreading. Some thought it was the site of a continuous orgy. Others heard it was more like an opium den, inhabited by people in a drug-induced cloud. Still others whispered about poetry readings: secular poetry, that is, writing that mentions ideas and desires unthinkable within the Lubavitch tradition.

The reality was less flamboyant than the rumors. Actually, the apartment known affectionately as "888" was a gathering spot for young Lubavitch dissenters. Aviva and Devorie—two Lubavitch young women who had run away from their families—lived there, and they opened their home every night to assorted friends and hangers-on. Their two friends Rochel and Miriam half lived at 888 as well; they were there virtually every night. On a typical evening, about twelve young men and women in their late teens and twenties would gather at 888. Of course, the mixed-gender social setting was in itself highly significant. Some of these Hasidim had lost all belief; some believed wholeheartedly but yearned for outside knowledge and experience; some were exploring and were not quite sure what to think at this point. Most prided themselves on their willingness to buck prevailing trends. As Rochel said many times, "My mother claims that I hang out with the lowest elements in Crown Heights, but really we're the highest." To Crown Heights at large, they were benighted, horribly misguided young people, but they saw themselves as the few proud souls who ferreted out the truth.

The predominant activity was intellectual banter. These people craved secular knowledge and culture: philosophy, literature, music, and film. Every new book read or thought pondered was an event to share, discuss, and argue over. "I *loved* that book. You *have* to read it," people would continually inform each other. Many of them also wrote, and they often shared their work with their friends. Most felt bitter about their lack of exposure to secular ideas and trends, and they were trying to make it all up fast.

Their passionate discussions would have delighted the typical college instructor; students at the most elite universities rarely tackle ideas with this sort of energy. Lubavitch community leaders, however, would have been horrified. Discussions at 888 were a traditional Lubavitcher's worst nightmare of the dangers of secular knowledge. Not only were these young scholars taking time away from Jewish studies to explore secular ideas, but they engaged head-on with writers ranging from the Christian Kierkegaard to the existentialist Camus, viewing those thinkers as potential sources of truth as they struggled to define life-driving worldviews. Hasidic Jews believe that the Torah encompasses all knowledge and wisdom; any ideas that contradict the Torah are heresy.

A quick survey of the apartment revealed seeming contradictions that made perfect sense if you knew where these people came from and what they were going through. A poster of John Lennon dangling a large cigarette from his mouth shared wall space with pictures of little boys with big yarmulkes—Devorie's brothers. The huge bookshelf housed works ranging from philosophical and literary classics to *The Joy of Gay Sex* to mountains of books on Jewish history and thought. A large mezuzah, an encased biblical parchment observant Jews attach to their doors, was placed prominently outside the apartment. Inside, religious rituals were shed.

As for drugs and sex, often one of the young men would roll a joint to liven up the festivities. The guys showed more interest than the girls, who would take perfunctory puffs that rarely altered their moods. I never witnessed anything remotely resembling an orgy. I did see yeshiva boys reaching out awkwardly, hungrily, to hug the girls, a weighty act in a culture that forbids males and females to touch. Miriam and 888 regular Dovid had been dating for months; they had long surpassed the awkward groping stage. Devorie, who called herself "promiscuous by anyone's standards," worked as a waitress at a strip club, but she was not one of the strippers and said she would never disrobe for money.

Male homosexuality was a common topic at 888, and a few of the girls hinted at lesbian desires. Because the traditional family is the nucleus of Lubavitch life, homosexuality would place a Lubavitcher beyond all boundaries of acceptability. Some Lubavitchers submerge homosexual attractions and carry out their duty to marry and start families. For the few who cannot or will not do so, alienation from the community is inevitable.[17]

So far, this may sound much like any artsy-intellectual-eccentric crowd at a secular American college. But the 888ers' Lubavitch upbringing defined and shaped them. Most of the guys sported the black pants, white shirt, ritual fringes, yarmulke, and beard of the typical Lubavitch man, even inside 888. My first glimpse of one of these rabbinical-looking figures puffing on a joint seemed surreal. These young men and women peppered their speech with Yiddish words and phrases. Perhaps most telling, they retained a zest for Jewish learning, a strong penchant for discussing Jewish issues, a hearty pride in their heritage, a love of Judaic culture, and a desire to spread their religious knowledge to secular Jews.

One evening I spent with them at Wetlands, a neohippie club in Manhattan, showed me how thoroughly Lubavitch these dissidents remained. Like their more traditional peers who searched out Jews on the streets to inform them of upcoming Jewish holidays, their Jewish radar was fine-tuned. When Rochel discovered two yarmulke-topped heads in the crowd, she said sarcastically: "Look. Jew boys." But she zoomed over to meet them and was thrilled to discover that they had been to the Boston Chabad House, a branch of the international Lubavitch outreach network. Soon, the 888ers began singing Hasidic tunes and attracting a little following of curious Jewish men. They were eager to let other Jews into their circle and share their songs. Here, in this club that broke practically every existing law of Jewish modesty, the 888ers had found their *shlichus* (Lubavitch outreach) activity. In the most unlikely of places, they were spreading Hasidic culture. They proudly announced to anyone who cared to know that they were Lubavitchers; Devorie added that many of them came from old, prestigious families.

After going on to a Russian café, they showed their Lubavitch hearts. Lubavitch is a magnet for troubled Jews. Many families host lonely lost souls for Shabbos meals; a few even invite homeless people to live with them. Lubavitch emphasizes the innate holiness of all Jews, regardless of external circumstances. At a nonkosher restaurant, these young questioners showed that they had assimilated the lesson of *ahavas yisroel* (love for fellow Jews). A haunted man with a put-on Australian-sounding accent followed us to the café. "At least you're talking to me. Earlier, people were treating me like I have some sort of social disease," he told us. He joined us as we ate, and afterward, the young man with the car offered to drive him to his subway stop: a friendly, trusting gesture toward a man who was clearly a bit unstable.

The 888ers seemed quite certain that they were unique in the history of Crown Heights. There have been other nonconformist cliques, to be sure. Everyone at 888 laughed about fast-track rebels who pull credit card scams, gobble down cheeseburgers, and tear around the city in stolen cars. The 888 crowd stressed that intellectual searching fueled their disenchantment with Lubavitch. Therein lay their uniqueness. Other nonconforming cliques rebel just to rebel. When their members mature and calm down, they typically ease back into Orthodoxy. Rochel speculated: "They probably just give up after a while because they have nothing to replace Judaism with. They haven't thought out why they're doing what they're doing. Your whole life can't be based on: 'Oh boy. I can eat bacon and drive on Shabbos.'[18] When that gets old, they become observant again, for lack of anything better."

The 888ers were not simply acting out. Their questions touched the core of Lubavitch ideology, and their noncompliance with Jewish law often stemmed from heartfelt conviction. Many said they could never live like mainstream Lubavitchers again.

The 888 group is now defunct in name, if not in spirit. The four young women who held it together—Devorie, Aviva, Miriam, and Rochel—have moved from Crown Heights to a grimy Manhattan neighborhood a few subway stops away from Hunter, the city-run secular college they now attend. The year before, Devorie and Aviva had gone to Touro, an ultra-Orthodox Jewish college that has become increasingly popular among Lubavitch youth who worry about the financially precarious combination of no college education and large families. Rochel, the most outwardly traditional of the group, was in seminary. Devorie and Aviva felt intellectually constricted in an atmosphere where students wanted a painless degree, not a mental challenge. And Rochel could no longer bear the pressure of a double life; she loved Judaic studies but simply did not accept the ideas she was exploring. So they all decided to join Miriam at Hunter.

Of course, they could have stayed in Crown Heights and commuted to school, but the community's inflexible expectations had begun to seem unbearable. They wanted to wear their jeans outside (only Devorie had the gumption to do this on Crown Heights streets). They didn't enjoy slinking around with their nonkosher food. They wished they could acknowledge their male friends in public. Above all, they longed to break cleanly and decisively from Crown Heights. It was hard, especially because they all had wonderful friends in the community, but they felt it was necessary. Aviva captured the predominant sentiment well: "I have great friends here, but I can't be myself. I'm constantly hiding so many things, and that sucks." Now in Manhattan, everybody combines school and long hours of work; no one receives money from home.

These young women's backgrounds reflect the diversity of Crown Heights Lubavitchers. Outreach to secular Jews has created some heterogeneity at the fringes of this community. Miriam's parents are *baalei teshuvah* who became religious as young adults. They have been divorced for many years, and Miriam lived with her mother until moving to Manhattan. Aviva's mother became religious shortly after Aviva was born. Her father, non-Jewish and black, had no place in this new life. Her parents were never married, and they drifted apart. Aviva has only recently begun repairing her relationship with her father. Devorie and Rochel hail from old, established Lubavitch families.

Both Aviva and Miriam felt stigmatized growing up. They were oddballs in a community where broken homes were rare, and Aviva shuddered when she heard the constant lambasting of black people that reverberated throughout this racially tense neighborhood. There was one other black girl in school, the product of her Lubavitch mother's rebellious fling, but Aviva was the only one in her grade. Clearly, overt marginality helped spur Miriam and Aviva to question, but Devorie and Rochel had elite lineage and intact, admired families. Their nonconformity seems to stem from inherent tendencies toward independence both in action and in thought. They each remember simply not accepting basic Lubavitch beliefs early in life, and both moved through childhood with bold disregard for behavioral expectations. Rochel admitted her lack of faith in front of her entire class; Devorie palled around town with a non-Jewish neighbor and experimented early with sex.

Though diverse in background, these young women have nurtured a profoundly sensitive friendship. They know just what to say to help each other surmount stress and insecurity. The group has nurtured Rochel through her estrangement from her parents, offered stability to Miriam and Aviva as they struggled with broken families, and helped Devorie through several failed romances. After years of feeling freakish, they have found like-minded companions.

I know these young women extremely well. As outcasts from the Crown Heights scene, they were the most open to the friendship of an outsider. I have interviewed them and spent many informal hours with them. Ranging in age from nineteen to twenty-three, they may seem just beyond the adolescent period, but their stage in life epitomizes adolescence. They are striving to define themselves, their life-driving beliefs, their goals and values: what to salvage from their rich upbringing, what to rework, and what to renounce.

I hope this introduction to the Crown Heights Lubavitch girls offers some sense of the tremendous range of personalities I encountered. Now that I have laid out intricate descriptions of different types, I must emphasize a crucial caveat: every one of these girls transcends these classifications; my road map offers only a surface orientation to the young women's indefinable minds and hearts. What's more, the categories are not inert. People shift and grow as they mature, and while basic orientations usually remain intact, crises of faith, mystical experiences, and the profound influence of friends, family members, or teachers can alter the course of a girl's life. A former hellion can become a model Hasid; a quiet, passionately observant girl can start to question.

The most fascinating part of this project was the intersection of background and personality: the interplay of religion, culture, rules, the ever-present outside world, and personal voice. Occasionally overt tensions surface, but more typically Lubavitch philosophy and personality interweave with grace. The analogy of two transparencies, one overlaying the other, seems apt. On top, for everyone, is Lubavitch culture. Beneath is a diagram of the individual psyche. The ink is wet, allowing for continuous seepage from one layer onto the other; every psyche is somehow shaped by its culture, and all cultures are defined by the individuals within them. It's a dynamic relationship, with the culture helping to shape the girls, and the girls, as the rising generation of adult Hasidic women, helping to define the future of Lubavitch. For a few, the psyche is drawn in bold, sweeping strokes. It is obvious at first glance, and it seems to clash with the upper layer in some fundamental way. For the vast majority, the psyche, while no less intricate, is fainter. It melds with the top layer, and the two transparencies together project a harmonious image. But each psyche, combined with Lubavitch culture, creates a unique and elaborate picture.

Hasidim have known this all along; it is hardly a revelation to them that they develop independent, complicated personalities. But for many in mainstream America, these girls' delightfully idiosyncratic minds and lives may seem surprising. When sharing anecdotes about my Crown Heights year, I find that the most routine evidence of the young women's intricate personalities rivets my audience, since people often do not think about Hasidic girls as complex, active characters. "You met a girl who had a *crush*?" a friend asked, and from her tone she might have been reacting to a monthlong orgy on the synagogue steps.

Perhaps Americans tend to dehumanize Hasidim because of their marginality in contemporary culture. The issue is not life-defining religiosity per se; few express astonishment that historical women with traditional religious rearing and conviction had singular desires and thoughts. But today, in a world where most teenage girls wear pants and many have boyfriends, Hasidic girls can seem more like anachronistic relics than the struggling, triumphing, giggling, brooding, hating, loving human beings who, of course, they are.

2

The Cast

THIS PROJECT INUNDATED ME with intriguing characters; Hasidic girls are endlessly fascinating. The interaction of quirky personalities, typical teenage hang-ups, entrenched religious doctrine, and a world-view infused with mystical notions gives these adolescents complexity and mystery. I made scores of young friends in Crown Heights, and every one could inspire a rich study. If the Messiah comes and perfects the world, as most Lubavitchers believe he surely will, some writer touched by God will write hundreds of books, capturing the beauty and spirit of every last girl in Crown Heights. Alas, that divinely inspired artist is not among us. You must bear with a well-meaning but imperfect woman who can complete only one book at a time.

A large question looms: How did I condense all that I learned and experienced into a single project? I could have written broad, thematic chapters on topics like "school," "home," and "time with friends." This setup would have allowed me to introduce many girls briefly, offering hundreds of cameo appearances to illustrate the subject at hand. But my focus was the girls themselves, and my driving goal was to know them in a profound sense, to delve into their minds and souls. From the beginning, I envisioned chapters that spotlight individual girls, portraits that give readers intimate knowledge of the young women's idiosyncrasies.

Of course, this strategy involved a difficult selection process. Fifty portraits make an unwieldy book; a few girls must suffice. How did I choose the people who will, for better or worse, come to symbolize Lubavitch teenage girlhood in my readers' minds?

My central interests helped to shape my choices. The girls' personalities and thoughts—how they manifest themselves within the framework of Hasidic norms and how far they can develop before they break the boundaries of acceptability—undergird this project. My fascination with boundary pushing has landed several limit stretchers in these pages. A random sampling of seven Lubavitch girls would surely not yield a future doctor *and* an infidel banned from her home *and* an adventurer who checks out a strip club. An entire Bais Rivka grade of over one hundred students might contain only five members who are that marginal.

Still, I did try to portray a range of backgrounds and religious orientations. Most estimates suggest that children of *baalei teshuvah* now form a slim majority in Lubavitch schools. And while most Bais Rivka students are Brooklyn natives, many girls come to Crown Heights after years of emissary work around the world. My profiles suggest the diversity of Bais Rivka society, with Crown Heights old-timers and denizens of remote Lubavitch outposts, children of old-line Hasidim and new recruits' kids. Rebels and questioners are disproportionate, but more typical Lubavitchers have a substantial and varied showing: a likable young woman whose susceptibility to peer pressure can ensnare her in some humorous scrapes, a charismatic school leader with an infectious adoration for Hasidism, an intensely spiritual soul who tries to subsume all her desires within Lubavitch aspirations (the very force of her religious conviction makes her unusual, and her quest for mystical enlightenment is every bit as much a battle to express independent voice as her neighbor's attempt to master secular philosophy). I want my readers to have a deep appreciation for the diversity of people who make up this seemingly monolithic group.

I must make one point clear: in no way are the girls I profile in the following pages "representative" of other people. It may be tempting to see these young women primarily as types: a *chassidishe* girl, a questioner, a normal girl, a rebel. But these classifications offer only a faint glimmer of Lubavitch girls' lives. Not all of these young women fall neatly into categories. I remember Dini—passionately spiritual like the most *chassidishe* girls, popular and playful like the "normal" contingent, an unabashedly independent thinker like the die-hard questioners. Even the people who seem to fit nicely into a type are distinct human beings. I do not believe that one person can represent another; these girls have unique ideas, personalities, styles of behavior, modes of thought. One popular young woman does not speak for all her popular peers; a particular questioner offers only an individual struggle with Hasidic norms.

I have tried to craft descriptions that present these girls in all their idiosyncratic splendor. I quote from intimate conversations, describe private moments, re-create scenes from their daily lives. Though I do my utmost to capture the true essence of each young woman, details have been changed. I have altered names, family backgrounds, particulars of interactions and events, ages, physical qualities, and other identifying characteristics of everyone I describe in this book. Identities are completely disguised. One girl and her family did give me permission to share some potentially revealing details; the very basics of her life goals are central to her character but unusual enough to spark recognition. Even with her, I changed several pieces of information. I hope to share these girls' quirks and quandaries without destroying their privacy.

Core concerns converge for many of these young Hasidim despite their diversity. This was yet another impetus to choose them; they show the range of reactions one issue can inspire among Lubavitch girls. I think of four young women wrestling with the role of the Hasidic female. Leah is an ardently religious soul who longs for the life of a male scholar; Dini is a well-liked, athletic, self-described tomboy mystified by her friends' love of clothes shopping; Malkie is a proud Lubavitcher with a weakness for using men's deodorant and a desire for a high-powered career; Rochel's anger about gender disparities in religious ritual and education helped spur her to renounce Orthodox Judaism.

Placed together in a dormitory suite, these four would probably go insane, but a central conflict binds them all. Take Rochel and Leah, ostensible opposites. Rochel seems the consummate questioner in her combat boots and cut-off shorts; Leah exemplifies Lubavitch ideals, from her unfailingly modest dress to her impassioned desire to bring as many Jews as possible around to the Hasidic way.

Rochel's sensitive, rigorous intellect led her to leave Lubavitch. She eventually realized that Hasidic doctrine did not square with her own logic, and, besides, she deeply resented her brothers' extensive exposure to the Talmud and preeminence in the public aspects of religious life. Males, it seemed, got to do all the things she longed to try in Lubavitch—spend long hours probing mystical texts, lead religious rituals, sing traditional songs in mixed-gender company (women's singing is banned in front of unrelated men, for fear of arousing male sexual desire). Rochel drifted away from Lubavitch and found herself enmeshed in a crowd more interested in erotic poetry and gaining admittance to secular college than in the Rebbe's directives.

Leah felt nearly as alienated from the traditional Lubavitch woman's role. She craved the life of the male scholar, with his utter devotion to the intellect and spiritual delving; the thought of dedicating her days to child care and housework made her shudder. Like Rochel, Leah thought and thought, read and read, trying to master the nuances of Hasidism's understanding of gender. Unlike Rochel, Leah eventually made peace with her role, figuring out ways of combining it with study and philosophical speculation, her true loves.

In Crown Heights circles, Rochel is seen as a brilliant bandit, Leah as a soft-spoken, saintly girl. These two young women started with very similar dissatisfactions but arrived at radically different conclusions. If the rebel in the red bandanna and the pious community volunteer met for pizza, they just might enjoy a rewarding conversation, for they have much in common. I am reminded of Rochel's comment to her lapsed Lubavitch friends: "If I believed, you'd all hate me; I'd be the most observant person around." The hellion could have been a saint.

Likewise, my main characters have merged unusual interests and Lubavitch upbringing in diverse ways. Gittel seamlessly combined medical training and Orthodox convictions. One minute she was studying Hasidic thought with two devout friends; the next, she was reviewing organic chemistry for the following day's exam. Her parents favored this sort of balance between this-worldly goals and Hasidic beliefs, so she never felt schizophrenic or freakish. This was life, hectic and frenzied at times, but perfectly reasonable.

An acquaintance of hers, Malkie, had ambitious though less defined dreams; she toyed with possibilities like academia and business, but she rarely discussed these ideas with her parents, devout *baalei teshuvah* who hoped their children would devote their lives completely to Lubavitch, with no interference from outside interests or concerns. She was silent about her unusual goals at school as well; only a few trusted friends knew of her ambitions. Many knew only one side of her persona—a studious young woman with a powerful faith that the Rebbe will soon usher in the Messianic age. She plans to pursue her dreams quietly, in combination with her desire to devote a large part of her life to recruiting new Lubavitchers.

Other girls felt more blatant rifts between their passions and Lubavitch expectations. Chaya's musical talent helped to alienate her from Lubavitch for a time; her beloved rock and roll is an anathema in

Hasidic circles. But she is slowly finding her way back to Hasidism, intending to combine her musical interests and an Orthodox lifestyle. She hopes to find a Hasidic husband who will respect her gift and allow her time to cultivate it, a breed she says is "rare but certainly around."

Finally, Rochel's immersion in secular philosophy and literature was a key factor in ousting her once and for all from Lubavitch life. When she told her parents about her plan to attend a secular college, they kicked her out of the house, for fear that she would influence her brothers and sisters. She moved away from Crown Heights, swearing off Hasidic life.

Different people, different personalities, reacting to various family dynamics and levels of commitment to Lubavitch ideals: this group hints at the tremendous range of girls I encountered in Crown Heights. Even young women who share the crucial bond of nonconformity have found diverse ways of handling their unusual talents and desires.

Yet every one of the girls I profiled experienced a Lubavitch upbringing. They were all raised by people who believe in the mystical power of Jewish rituals, in the Rebbe's holiness, in the urgency of sharing spiritual knowledge with Jews around the world. In the midst of their differences, profound similarities emerge. Each one of these girls quotes from the *Tanya,* the preeminent text of Lubavitch philosophy, in describing her life. They all have an acute awareness of Lubavitch's emphasis on the Messianic era, even if, in Rochel's case, scorn is the strongest reaction that emerges. Jewish thought infuses their self-conceptions; they have, after all, been engaging with it since birth. These girls share a passion, an awe, and a sense of the mystical importance of their actions that surely derive from their religious training.

Estie, for instance, was a fun-loving sort with a quietly winning personality. High school for her often seemed like a whirlwind of social gatherings and expeditions into Manhattan with her closest pals. She was easygoing, casual, nonbrooding. But, in the midst of all the pleasure, Estie was constantly weighing spiritual considerations. An evening with her friends in Manhattan spurred a reverie on divinely chosen mates; as she slipped into a funky outfit for a neighbor's engagement party, she contemplated the Rebbe's powers and longed for his return to earth as the Messiah. She is typical of her peers in this respect—most Lubavitch girls have an uncanny ability to fuse the day-to-day and the godly. Indeed, every one of these young women presents a variation on the theme of nitty-gritty life and personal whims intermixed with sublime intentions and laws meant to help Jews touch holy realms.

But I have expounded long enough on my own thoughts; it is now time to meet the girls. These young women are all intriguing, thoughtful people whose stories can speak for themselves. I hope you enjoy getting to know them as much as I did.

3

Esther (Estie) Gutman

Wild Times and Holy Designs

ESTIE WAS TRAPPED. Unholy situations had been springing up throughout this strange night, but they were the minor, laugh-it-off kind, the sort that came with the territory if you wanted fun friends. This final quagmire loomed larger, for it would take the indiscretions of the evening and drive them, literally, back into Crown Heights. It could trash Estie's reputation if the wrong person saw, misunderstood, and, in the common manner of Crown Heights, spread word around. Slanderous gossip is a serious sin, one that can inflict severe harm on the perpetrator, the subject, and the listener through the inexplicable powers of hidden mystical forces. Hasidism teaches that the smallest of actions unleashes potent spiritual consequences. Rumormongers inflict foul energy upon the world and upon themselves; God only knows what disaster might plague the woman who badmouths her neighbor. But this sort of misfortune is common in Crown Heights, as it is in any tight-knit community where people have tongues and curious minds.

The day had started out innocently enough. Bais Rivka was on Hanukkah break, and two of Estie's friends from her twelfth-grade class had invited her to go clothes shopping in Manhattan. Shopping went well; Estie found a long denim skirt and a pair of blue and white striped sneakers. Then the girls stopped off to play a few rounds of pool at a nearby hall. The people there were hardly Orthodox specimens. Not many were Jewish at all, judging from the looks of them; they fit Estie's vision of the *goyim*, the non-Jewish nations. There were lots of *goyishe* men with muscular, tattooed arms who chugged beer and flirted with women. The place stank a bit from all the beer. One guy even came over and winked at Estie's friend Bayla, a black-haired, brown-skinned beauty. "I'll buy you a drink, Love. Any time you want," he offered. But the girls laughed and waved him away; they surely did not want any

73

part of his generosity. Still, if their mothers knew. . . . Estie squelched that thought as soon as it entered her mind. They were just playing a game and unwinding with friends; there was nothing wrong with that.

When they got hungry, they found themselves at a kosher Chinese restaurant, feasting on egg rolls, mushroom lo mein, and diet Cokes. The food was a bit soggy and bland, but the religious Jewish owners tried hard to please, and the girls enjoyed the meal; it wasn't as if they had ever tried authentic Chinese cooking. This was adventure enough, with the little containers of duck sauce for dipping and menu choices like egg foo young and sweet-and-sour chicken delight.

All the area yeshivas were on vacation, so the restaurant was filled with modern Orthodox kids. Many of the girls had rolled their sleeves above their elbows, and the guys had knitted yarmulkes and clean-shaven faces; they looked like typical American boys, unlike the black-hatted, scraggly-faced young men Estie was used to from Crown Heights. The boys and the girls talked and teased each other, a very different scenario from the gender-segregated world of Crown Heights. Estie noticed a guy she thought was cute—a slim young man with a little knitted yarmulke clipped onto a thick bush of brown curly hair.

Quickly, she looked away from him and concentrated on her friends, who were entertaining enough that she could avoid focusing on forbidden fruits. Shula was loudly talking about her time at camp the previous year, swishing her long brown hair as she disclosed incriminating details about one of the snootiest girls in her bunk: "If she thought your sneakers were a little *nebby* or something, she wouldn't even greet you if she saw you outside. Like, hello, *nebby* sneakers are not a contagious disease." Bayla screeched with delight. Estie laughed, too, quietly at first but then almost as loudly as Bayla. Estie wished she had the discipline to act more like a *bas Chabad,* a true daughter of Lubavitch, someone who would behave more modestly in public, mixed-gender settings like this one. But it was so relaxing and pleasant here, just letting loose with her buddies, that she didn't try as hard as she might have.

They talked and talked, laughed and laughed, and soon it was after midnight, time to think about getting back to Crown Heights. Taking the subway back at that time scared them all a bit, but a taxi would cost a fortune, so they resigned themselves to a late-night subway ride. Then Bayla spied her cousin Mayer, a handsome fellow of about twenty, just a few years older than the girls. He recognized her, too, and came to the table to say hello. Mayer didn't sit with them—that would have been immodest—but they all exchanged pleasantries about the weather, school, and the like. "So how you getting home?" he asked them.

"Oh, the subway. It's a little seedy at night, but we'll live."

"Well, I have a car. You can come with me."

It was quite a proposition. Sure, Mayer was Bayla's relative, but only a third cousin or something like that; she couldn't remember exactly. He was certainly not part of her immediate family, so Bayla and he would have to observe all codes of modesty, which would by no means allow sharing a car without adult supervision. And Estie and Shula were not even related to him. It would be a very un-*chassidishe* thing to do.

Then again, the subway was dangerous so late at night, and adventures like this didn't come up very often.

The girls were silent for about a minute before Bayla piped up, "Sure, why not?"

Shula immediately agreed.

Estie held out a little longer. She wished she were at home; she did not like the way this evening was turning out at all. This behavior was completely unbecoming to a Lubavitch young woman. It was wrong, and it could ruin her reputation if anyone found out. The dating and marriage process was not far away for her, and if anyone saw her driving into Crown Heights with this young man, her chances of finding a good match would plummet. She could just picture it: some nice boy's mother would mention Estie's name to the matchmaker, who would harrumph and hesitate and finally say: "Possibly. . . . But keep in mind that she was spotted one night driving home with a single young man." That would be that. The doting mother would not want this match for her darling son; who knows what sort of stunt such a woman might play in the future?

Faith in an omnipotent God can breed sluggishness about our own part in shaping the world, a feeling that, if everything is in divine hands, we might as well sit back and enjoy the show. Not in Lubavitch. Certainly not when marriage looms. People take their decisions very seriously, and marriage is the defining event in a Hasidic life. Hasidism teaches that all Jews have divinely ordained mates whom they will marry in the course of events, who on a spiritual level will complete their personalities. But this belief does not create complacency when it comes to the marriage process. People monitor their behavior meticulously to ensure that they land the best possible spouses, and parents work the phone lines and gossipmongers every bit as hard as their prayer sessions when their children are ready to marry.

This fling could give the mighty talebearers rich fodder. The prospect was not enticing. It was rather unfair, too, for the young man himself, the one who had instigated this whole sorry affair, would get off much more easily. People would chuckle about him and think, "Oh, he's a good boy. He just experimented a teeny bit." A girl does not get away as freely; one bad move and her good name could die.

These thoughts flitted through Estie's mind for about thirty seconds before she agreed: "Sure, I'll go with you guys." She was not one to buck her friends. If someone else had balked, Estie would have sided with her immediately. But alone, she went with the flow, never wanting to risk social alienation or bad vibes.

So all three girls hopped into Mayer's cranky old Buick sedan, and, when they neared the Crown Heights neighborhood, slunk down in their seats so nobody would see them, giggling all the while. The young man behind the wheel intrigued Estie; this was the first time she had ever seen a boy outside her family in such tight quarters. She stared at his thin reddish beard, his bony hands, his foot that floored the gas pedal hard and lurched them into motion, his bobbing Adam's apple as he yelled "Shmuck!" at a weaving car. She was surprised to find that, after his cowboy-like start, Mayer was a careful driver who got everyone home safely and, seemingly, with no repercussions.

Afterward, Estie felt a little guilty, but she is not one to obsess. Riding home with this guy wasn't the most saintly thing to have done, but she tries hard to behave according to her community's expectations, and if she backslides occasionally, she forgives herself and resolves to adhere to higher standards in the future.

Estie told me this story as we sat on the porch of her family's attached brick house—a fairly large home whose thirteen occupants can make it feel cramped at times. It was a humorous, emotional tale, and I think I did a reasonable job of mustering the appropriate surprise. The truth is, I had heard it before from Brocha Greenspan, a Bais Rivka teacher, though not in nearly as much detail and with some slightly different twists and elements.

Brocha's parents had invited me for Shabbos lunch, and when I heard that Brocha taught at Bais Rivka, I decided to pick her brain. I asked how she, as a fairly young teacher, would define that elusive term "normal girl" that was bandied about quite a bit at Bais Rivka. She asked me if I knew Estie and her friend Shula. At that point, I had not met either one. "They're it," she said, laughing. "They're the 'normal girl.' They're basically good kids, lively, active, popular, cute looking, well-dressed, strong students. Occasionally they get themselves into some mischief and find themselves in situations that the most *chassidishe* girls wouldn't dream of."

"Like what, for example?" I asked, salivating. It was early in my Crown Heights year, and I was hungry for some juicy material.

Brocha told me a spirited story about three Hasidic girls' day and night in Manhattan. She even knew that Estie had been the one to hesitate, for just a few seconds, before she went along with her friends: "Estie is sort of a 'nice girl' follower type. She's perhaps a bit stronger spiritually on her own than some of her friends, but she gives into peer pressure every time." I asked how Brocha had heard about this spree, and she told me: "Shula started bragging about it to some of her friends at school, and some of the teachers overheard." So much for secrets. But the rumor grapevine can be multifaceted. Estie was not blackballed for her complicity in the escapade; people understood that she's a good kid whose craving for popularity and horror of stirring tension inspired her indiscretion.

Estie's willingness to go with her friends' flow is both a weakness and a talent. A more independent, confident young woman would set her own boundaries, but she would frequently antagonize people, as all strong personalities do. Estie is rarely prickly; she enjoys an unusual gift—universal likability. She has a tempered charm that endears people without intimidating or overpowering them: confident with an edge of insecurity, quietly friendly, cute in a quirky sort of way, bright but not intensely intellectual. Her crewneck sweatshirts, denim skirts, and thick-soled striped sneakers fit right into Lubavitch after-school style. Estie's clothes, like her persona, are appealing but subdued; she fits in easily and unremarkably wherever she goes in Crown Heights.

Sociability is as inherent to Estie's nature as curly hair or large brown eyes. I spent an evening with her on the front porch outside her home, and she was constantly calling out greetings to friends as they passed by, often on their way to one of the many engagement celebrations always springing up in this community. She kept a cordless phone by her side, and I felt like a killjoy as the number of conversations postponed by our discussion mounted. I wondered why, if she didn't want to talk, she answered at all; she could have let her family take messages for her. But whenever one of her many friends called, the mystery was solved anew. She would light up, in a slightly different way for each pal, relishing the brief contact: "Hey, Hindele, I'm in the middle of a great conversation with Stephanie—you know, the one who's writing the book—but I'll talk to you really soon. Great to hear your voice." It was Estie's senior year of high school, and she seemed to want to savor her friends for a few last months before everyone headed off for seminaries around the world.

Her parents are the kind of *baalei teshuvah* who could grace a promotion brochure for Lubavitch. Yitzchok and Bassy Gutman have cultivated an ease in navigating Hasidic life that sometimes eludes newcomers to this world (though, amazingly, often does develop despite the tremendous overhaul in lifestyle and values that accompanies a transformation from secular American Jew to Hasid), and their active involvement in community affairs has given them an insider status that is unusual among the newly religious. Yitzchok is a dentist, a remnant of his middle-class secular Jewish upbringing. He made the final plunge into Hasidism shortly after dental school, following years of intense interest in observant Judaism inspired by dedicated Lubavitch mentors who worked with students at his upstate New York college. Bassy is a homemaker and child raiser responsible for eleven children— a challenging job that calls on her uncanny ability to shift effortlessly from psychologist to housecleaner to money manager to social director.

The Gutmans raise their eleven children, including their middle daughter, Estie, with affectionate strictness. They seem to have mastered the tricky balance of loving but not smothering their children. During my marathon conversation with Estie on the porch, both parents peeked out, smiled, and then quickly vanished inside the house in their characteristic involved but not overbearing fashion.

Estie's father, a hefty, jovial man with an infectious grin, seemed relieved when he heard my obviously Jewish last name. This was a boon throughout the project; I was a snoop, but I was a Jewish snoop, and in this community, that one fact catapults a person from stranger to kindred soul. I was embraced much more often than feared.

The Gutmans showed extensive hospitality toward this wayward but curious Jew; I have spent several Shabbos meals at their home. Bassy Gutman makes delicious holiday feasts, with traditional favorites like baked chicken and noodle pudding combined with slightly more exotic fare—eggplant spread, apricot sauce for the chicken, poached salmon. She brings out her creations quietly, with little commotion, as if they took no effort at all to prepare. No frenzy erupts at mealtime; Bassy has the whole production down cold. Holiday discussions here are relaxed but spirited. Parents, children, and guests take the time to catch up on each other's interests and concerns.

One Shabbos I arrived a bit before most of the family had come home from synagogue and spent some time talking with Bassy. She had endured a difficult childhood: her parents had nearly continuous health and financial problems, and the family was always in flux, moving from place to place in search of miracle doctors and jobs that could accommodate her parents' illnesses. I asked if she thought the stability of Hasidism was part of its appeal for her; she had found Lubavitch in college, just as she was breaking away from her family and working to develop a plan for her own life. She said, "No, no. I was attracted to Lubavitch because it was the truth. There was no reason other than the fact that my *neshama* [Jewish soul] responded to the truth." Still, as I looked at the dining room table with the candles flickering, adding a peaceful glow to the bookshelf packed with works on Jewish law and Lubavitch customs, I felt the serenity and predictability that Bassy most likely lacked as a child.

Of course, little glitches came up throughout the evening. The Gutmans' teenage son Eli, home for a short break from yeshiva in Australia, popped in and announced that he would be having Shabbos dinner with a school friend. Bassy was not pleased: "You're home for one Shabbos and you don't have dinner with your family?"

Eli clicked his tongue and scowled with relish. "I'll be here tomorrow," he muttered as he went on his way, checking out his new black hat in the hallway mirror. It was a typical adolescent scene, Hasidic style. The youngest Gutmans, wound up from synagogue, frisked about, knocking toys and, in one unfortunate swoop, spilling a bottle of grape juice. But Bassy adroitly cleaned up and quieted her children; it was all part of the normal course of events. Bassy and Yitzchok had perfected the art of peaceful living among children of all ages.

Bassy's easygoing manner offers no hint of a burdensome background. At this point in her life, she is settled and content. She has merged her past and present unusually well; she still carries herself with a hippie tinge that betrays her history of student activism. Her wigs are long and flowing, not like the typical Hasidic woman's thick shoulder-length style, and she often wears chunky clogs the likes of which would be difficult to find among the conservatively dressed life-long Lubavitchers. Many old interests have dissipated. Bassy no longer indulges in secular music or literature—she wants her soul to bask in purely Jewish pursuits. She doesn't seem to miss them; her life is full enough between her family and her loyal assistance with the many talks, gatherings, and publications the community sponsors for Lubavitch women.

Yitzchok, like the vast majority of Lubavitch men (there are exceptions among the *baalei teshuvah,* but they're rare), looks indistinguishable from his brethren who were always religious, with his black coat, hat, and beard. His speech pattern is a different story; exciting situations are "cool" or, in extreme cases, "a real trip." He comes from a supportive, middle-class secular Jewish family with few major problems, but their life seemed empty to him next to the spiritual depth of Lubavitch.

Estie feels she has been shaped by her parents' histories as *baalei teshuvah.* She has noticed that girls with *baal teshuvah* parents often bring more wonder and appreciation to Judaism than do girls whose families have been Hasidic for generations. They are less likely to take it for granted, for their own parents' lives were refashioned by its power: "I think personally that the girls that are born from *baalei teshuvah* are on a higher standard. They have more love for *Yiddishkeit* [Judaism]. They take it more as something that they love and not something that's just natural." She has also noticed that *baal teshuvah* parents tend to be a bit stricter, since they have witnessed firsthand the unsavory influences from which they hope to shield their children: "I think that since our parents are coming from there they sort of try to keep us more away from it, so that we shouldn't fall into it."

Ever the amenable pal, Estie has friends from all different Lubavitch backgrounds; she must often modulate her own standards to accommodate her friends' preferences. One afternoon I joined Estie at her friend Chani Silverman's house. There Estie encountered standards very different from her own and, in characteristic fashion, went along. Rock music blasted through the spacious top floor of the Silverman home, a stately brick mansion in the most affluent pocket of Crown Heights. Chani, the oldest daughter, was pounding away on the treadmill, spurred on by a popular New York rock station's lively tunes. Her sweatshirt was saturated with sweat. Chani is a petite young woman, short and wiry, with a sleekness to her body that suggests regular, heavy exercise. "Sorry! My workout will be over in about five minutes," she called out when she saw us. Listening to rock music is common among Lubavitch teenage girls, but it's typically a surreptitious pleasure, for the Rebbe had condemned all non-Jewish music as corrosive to the soul, particularly rock songs, whose lyrics are often deeply offensive to Hasidic sensibilities. In this house, there is no subterfuge. It's not necessary; Fradie and Moshe Silverman are confident that rock's hold on their children will pass, just as it did for them.

The Silvermans' relative permissiveness seems to stem from an optimism bred by opulence and an easy comfort with Lubavitch life. They both hail from a long line of elite Lubavitchers, and Judaism's complex array of observances has the comfort of a worn pair of sneakers. Moshe's jewelry business, inherited from his father, has enjoyed consistent success. Moshe and Fradie are sure that life will work out for their children, too, that a little freedom along the way won't harm them.

Meanwhile, Estie couldn't figure out whether to revel or cringe as she listened to the loud music that seemed to overtake the room. She would grin, nodding her head to the beat, then she would stiffen and look at her feet. Finally, the buzzer sounded, and Chani, soaked with sweat, stepped down from the treadmill. She bobbed a bit to the music before switching it off. To her it was a small, almost harmless indulgence. The music snapped off, and Estie exhaled loudly, in a curious combination of relief and regret.

For Estie, secular music is a complex issue fraught with anxiety, ambivalence, and, to make matters worse, pleasure. Only tunes written by a Jew, with no lyrics that offend Orthodox sensibilities, are considered kosher. The proportion of popular music that fits these criteria is vanishingly small. Even hearing a snippet of a song once on the radio could weaken a young woman's spiritual fortitude; music has heady mystical powers. Estie wants to keep her mind pristine, but she loves listening to music and eventually tires of Orthodox Jewish options.

A tough battle of will emerges. Estie explained to me after our afternoon at Chani's:

> You know, there are a few good Jewish singers, and I know every last one of their tapes by heart, with all the music and everything and every little way they move their voice and everything. I love it. But then once you finish that, you've listened to everything. And I know it

all by heart and I enjoy listening to it. But after a while it gets boring when you listen, so it's hard to keep away from the non-Jewish music. I try very hard.

She would never dictate the religious level in someone else's house, and, besides, it feels downright blissful to hear music that differs from the typical Orthodox tunes for a change. But she doesn't listen at home; when she is on her own, she tries hard to make decisions that will help her soul flourish.

Estie views the whole struggle as a slow upward climb. She is constantly trying to set higher standards for herself, to fall ever further along the side of strictness. Though she occasionally backslides, she keeps striving for that elusive goal of holiness: "You have to more or less set your own standards, you know, live up to where you want to go. And I mean you always have to strive for something higher. That's what a Jew is all about, a person is all about. Hashem [God] created human beings always to strive for a higher thing." She smiled and slung her leg over the porch banister. This is not an overwhelming, all-encompassing directive for her. She does what she comfortably can, trying to set progressively higher standards for herself as she matures. But if she fails at times, so be it; she has a whole lifetime to perfect herself.

Estie's familiar tug-of-war between spiritual passion and attachment to the mundane world has her a bit conflicted about her goals for the next few years. She enjoys religious studies, particularly the mystical aspects intrinsic to Lubavitch education, and she poignantly described Lubavitch's ability to imbue all aspects of Judaism with intellectual and emotional profoundness, to create an interrelated tapestry bound together by Hasidic thought: "I like the richness in Bais Rivka's Hebrew studies. You know, everything that you learn is integrated with *chassidus* [Hasidic philosophy] and the Rebbe's opinion, and all the previous Rebbes, and, you know, the *chassidus* outlook. And it's just so beautiful. You get such richness out of it. It's not just learning a plain story, blah, blah, blah." She offered a striking example:

It's so hard when you learn that Moshe [Moses] sinned. He was such a great *tzaddick* [spiritually perfected man]. How could he have sinned? And then you learn it according to *chassidus,* what it means on his level and what the sin meant. They put it in a whole different outlook and you look at it in such a positive light. I think that's the most beautiful thing about school, is that it's a Lubavitch school and that it teaches you this whole new rich world.

Lubavitch's exploration of Moses' psyche captures the power of this group's religious studies program. Issues are explored layer by layer, with a careful consideration of how human physical, emotional, and spiritual drives interact with the divine power that shapes every particle of the universe. Even the most lackadaisical students often feel personally galvanized by the classes on Hasidic philosophy and find that the biblical characters and Rebbes they study carry penetrating lessons for their own lives. There may be a lot of chattering, giggling, and practical jokes throughout school, but in the midst of it all, students pick up incisive lessons and insights that will inspire them for years to come. The same girls who stir pandemonium during school quote liberally from the *Tanya* when trying to make sense of their opinions, plans, ideas, and self-conceptions.

Seminary focuses solely on Judaic studies from a Lubavitch perspective, so the classes should captivate Estie. Nonetheless, the thought of two full years of this sort of schooling overwhelms her at times. "I can't think about two years of seminary right now. I just don't want to picture it," she told me when I asked about her future plans. We were walking outside on a sunny June day, and Estie cupped her hand over her eyes and stared intently into the distance, as if trying to divine her future from the expanse of urban buildings before us.

Her mother wants her to complete a full two-year seminary program, but Estie enjoys computers and has considered getting trained as a programmer at Touro College, an ultra-Orthodox school with gender-segregated classes, after one seminary year. As much as Hasidic thought enthralls Estie, her more practical, earthy side loves the nitty-gritty challenges of computers and math, her two favorite subjects in school.

As in so many realms, there is the spiritual ideal, and then there are Estie's desires, which fall just short. When I asked her about college, her ambivalence was palpable. She bit her nails and then grinned. It was a tough one: "You shouldn't go to college, especially not till after you're married and you have children [presumably, people are then less vulnerable to temptation and unholy influences]. The Rebbe doesn't think it's right for children or young adults. But we'll see. I mean, with Touro having separate girls' classes and all that . . ."

Her voice trailed off, cryptically. In the same breath, without hesitation, Estie jumped from the Rebbe's model of no college, at least before marriage and children, to the possibility of attending Touro. She told me later that she was strongly considering doing one year of seminary and then beginning Touro. Yet another ethical juggling act has emerged. As always, Estie was calm about the dilemma. She told her mother: "We'll say one year of seminary right now. I'll do seminary this year and then after that, toward the end of next year, we'll decide what's gonna be next."

This tension between God's ideals and the tempting world of friends, pleasures, and idiosyncratic interests is constant throughout Estie's life. She ended our longest conversation in the Janus-like way she lives—with one face turned toward each sphere. A large, laughing contingent of girls jogged by, and finally, the lure was too great. A party was going on for a friend's sister's engagement, and Estie loves parties. "Guys, I'll be over in a few minutes!" she called out.

"You can go now, if you want. It's okay," I told her.

"Wait. Just let me finish," she said, with urgency. She had been telling me about an experience she'd had with the Rebbe, after his death. Anxious about the summer, seminary, and the unexpected engagement of a friend, she went to the Ohel, the Rebbe's grave site, to pray. When she arrived back home, she opened a book of letters the Rebbe had written to various followers and elatedly discovered that the page she happened on discussed issues that were directly pertinent to all her major difficulties. As she changed into her silky new dress and sleek leather shoes, the perfect party outfit, she explained to me:

> I feel like I have a much closer connection to the Rebbe, now that he sort of answered me through what he was writing. I have this great love and admiration for him. He's just such a great person. All his miracles and all the love he shows us, even after Gimmel Tammuz [the date of the Rebbe's death] shows me that he really is Moshiach [the Messiah]. And I just hope that—this is my main prayer—that Moshiach comes soon and we have him back with us. That's what all Jews are waiting for, is for Moshiach to come. So it should be soon. That's all. It's important.

With that, she jumped up and hurried down the street to catch her friends. In an instant, she slipped out of the framework of mystical coincidences, reverence for the Rebbe, and longing for the Messianic age, and into party mode.

Some might say Estie has not quite honed her spiritual potential, that she needs to whittle down her worldly side somewhat. But Lubavitch's emphasis on outreach to secular Jews suggests another view. Estie would make a convincing messenger to the outside world. She brings impressive depth and energy to Judaism, but she's like you and me; she likes a great party, an evening with her friends in Manhattan, the sound of good music. Her friendliness and social sense could extend far beyond the Lubavitch domain.

About a year after I left Crown Heights, during a break from seminary, Estie invited me for a Shabbos meal at her house. Lisa, a tall, athletic New York University undergraduate on the path toward Orthodoxy, ate with us as well. The two young women bonded easily. Although one grew up in suburban California, went to prep school, and played varsity tennis, and the other hailed from Hasidic Crown Heights, they had core common ground: a love of Manhattan, the pain and excitement of leaving high school, even a shared taste in music (which Estie conveyed quietly while her mother was in the kitchen).

As for their differences, mutual fascination reigned. Estie listened with rapt attention to Lisa's descriptions of tennis tournaments around the country and her new boyfriend. I glanced over at Mr. and Mrs. Gutman. Boyfriends and girlfriends are not a Lubavitch concept—people date for the sole purpose of getting married. I thought, perhaps, they would not want their children to hear about such matters. But they just smiled and nodded at Lisa to continue. The young Gutmans would be out in the trenches trying to influence secular Jews soon enough; some exposure to their typical concerns would be crucial.

Lisa relished the opportunity to hear about Estie's Lubavitch childhood. She wanted to get the whole lowdown: "What is it like to go to school with only girls? What do you do for fun? Do you like Crown Heights?"

Estie gave the sort of answers a spiritually searching young woman with a strong desire to enjoy life would want to hear: "Life here is so great. You've got your friends, a great social life, the Rebbe's constant *brocha* [blessing], and Yiddishkeit [Judaism] everywhere." In other words, it is a deeply religious life, but that certainly doesn't preclude wonderful times with friends.

For a minute, Lisa was hooked: "It sounds just awesome." But she wasn't quite sure she could follow such stringent religious standards. At the moment, she was having some problems in the kosher department. She wanted to join her friends when they met in restaurants and admitted that, on occasion, she ate vegetarian food in nonkosher places—not as bad as eating nonkosher meat, but still a tremendous violation from a Lubavitch perspective.

"I *know* it's hard," Estie told her, with such conviction that her own temptations seemed to sizzle beneath her words, "but it's important. When you eat nonkosher, it hurts your soul. All the Jewish laws have their reasons. Something may seem stupid, but if it's in the Torah, it's all part of Hashem's plan." She twisted a few strands of her thick hair, carefully groping for the right words to influence Lisa. "It's like you have all these different invisible eyes, and each one can see a different part of spiritual life and appreciate a different aspect of Hashem. Whenever you eat nonkosher food, one of those eyes is blinded. The dietary laws are meant to increase the spiritual ability of all Jews."

Lisa listened solemnly, cradling her head in her hands. This evening had fascinated her. When she had made her weekend plans, she had known that the Gutmans had a daughter around her age. She had expected a very nice, very holy young woman who had no clue about life, or how to carry on a decent conversation. It was an utter miscalculation. Lisa could talk to Estie for hours, joking and exploring like she did with her closest friends. This Hasidic girl even liked the new Madonna song. Of course, she didn't know who sang it, let alone the significance of the singer's name, but at least she had some sense of what was going on in the world.

The young tennis star had to admit that Estie's thoughts about keeping kosher were compelling. She sat quietly, mulling them over, before resolving: "Dude, I'll do my best."

4

Rochel Lehrer

Evolving, Not Rebelling

WHEN I ENTERED nineteen-year-old Rochel's room, a huge picture of a toddler glowered at me from the back wall. She was frowning, with her head cocked and her dark eyes wide and blazing. Her angry misery came through in an instant; the festive pink party dress seemed almost a mockery. With her upturned nose and deep-set eyes, the girl was un-mistakably Rochel—one of those people whose basic features will never change. "I *love* that picture," Rochel told me, laughing morosely. "It totally sums me up." The room was tiny, but it was her own. Her four siblings all shared bedrooms, a situation that may appear unfair, but Rochel is a master at getting what she needs, and she truly required her own space. Logistics demanded it—her room was loaded with books that would have horrified her devout Lubavitch sister. So did her emotional fragility. She read alone for several hours each day, every-thing from Philip Roth to Nietzsche, and this refuge from the bustle of her large family helped her maintain her sanity.

It was early in the morning, perhaps around five. We had spent the night with Rochel's friends, young men and women who, to varying degrees, had sworn off Lubavitch beliefs, rules, and customs. Rochel wanted to show me her room because she felt it would help me under-stand her. It was messy, with clothes and books strewn on the floor, but she navigated her way knowingly, locating whatever she needed with-out hesitation. Her books, like her mind, ranged widely. *My Name Is Asher Lev,* Chaim Potok's exploration of the life of a Hasidic boy whose passion for art alienates him from his community, lay open on her bed, between a dog-eared, marked-up Western philosophy textbook and the *Tanya,* the classic Lubavitch explication of Jewish mysticism and psy-chological insight. Rochel motioned to her bed: "I'm reading them all. I kind of alternate between them. I read like three hours a day at least."

Then she showed me her yearbook, pointing out her friends and giggling, reminiscing about good times.

"So you liked high school, then, in some ways?" I asked.

Rochel was aghast. "Have I shown you my writing?" She jumped up and found a black composition notebook she had filled during high school. I thumbed through it, struck by the repeated references to loneliness, emotional pain, and hope that her troubles would soon end. She might have been alluding to suicidal thoughts; she might have been hinting that she would escape her morass and search for contentment. In fact, she had attempted suicide shortly before completing that journal, and she has hinted at death's allure many times since I have known her. She has also managed to find a group of friends who understand her lack of faith and her rage at a social system she finds stifling. Not long ago, she moved away from her family and fulfilled her dream of enrolling in a secular college—taboos that required tremendous emotional fortitude to carry out. Rochel is a brooder, but she is also strong.

I looked again at the small, narrow bed with its pillow scrunched in a corner. Though it was covered with books Rochel loved, it looked forbidding somehow, perhaps from absorbing the accumulated energy of years of bedtime sobbing. Rochel's childhood was miserable. She seemed like the sort of person anyone would want to be: self-assured, funny, charismatic, known throughout the community for her intellectual brilliance. But in a world of certainty, holiness, and sacred purpose, she lacked faith, and until she found a group of like-minded friends, she thought she was insane. Again and again, through tears, she would ask: "Why can't I just accept it? Why do I have to have all these questions? Why don't other people have them? I'm not that different."

I had first talked to Rochel on the phone a few days earlier, after another young woman had told me about the infamous 888 Montgomery Street apartment where young Lubavitch questioners converged. It was like a club, affectionately dubbed "888." Rochel was excited about the chance to contribute to a research project and invited me to come over and meet the group for myself. Then she asked, "Wanna join us at a lesbian bar?" My journalistic instincts rejoiced at the prospect—Hasidic girls at a lesbian bar!—and I eagerly offered my company. But this was not a serious invitation; it was an attempt to shock, which Rochel loves to do. A few months later, she would begin experimenting sexually, with the same penchant for flouting conventionality she brought to all other realms of her life. She found a Catholic boyfriend; she wondered whom she might love if she turned out to be lesbian. For now, though, intellectual questioning provided more than enough challenge. When I arrived at 888, Rochel was much more eager to teach me about her life than to go out anywhere.

I met some of the 888 regulars, Rochel's closest friends. Miriam, a study in black from her long, thick hair to her shiny leather boots, was thrilled to meet a real live graduate student (it's amazing how *anything* can be exciting if it differs radically from your usual routine) and told me she hoped to get a Ph.D. in philosophy at an elite school, maybe Berkeley. Behind her, fondling her back, was her boyfriend Dovid, whom everyone revered as a genius. Dovid had a memory so precise that while the Rebbe was alive, he memorized Rabbi Schneerson's extemporaneous Shabbos talks and wrote them out word for word later on: a highly prized ability, since writing and tape-recording are forbidden on Shabbos. His yarmulke and beard were a bit deceiving, for he had completely lost faith in the tenets of Orthodox Judaism. Devorah (Devorie for short) wore a snug, sleeveless T-shirt emblazoned with the words "Queen of the Fucking Universe." Petite and cute in a way that somehow combined boyishness and feminine allure, Devorie was financially quite productive as a strip club waitress, a job she combined with college, where she maintained a perfect 4.0 average. Aviva, a light-skinned black young woman (her father is black; her mother is Jewish and became Lubavitch in her twenties), sported dreadlocks and a multicolored tie-dyed shirt. She told me proudly that she had been selected to edit her college's poetry journal, and her friends raved about her brilliant poems.

It was a tantalizing group of people, and I would have plenty of opportunity to get to know them all better; this gathering was a ritual more or less repeated every night, and everyone made it clear that I was welcome any time. The cozy living room—strewn with open copies of the Talmud and ashtrays heaped with remnants from pot and cigarettes—became my counterpoint to the Lubavitch world, a place where I, just like the real 888ers, could slip on a pair of jeans and share my evolving thoughts on Lubavitch.

For me, it was another world within another world. The people seemed similar enough to friends back home, but they were anomalies here among their peers whose main concerns were finishing seminary, finding suitable spouses, and getting on with the next stage of their Hasidic lives. For many of the 888 regulars, Hasidic life was about to end;

they lacked faith and shared a boundless curiosity about the non-Lubavitch universe. By the time I left Crown Heights, they were out of Brooklyn, enrolled in college, and sharing a cramped but welcoming apartment in Manhattan, free at last. At the moment, they were plowing through a sort of limbo—living in Crown Heights while struggling with thoughts and feelings that defied Lubavitch boundaries of acceptability.

Freedom was as painful as it was exhilarating to Rochel. She was "evolving, not rebelling," a distinction she has made several times. Though she has veered radically from accepted Lubavitch thought and behavior, she explained: "Who I am now is not an act of rebellion. It's a thought-out process. I've not rebelled against religion." For Rochel, the word "rebellion" implies a carefree slap in convention's face, a "screw it all" just for the fun of it. Rochel's evolution has tormented her. She sees beauty and security in much of Jewish tradition, and she longs to join her peers as they begin to marry, start families, and ease into Lubavitch womanhood. In her blunt words: "And still today it would be a nice dream, although I really know that I will never believe in it. It would have been such a nice dream to say, 'Yes. It's perfect. Religion works.' But it doesn't."

When I arrived at 888, Rochel was sprawled on the living room's deep couch that often doubled as a bed after long nights of talking. Like most furniture in the apartment, someone had rescued it from the garbage; the group had well-trained eyes for odd castoffs that suited their needs. Rochel was chain-smoking, as she does much of the time, sucking the smoke in hungrily as if it were her lifeline. She wore cut-off shorts, a T-shirt, and a bright red bandanna tied around her forehead. "I will not walk out of the house like this. I will put the skirt back on," she explained—a concrete symbol of her double existence.

Rochel had invited me, so she took the role of host, offering me iced tea and cookies, assuring me that it was all kosher. "We keep separate stuff just in case. Everything was bought right here in Crown Heights," she told me, with a worried edge to her voice. She seemed concerned that no Lubavitcher would accept food from the likes of her, that she had become consummately untrustworthy to any observant Jew. When I told her I didn't keep kosher, she looked relieved.

Then I admitted my penchant for pork ribs from the Chinese place around the corner and pleaded, "Please don't tell anyone at Bais Rivka.

They'd probably kick me out." I received high fives and back slaps all around; I was, in a sense, on their side, a rebel with secrets and a vested interest in not antagonizing the Crown Heights establishment.

Even among this group of close friends, Rochel's charisma was obvious. Compliments were constantly coming her way. "You look great, Rochel! Your hair looks amazing," Aviva called out, randomly. Rochel had not said anything for several minutes, but it was somehow impossible to forget her, no matter how quiet she might be. And when she spoke, she commanded immediate attention, whether she was sharing a literary reference or complaining about her mother; she never seemed to endure the subtly embarrassing experience of saying something in a group and receiving no response.

The conversation switched, as it often did, to Lubavitch culture. These people were questioners, sure, but Hasidic values underlay their upbringing and, to a large degree, their psyches. "I have to admit, lots of what the Rebbe had to say about human nature is brilliant. He was a *holy* man," commented Miriam, who retained a streak of the mystical somewhere beyond her miniskirt and the philosophy-major jargon she had picked up from her secular college.

Devorie was a budding psychologist with a particular interest in helping observant Jews feel more comfortable with their bodies and their sexuality. Her response was swift:

> True, but look at the practical implications. The Rebbe may have had fascinating reasons for wanting women to wear wigs, but look at what that really means for them, with their heads always uncomfortable. I mean, how pathetic for a woman to be embarrassed to show her damn hair. It's a part of her. Those wigs can really damage women's confidence and body image.

Aviva, the consummate pacifist, just wanted to get on with her life without interference from her fiercely religious mother and the Crown Heights community:

> Some of those women seem pretty happy beneath their wigs, and if it works for them, great. I just wish they'd lay off me. Why do they think everyone has to do the same thing? Bunch of sheep! They're like the *frum* [religious] mafia.

Rochel's nostrils flared; this was a sensitive topic for her. Her questioning has been global and all-encompassing, but her sense of women's inferiority in Orthodox Judaism is her most painful point of contention. As usual, she spoke calmly and deliberately, but with an undercurrent of tension:

> Not only are some of them happy, most of them are, but that misses the point. Slaves can be happy if they're treated well. And women in this community are like slaves. I was just reading a Rambam [a commentary written by Maimonides, a renowned medieval Jewish scholar]. I had to find the source, because I don't want to believe everything I hear. So I looked it up and I found that a wife is obligated to do five things for her husband: make his bed; serve his meals; wash his hands, feet, and face; weave his clothing; . . . I think there's one more. And if not, he can beat her with a whip. I don't know if it's accepted as *halakha* [Jewish law], but this was written by someone that's accepted as an authority.

It is typical of Rochel to look up the traditional scholarship on the wife's role even though she never, ever plans to mold herself accordingly. She wants to understand, in the fullest way possible, just what it is that she is rejecting.

I found myself imagining Rochel as a young Lubavitch man, mentally chopping off her hair and dressing her in a black suit and yarmulke. A complicated question nagged at me: Would Rochel have been happy as a Lubavitch boy? His freewheeling mind, skeptical nature, and independent spirit may well have driven him to a similar place. But I could also envision a very different scenario—Rochel as a star, a brilliant young man who probes and pushes his teachers to the limit but who is sent to the most learned Talmudic scholars for answers. His analytical bent would surely compel him to question, but perhaps he would remain in the fold, satisfied with the responses of wise mentors, and use his submerged doubts to empathize with the less religious Jews he tries to win over to the Lubavitch mind-set. Maybe he would become the revered head of a Lubavitch outreach center, using his wit, charisma, and intellect to win over record numbers of secular Jews. He would marry a woman of formidable intelligence who would help with his work in attracting nonreligious Jews, and she would take care of the nitty-gritty household tasks—cooking for the massive numbers of guests, cleaning the house, changing children's diapers—that he found unappealing.

Even if he went through a starkly rebellious stage, he would be welcomed back. Rochel bitterly noted a double standard in this domain: "Boys, you come back, you learn six months in 770 [the synagogue], and everything's great. He's great. He experimented a bit perhaps, but then everything dies down and people respect him again. Whereas the girls, her quote unquote reputation will follow her" and damage her in terms of marriage prospects.

I can picture it vividly: Rochel the unruly, brilliant Talmudic scholar whose recalcitrant streak is accepted, even admired, because it melds so perfectly with a rare intellectual energy. Rochel as a man may have been a revered Lubavitcher. As a woman, she just could not find her niche. Gender disparities that barely fazed the overwhelming majority of her peers hurt her tremendously. Her father's place at the head of the table during holidays infuriated her, since it symbolized everything that seemed better about the boys' lives—their deeper exposure to Judaic studies, their reduced household chores, their increased travel opportunities. She told me, in a voice trembling with anger, that if she got married, she "would have a round table so that there would be no head of the table. Everyone's kind of equal around the table." Lubavitch mystical thought would have a profound answer for her, that everyone *is* equal, that the man's place at the head of the table in no way implies overarching superiority, but as far as Rochel is concerned, Lubavitch women are subordinate, pure and simple.

Rochel's brilliance in her present incarnation inspires both awe and horror. A young teacher at Bais Rivka who knows Rochel's family told me: "Rochel is the perfect example of why a parent might cry if their child is too brilliant." Twisting and twitching, uncomfortable at the mere mention of Rochel's name, the teacher refused to elaborate, explaining, "Anything I could say about Rochel Lehrer would be *loshon hora* [slanderous gossip]." She hesitated, then added the usual refrain: "But she's very, very bright." This woman summed up the conventional Crown Heights wisdom on Rochel: she is the symbol of a gifted mind gone awry. Disgust intertwines with profound respect. The community venerates intellectual talent but despises anything that threatens the Lubavitch way. Rochel, in characteristic fashion, has presented Crown Heights with a conundrum.

Contradiction and complexity defined Rochel's life. While she spent her evenings in an infamous center of blasphemy, she woke up in a house run by Hasidic parents whose elite lineage and intelligence won them unqualified community esteem. That night, after I had spent a few hours with the 888 gang, Rochel invited me back to her house to see her room and talk about her life in a quiet atmosphere. It was nearly 4:30 A.M., but in this crowd, that is a fine time to begin a new venture. To prepare herself for the walk outside, Rochel threw a loose skirt over her clothes with a scowl; all she needed was for some insomniac neighbor to report to her mother that she had seen Rochel on the street in a pair of shorts.

As we stepped out into the darkness, I recalled the admonitions of scores of family members: "You're gonna be *living* in Crown Heights? That place where all those riots happened? Just be safe about it. Don't do anything moronic, like walk around outside in the middle of the night." I looked up to the sky and soundlessly pleaded with the powers that be to protect us, a gesture I would repeat countless times as my friendship with the 888ers developed and I began to find myself on midnight treks around Crown Heights and 3:00 A.M. Manhattan-bound subways.

With Rochel, it was hard to be scared. She sauntered through those late-night streets, combat boots clicking solidly on the pavement, as if nothing bad could possibly happen here. In fact, the roads were pretty quiet. Scattered Hasidic teenage boys were walking home, books in hand, from late-night study sessions. A few drunk middle-aged men with thick Caribbean accents glared, spit, or leered in our direction, but they seemed more disoriented than dangerous. Women and girls were conspicuously absent; several Lubavitchers have told me that females here, as in many places, feel vulnerable outside in the wee hours. Walking along Albany Avenue from Montgomery Street to President Street, everything was closed, locked, and barred up: the Caribbean bakery, the kosher deli, the grimy snack shop that some say is really a front for drug dealing. In about fifteen uneventful minutes, we arrived at the Lehrers' stately red brick house on President Street.

This was prime real estate in a prime location, between the main thoroughfare of Kingston and Brooklyn Avenue, in the thick of the Lubavitch neighborhood. The area is heavily populated with old-line, elite Lubavitchers who have lived in Crown Heights for decades. Newcomers to Crown Heights are hard-pressed to find available property here; as the Crown Heights Lubavitch population has grown, Hasidim have fanned out over an increasingly wide space, covering several blocks up to and even slightly past the Caribbean-dominated Utica Avenue, four long blocks from Kingston. No den of rebellion could flourish near the Lehrer home; too many community paragons lurked about. Each night, Rochel's walk home took her from the farthest margins of Crown Heights Lubavitch society to the pinnacle of prestige and influence.

The house was dark and silent, and we tiptoed around as we whispered. Rochel pointed out everyone's room, smiling. Her brother was asleep on a chair. When she saw him, she grinned as she lightly patted his head, her face bearing the sort of familiar warmth that only a person you have known and loved for a long time can evoke. She seemed calm and carefree, in stark contrast to her daylight hours in this house, when the tension seethed between Rochel and her deeply religious, image-conscious mother. Now, as the rest of the family slept, Rochel could imbue the quiet house with the harmony and stability she wished it held for her when people were up and about. She was content. I never saw her quite that way again.

We climbed a thin, rickety staircase off the kitchen to the attic, where Rochel had staked out her private turf, and I found myself in the small room with the picture of the indignant little girl. Rochel's mood shifted immediately. This was, after all, the seat of her most intense brooding. Someone unfamiliar with Lubavitch culture might assume that this room, with its piles of books on Jewish thought, belonged to a traditional Hasidic Jew, but all sorts of little cues would let an experienced observer know that something was amiss, from the secular novels and philosophy books to the men's combat boots by the door.

Rochel straddled two worlds. Every night, she made the trek from her parents' house in a relatively safe, affluent pocket of Crown Heights to join her friends at 888 Montgomery Street, on the outskirts of the Lubavitch neighborhood. She spent her days at the seminary; she is the only young woman from the 888 crowd to complete the two-year seminary program. Rochel handled both universes with seeming ease. Her school friends adored her—if she threw a party, nearly the whole class would come, and the few no-shows would apologize profusely the next day. Her teachers marveled at her sharp mind. But just beneath this surface aplomb, she smoldered with confusion and pain.

We spent over an hour sitting on the floor, chatting in the small space Rochel had cleared amid the books and papers. It was a rare opportunity for Rochel to share her story with someone beyond her tight-knit circle of friends, and she relished it. We had a long, intense talk, and Rochel discussed the pain of growing up Hasidic without the faith that undergirds her community. Her speech was rapid and often tinged with passion. She spoke softly, since she did not want to wake anyone, but her energy was palpable.

Intensely curious and independent, Rochel had spent her childhood questioning, exploring, and examining. She wanted to *know,* and the answers she was offered did not satisfy her: "I just couldn't accept the absolute religion: just do it because you're told to do it, because your grandparents did it. A lot of things were not based in logic. It was just: accept it because it was written hundreds of years ago by people greater than you." She shuddered. This was heady stuff for a young woman from a long line of Hasidim, whose ancestors had risked their lives to follow religious dictates she was slowly renouncing. By the age of sixteen she had begun shedding her religious observance; it felt like a curtain of hypocrisy draping a fundamental disbelief.

An acute tension infuses Rochel's life. While she craves the warm embrace of her Lubavitch heritage, she perceives rampant intellectual shallowness, sexism, and intolerance in the culture of her upbringing. Practically in the same breath, she can describe love and disdain for Lubavitch:

There is a lot of beauty. There is a lot of beauty. There's a certain charm to the whole family sitting at the table together, and if there are no males that are not part of the family present, the whole family can sing together and eat a lot of soul food [women cannot sing in front of men outside their families]. There is a certain charm to us all standing around the menorah and lighting candles, which kind of have a beautiful flame, although I'm not a pyromaniac. [She chuckled.] So there's a lot of beauty in it. And there are partial answers, especially in *chassidus* [Hasidic philosophy], for a lot of your questions. Like, God is infinite. He doesn't want you to know. Your brain is limited; his is unlimited, so you can never understand fully. So if you can accept that, then here's your answer to just about all your questions.

Rochel smiled slightly, in a wistful sort of way, as if she were imagining herself as someone who believed, who could accept arguments like the limited human brain up against God's infinite wisdom, who could go about her business as a young Lubavitch woman. Her delight in the beauty of her culture resonates, but so does her resentment. Though Rochel's enthusiasm for the regular holiday meals that punctuated her childhood was heartfelt, as she hinted at the rule that a woman cannot sing in front of an unrelated man, her nostrils arched and her voice hardened.

We grinned at each other, as if we were sharing a deep secret. When I talk to a girl, I try to understand her triumphs and difficulties to the point of feeling them. This can be challenging. While I can honestly say that I liked all the girls who spoke to me, some of them discussed issues that rarely surfaced for me, and I was forced to rely more on my imagination than on actual experience. Identifying with Rochel was easy. I also adored the holidays: the family togetherness, the delicious meals, the religious rituals with their profound mystical significance. I, too, longed for a faith that would comfort me and place my worries within the context of a grand spiritual plan, but, like Rochel, I was unsure what I believed and struggling to assimilate my Crown Heights experiences into my worldview.

Rochel's reactions to Lubavitch were actually quite similar to my own, though our different relationships to the sect—curious outsider as opposed to the scion of a long line of Hasidim—made for an immense disparity in emotional valence. I could come and go as I pleased. My parents did not expect me to practice Orthodoxy; in fact, they much preferred that I continue in the ways of an infidel. Rochel's relationship to her community hinged on her remaining Lubavitch. If she veered too far, she risked alienation from her entire family and many of her friends.

The prospect horrified her. She showed me photographs of her family spanning a wide range of time, pointing out again and again how the Lehrer kids look basically alike, with their upturned noses and flashing eyes. I asked if she got along with her siblings, and she said, with a sweetness that seemed incongruous in this tough young woman who stormed the night streets in her combat boots, "I love them all very much."

She turned the page and found a recent picture of her parents: a forceful-looking, large-boned mother and a slight father with a wisp of a grin peeking out behind his bushy beard. Rochel's parents did not quite know what to do about her. They are from old, elite Lubavitch stock. The term used among insiders is *geszha,* which Rochel explained with the peculiar sarcasm of privilege. She comes from this background, so she can mock it without seeming bitter: "'*Geszha*' is the Hebrew word '*geza*,' which means 'root,' which means you're the root of Lubavitch. The Russians can't pronounce the 'z' sound, so they say 'szha.' It's kind of funny. This is the mispronounced word that's come to mean so much." Rabbi and Mrs. Lehrer have never known any way of life other than Lubavitch; as far back as anyone can remember, the entire clan on both sides was Hasidic.

This illustrious lineage yielded advantages for Rochel. She is sure that she was able to ask her theological questions at school with no social repercussions because she came from such a "good family." In high school she accomplished the amazing feat of branding Lubavitchers' reverence for the Rebbe "idol worship" right in class, and the next weekend throwing a party that drew nearly an entire grade's worth of admiring guests. She is also convinced that her teachers would have been more horrified if she had come from less prestigious stock. As it was, people could not fathom that she truly meant what she said; they often believed she was just trying to get attention: "People from my background don't have those questions."

The perk is double-edged. People assume Rochel's family is holy and pure—useful as far as it goes—but she can no longer hide under the umbrella of borrowed sanctity. Now that her nonconformity has progressed far beyond the point of ostensibly innocent questions, her parents fear that their daughter will tarnish the family's pristine reputation. They see Rochel as a break in a generations-long chain of tradition. Since she is the oldest child, they worry that she will contaminate her younger siblings with her ideas.

When Rochel told her parents she planned to attend a secular college (banned because of the social atmosphere and the exposure to ideas that conflict with Lubavitch doctrine), they balked. If she went to any college other than Touro, a school geared particularly toward ultra-Orthodox Jews, she would have to move out of the house. If she did move out, she could never go back, even to visit:

> They've threatened me. They've kind of told me that if I ever moved
> out, it's not done. A girl lives with her parents and then with her hus-

band. [They told her]: "We're not gonna talk to you. We won't let the children see you, not because we don't want them to see you but just because we don't want them to have ideas of that kind."

This situation confused Rochel. She was unsure how to feel or how much to care for these people who brought her into the world yet seemed ready to abandon her. She told me, in a tone that somehow managed to combine steeliness and pain:

> I do care about my parents, and I don't want to hurt them more than necessary. Although, *although,* on the flip side of that, I really don't care how much I hurt them because they put me into this world. They created a separate entity, and they have no right to expect anything from me. But at the same time it's not necessary to hurt them and hit them with the whole blunt truth all at once.

So the edginess works both ways: Rochel's parents baffle her about as much as she baffles them. Her mood toward them can shift radically in seconds. She doesn't want to hurt her parents, then she doesn't care if she hurts them. At bottom, she does care for them, but at the same time she is angry.

Rochel has a particularly troubled relationship with her mother, who is strong-willed and very concerned with public appearances. Her father is softer and calmer. It was her mother who orchestrated the ultimatum on secular college; Rochel thinks her father, on his own, would be more flexible. Rochel's mother rarely shows her affection. Commanding and well organized, she has an easier time exerting control than expressing warmth. Mrs. Lehrer's love seems wholly contingent upon religious faith and observance, and this torments Rochel. She recounted a conversation that particularly horrified her, one that encapsulated her fundamental quarrel with her mother—conditional love:

> I said, "Can't you love me for whoever I am?"
> And she says, "Does a mother love a son who's a mass murderer?" She did say she wasn't equating my situation with murder, but that was her example.
> And I said, "Yeah, she should. A mother should not bring a child into this world unless she's prepared to give him unconditional love." And she said that I'm wrong on that point and that her love for me

would be conditional. And I said, "So your love for me is based on religion." She kind of had to agree that that's what she was saying. So that was extremely disturbing, that, Mom, religion comes before me? What the fuck did you put me into this world for? If you're not prepared to stand by me, you shouldn't have had me. It was very painful. I was completely in a daze afterward.

I met Rochel's mother, Tzipi, once, briefly, after hearing this story for the third time. Immediately, I saw why it dominated Rochel's thoughts. Its main theme—Rochel's hunger for a mother's adoration and Tzipi's steadfast refusal to offer it under the circumstances—is played out daily.

Tzipi is a broad-shouldered woman, similarly built to Rochel but a bit taller, as if to demonstrate on a physical level that she is still the mother and still wields the power, even though Rochel has reached young adulthood. Tzipi had just finished her morning prayers; she kissed her prayer book in the customary manner and closed it. Rochel tried to introduce me: "Mom, this is Stephanie. She really wants to meet you." Tzipi pursed her lips and stared at the prayer book. Her eyes met mine for a second and then darted back to her book. "I guess we'll talk later then," Rochel told her. Her mother did not respond with even a slight gesture. Tzipi was suspicious of all of Rochel's friends; she probably thought I was a rebellious ex-Lubavitcher who had lured her daughter into drug experimentation or heretical thinking.

Rochel's younger sister walked in, and her mother grinned at her, motioning with her hand toward the fruit and cold cereal on the kitchen table. The disparity was striking. This is clearly not a woman who makes a habit of ignoring her children, but Rochel has pushed her too far. Tzipi takes tremendous pride in her children and wants them to achieve community-wide respect. She fears that Rochel has damaged her own reputation and tainted the standing of her family as a whole. She also may well feel that the tough-love approach will win her oldest daughter back, that if she is harsh, Rochel will fold and return to her rightful place as a Lubavitch young woman. Within Tzipi's worldview, seeming cruelty deriving from love would be a small price for the mooring of her daughter's anguished soul.

We moved into the next room, and Rochel tried to joke about her mother's coolness. "She's in a great mood today, huh?" she said, laughing softly. Still, the situation disturbed her tremendously. She managed to maintain a close relationship with her father, a bright, easygoing man who loves to debate with her about theological issues, but her more aggressive mother controlled the atmosphere in the house.

Rochel teetered on the point of no return, refusing to compromise her own beliefs and values but hoping, somehow, to keep her family even so. At times she did bend, like when she agreed to the date. Many Lubavitch girls begin the marriage search in their second year of seminary, but there was no place for a Hasidic husband in Rochel's plans. In fact, at the moment, sexuality in general was simply not on her agenda. She told me that night: "My friends and mother tell me that I put up this invisible barrier around myself that says: 'I'm just human; I'm not female.' I'm not into sex or any of that." Her man's T-shirt and combat boots reflected this androgynous image.

To placate her parents, she did consent to one date with a Crown Heights boy. The gossip grapevine had divined that this young man was unusually "modern," a code word in Lubavitch circles that connotes an atypical interest in secular culture and, sometimes, a hint of rebellion. A community matchmaker thought he might be compatible with Rochel and passed his name along to her parents. The potential couple met at a hotel lobby, a common place for a Lubavitch date, so they could talk. If they had both been willing, they would have met again to develop a deeper sense for each other's personalities and priorities. The young people do not tell each other their reactions; they tell their parents, who then relay the information to the matchmaker. The idea is that nobody should be hurt or embarrassed by up-front disclosures.

In this case, the process was wise indeed; Rochel's reaction to her date could only have damaged his self-esteem. For several evenings after the big night, Rochel hooted about him with her friends: "He has no experience outside of learning at 770, he hasn't read, he hasn't traveled. He ordered a drink and thought he was so cool, but he only managed to have a few sips. I told him he should read and travel, and he just smiled. But I was very nice. I even put on a clean shirt," she said, her eyes streaming as she laughed.

None of the other 888 regulars would have considered even playing at the Lubavitch dating scene. As with her resolve to graduate from the seminary despite her utter lack of faith in her teachers' theological messages, Rochel tried, armed with equal doses of sarcasm and longing for the comfort of home, to go along. She failed.

The sarcasm and the longing, the brazen confidence and the distress about everything she will lose as her questioning proceeds, are her yin and yang, embroiling her life and spirit in a continuous tug-of-war. In her words: "I'm not like a happy person in general. Actually I'm more into misery. But I actually do like myself, just in general." Rochel's college application and decision saga highlighted her mood swings. When I first met her, she had planned to apply to a joint program at the Jewish Theological Seminary (JTS) and Columbia University. JTS is run by the Conservative branch of Judaism, disdained by Orthodoxy for its more lenient interpretations of Jewish law. Rochel didn't especially identify with Conservative Judaism, but she wanted to study the Talmud on an equal footing with men, which she would not have been able to do in a Lubavitch context.

For a while, Rochel exuded enthusiasm about the plan. She was sure she could learn Talmud as competently as the most talented men, and she saw Columbia as a magnet for exciting ideas and scholars in secular studies. Rochel has always enjoyed learning and reading. Particular interests include Judaic studies, literature, languages, and history. Still, in keeping with her individualistic spirit, her grades have ranged from stellar (when she is captivated by a subject) to poor (when a class seems a waste of her time).

Hoping to ensure admission to the JTS/Columbia program, she pored over her application essay. Her friends at 888 helped her brainstorm and edit. Then she discovered a conflict in the essay: she abhorred the Talmud's views on women, yet wanted to devote years of her life to studying it. Suddenly her plan cracked. All of her contained doubts, hidden so well under the confident veneer, began to torment her: she was not qualified for such prestigious schools anyway; people at competitive schools scare her; if she went and didn't maintain a perfect 4.0 average, she would be crushed. She spent the evening on the old 888 couch, curled up in a fetal position, with her thumb in her mouth. "You can put this in the book, that I'm not going to JTS," she told me, on the verge of tears.

Rochel never applied to the JTS/Columbia program, but she did wind up joining her friends at Hunter College and lives with them in a grimy Manhattan neighborhood south of the school. True to their word, her parents began the year by ostracizing her and refusing to allow her in the family house. Rochel was able to sneak back periodically to see her siblings until she broke it to her parents, in response to a direct question, that she was no longer religious. Appalled, they strengthened their resolve to keep Rochel away from their other children. Rochel managed successfully on her own. She did well in classes and worked nearly full-time to support herself, first as a waitress, then as an assistant in an engineering firm. Her parents softened a bit after she devoted much of her already overextended time to nursing her younger brother as he recovered from a bicycle accident. After her brother left the hospital, Rochel's parents began allowing her in the house occasionally.

A year after I first met Rochel—she was now out of the house and enrolled in college—her depressive strain lingered right along with the energy and gumption that carried her through her new life. She joked about wanting to take Prozac and claimed one evening with solemn finality: "I will never be satisfied with my lot. There is no point to my existence. I don't even know why I'm here."

Rochel's relationship with her first boyfriend, a young man from a Catholic home, epitomized her way of handling her world: self-preservation in the midst of turmoil. Eric's psychological depth, scope of knowledge, and independent mind-set mirrored Rochel's. Unfortunately, his tendency toward melancholy was more debilitating than hers. He never graduated from college despite his intellectual gifts and had not been able to keep a job. His precarious emotional state at times pushed him into offensive behavior. For a few months, Rochel adored her new lover. Then he began flirting with other young women and treating her coldly. The last time I saw her, she planned to break up with him: "It *hurts*. I loved him, the old him. I don't recognize this new person. I don't know who he is." She agonized over the decision to leave him, but her anger and conviction that she deserved more overshadowed her gloom.

Rochel's trademark bouts of depression never do manage to crush her fundamental optimism and self-assurance. Somehow, she forges on with enviable confidence. School and work go well, and she is slowly recultivating a connection to her family. Thankfully, Rochel has a stable group of friends who have given her "a lot of courage and support." They have offered her some semblance of family now that her ties to her real family are precarious. They are the kind of friends who truly care, who empathize to the point of agonizing right along with her. Rochel needs this. For all her independence, she craves closeness with others.

She once told me, with feigned detachment, that she and her friends "might not even perpetuate as a group. We might each go our separate ways, and that will probably happen." But later that summer, when the 888 group seemed to be disbanding—one of the guys had settled alone in Manhattan; Rochel and her closest friends were planning a move together elsewhere in Manhattan; most people were staying in Crown Heights—Rochel was distraught. "I always thought of you all as my friends. I really hope I was right. I really hope we all keep in touch," she kept saying.

The end of 888 was particularly difficult for Rochel, since it offered a beacon of interpersonal stability in the midst of her family turmoil. She is now living with her closest friends from there, so the blow has been manageable. Rochel compares her relationship with her roommates to a short-term marriage, referring both to the inevitable squabbles and to the love. She said: "I love every single person here 'cause they understand a lot of what I feel and question. Most of them have gone through similar or the same things. I wouldn't say they have the same questions, but the idea of questioning is so foreign to Crown Heights. You know, you don't question." Meeting these friends helped Rochel maintain her sanity. Finally, she was able to fall asleep at night without crying. She was no longer a freak; she had found a community of questioners. Rochel's friends have buoyed her optimism and helped her control her depression.

During all of Rochel's major traumas—when her parents kicked her out, when her college plans wavered, when her relationship crumbled—her friends spent hours talking with her, joking with her, doing their part to ensure that she coped. I can still picture Rochel, Devorie, Aviva, and Miriam on the floor of their new Manhattan apartment, their faces faintly glowing from the low lamps positioned around the living room, meticulously working out the pros and cons of Rochel's relationship with Eric: "Maybe he'll be better if he starts taking the new medicine his psychiatrist gave him."

Rochel's speculation was quickly trounced with a chorus of "Oh, please!" It went on like this for hours. Patience is not quite the right word for it; patience implies a hint of annoyance, a conscious concession to help someone when you would really rather be elsewhere. I got the feeling Aviva, Miriam, and Devorie cared about reaching the right decision every bit as much as Rochel did.

Still, Rochel is not content. She is filled with an intensity that creates an inevitable restlessness. Part of her longs for the spiritual comfort of her upbringing. She no longer keeps kosher or observes Shabbos, but every Friday night she lights Shabbos candles in accordance with Jewish law. Often she will comment, with a strange combination of sarcasm and wistfulness, "I could have had some semblance of a life in Crown Heights."

Conceivably, the same passion that drove her away from Lubavitch could lure her back. She recently spoke with a young man who defected from Satmar, a more cloistered Hasidic sect, who is no longer religious but still believes. At this time in his life, he doesn't have the discipline to follow Jewish law. "I have absolutely no respect for him. If I believed, I'd be the most religious person around," she told me. A fervid inner quest for truth drove Rochel away from Lubavitch. The same search could have catapulted her deep within Lubavitch mystical teachings and imbued her with an urgent drive to carry out all of Jewish law in the fullest possible way.

I am reminded of a practical joke I watched Rochel play. It was the anniversary of the Rebbe's death. Politics festered and energy sizzled. Two separate community gatherings had formed: The *meshichists*, those convinced the Rebbe will come back to life and proclaim himself the Messiah, leaped and danced at the main synagogue. They hoped Rabbi Schneerson might choose this holy day to return. The doubters and naysayers held a more somber party at a local yeshiva. Rochel traipsed off to the main synagogue with her tambourine: women are supposed to carry tambourines to herald the coming of the Messiah. This was a sign of supreme faith; few of the other women had brought tambourines. It was the ultimate act of mockery for a girl who had called the Lubavitchers' reverence for the Rebbe a form of idol worship.

We arrived around 1:00 A.M. A few stragglers were left in the women's section, dancing wild-eyed, yearning for the Rebbe's return. They ranged from Chana Goldstein, a distant relative of Rabbi Schneerson's who manages to show up at every Messiah-related event and stay until the very last minute despite her large family (her youngest was with her, sleeping soundly in a baby carriage amid all the commotion), to Leah Levy, a homeless *baal teshuvah* whose love for the Rebbe fills an otherwise lonely existence.

Rochel joined in, shaking her tambourine. Some of the women told her she was too late, that the Messiah had not come. "I want to be ready whenever he gets here," she responded. The women whispered among themselves that they should all learn and grow from this girl's faith. Rochel pranced around and pounded her tambourine. Her eyes burned with scorn and, for a split second, a touch of bliss.

5

Nechama Dina (Dini) Rockoff

Chutzpah and Holiness

BAIS RIVKA'S SENIOR CLASS, about to set off for Washington, D.C., needed to settle a crucial question: Who would sit with whom? Clusters of girls arrived, jittery and excited, often with mothers in tow, hoping to give their daughters one last kiss before the trip. The big tour bus, inviting from the outside with its plush brown seats and its grinning faces at the windows, thrust many girls into a world far different from that of a mother's love. The ride was long. People did not want to get stuck next to a total *neb,* or someone who would talk too much, or make crumbs, or play with her hangnails. Lubavitch's emphasis on loving all of one's fellow Jews notwithstanding, the situation called for some frank brush-offs. A refrain, said with the necessary combination of forced politeness and I-mean-business firmness, swept through the air: "I'm sorry, but this seat's saved."

For many, the situation was calm and clear. They settled in next to their best buddies, looking forward to a long ride together. Others had less luck. One girl, a dreamy, self-absorbed type whose knotted hair and awkward giggle were marked danger signs, received a steady string of rejections before choosing a seat next to that strange graduate student who was writing a book about the girls. She cried for just a second, then took a deep breath and made the best of it. "No offense," she assured me. "I've just been thinking I should have more friends my own age." Older people often appreciated her eccentricity and sweetness, but her peers recoiled from her oddness. "Look at my earrings, how they sparkle in the sun," she implored two girls in front of her, interrupting their earnest discussion about the most popular shoe styles in the Crown Heights shops. They furrowed their eyebrows and smirked at each other before picking up the conversation just where they had left off, as if nothing at all had been said to them.

The driver, not Lubavitch and probably not Jewish, flipped the radio to a local rock station. Predictable factions materialized; the permissibility of popular music is a highly contentious Bais Rivka issue. A slight young woman, who wore long sleeves and buttoned her shirt up to the top even on this warm day, called out: "Please turn that off! We only listen to Jewish music." Her friends echoed the sentiment: "Yeah. Please. We can't hear that stuff." A group of girls near the back in funky jumpers and leather beaded necklaces groaned loudly; they had been singing along with delight. "It's gonna be a loooong trip," one of them called out.

Dini Rockoff, a tall, broad-shouldered young woman, was just stepping on when the wrangle erupted. She stood at the front of the bus, observing the tension, laughing and winking at girls from both sides of the controversy, who responded with warm, gratified smiles. The music neither tantalized nor horrified Dini; it simply did not interest her. I learned later that she had spent her pre–high school years in suburban Pennsylvania, where she'd had her fill of secular music, mainstream movies, and the like. Her parents were emissaries of the Rebbe working hard to influence secular Jews in the area. Dini had gone to a non-Hasidic Jewish day school; in her friends' houses, music like this had been rampant. Now she was beyond it. These songs held no mystery or appeal for her.

The tension did not abate when the driver turned off the radio, for someone noticed the video screen at the front of the bus and suggested that everyone watch *Fiddler on the Roof*, a musical about an early twentieth-century Jewish community in eastern Europe. She had selected it from her parents' library for the long journey; before they became Lubavitch, her *baal teshuvah* parents had been avid Broadway music lovers. "There's nothing wrong with it. It's nice. It's about Jews, and there's nothing dirty," she said, anticipating the objections.

One of the teachers had boarded by this time, a stocky, freckled young woman who would probably still have been a college student if she had grown up in a less religious family. She stood on her toes to assert her authority and promptly quashed *Fiddler*'s hopes of making it onto the screen: "I'm sorry, but that's not a *frum* [Orthodox] movie. We can't watch that here." Again, groaning ensued, along with several relieved sighs. Anyone who clings to the notion that all Hasidim follow identical codes of behavior should join a Bais Rivka class trip for ten minutes.

"Oh, lighten up. *Fiddler on the Roof,* Shmiddler on the Roof. What difference does it make, anyway?" Dini added her take on the situation before taking the plunge and claiming a seat. Everyone hushed, just for a second. Dini made her way down the aisle, glancing at her various options for seating partners. It was clear that she would have her choice; nobody would pull a "Sorry, this seat's saved" on her. Girls ranging from the intensely religious Sheva Adler to the easygoing, popular Miriam Bloom to the rebellious Sara Wexler looked at Dini expectantly, happily poised to move their things and make room for her. Finally, Dini chose Sheva.

One glance at Dini suggested what I would learn as I got to know her: she fit no categories. She was wearing a long, loose cotton skirt; nondescript white sneakers; and a long-sleeved plaid button-down shirt. She was extracovered, like the most observant girls—no slivers of knees or elbows peeked through on Dini. Her clothes reflected her religious commitment; in her own way, she was passionately observant, even by Lubavitch standards, with definite plans to devote her life to spreading Lubavitch teachings and customs anywhere in the world she is needed. But her plaid, boyish shirt was nothing like the typical Bais Rivka religious conservative's old-fashioned, feminine, almost frilly style. For that matter, her propensity to be, in her words, "*chutzpadick* [exuding chutzpah] with all the teachers," a tendency that surfaces with nonteachers as well, veers far from the stereotypical *chassidishe* mold.

I had noticed Dini many times around school. She has one of those powerhouse personalities you just can't overlook, an easy, innate charisma. If she's there, she's *there*. She may be teasing a teacher or steering a class discussion. Almost certainly, she is not languishing in the background.

Away from Bais Rivka, Dini's spirit was unbridled as ever. At the large Maryland Chabad House that housed the girls during their trip, one of the teacher-chaperones decided to try an art project with the class. She transformed the dining room into a communal studio, with paints, crayons, and bare tambourines waiting to be decorated. Since Lubavitch teaches that Jewish women will greet the Messiah with tambourines, this was art with a purpose. Now the girls would have their own personalized instruments to usher in the Messianic era.

Most people were excited. They examined the crayons with their finely gradated labels, deciding whether they preferred "magenta," "lavender," or just plain "purple." They shook their tambourines and laughed. Most Bais Rivka students do not take organized art classes, though the yearly theatrical production does allow some girls to hone their artistic talents by painting scenery or organizing props. Tambourine making would be different and, with any luck, entertaining.

Some old insecurities arose; a baby-faced young woman lamented, "I don't know how this is going to work out. I'm really, really bad at stuff like this. I have like no talent." A few of her cronies shared her fears. But by and large the girls were glad at least to try.

The activity leader, a well-meaning but sometimes cranky middle-aged history teacher, explained that the girls should paint over the white surface with a color they liked and then add pictures and designs with the crayons. She showed an example: a tambourine with a sky blue base and a pink crown, emblazoned with the words "Melech HaMoshiach" (King Moshiach). Most girls nodded, about to set to work according to these instructions.

Dini did not care to follow these rules. She raised her hand coyly, her mouth twisted in a wry grin, and asked, "How about if we color them in crayon first, and then paint on the designs?"

"No. That would be messy."

"I don't think so. I think it would be interesting looking."

Soon some of the other girls joined in; Dini always has a following before long: "Yeah. I think Dini's right. That would look cool."

Finally, the teacher relented: "Do what you want, girls. But you're taking a big chance that it won't come out right."

Despite the warning, Dini created a sharp-looking tambourine, with a lovingly painted, wide-eyed rendition of the Rebbe over a light dusting of yellow crayon. I thought of this scene weeks later when Dini told me, "I'm like the teacher's kind of nightmare. I come into the class, cause problems in the class, and do well on the test anyway."

This tendency seems to extend beyond the academic classroom. Dini stirs trouble but still excels. And when she incites tension, she also harnesses other girls' energy, which can be channeled into holy realms. Many of her classmates are convinced that she will someday be an ideal spokeswoman for Lubavitch, the sort who wins scores of new Hasidim each year. At bottom, to instigate is to inspire; Dini is the ideal cutup because she has such a potent ability to influence others. She can be difficult, but she can also add a delightful spark.

One spring afternoon I sat in on her English class's public speaking unit. The teacher, sixtyish, chunky *Morah* (teacher) Schwartz, handled

her lively crew beautifully, funneling the girls' energy into some entertaining speeches. Occasionally the students became overexcited, speaking all at once or screaming out, but Schwartz gently redirected things
to a more controllable level. The girls had an assignment to give a five-
minute talk on a topic of their choice. Subjects and demeanors ran the
gamut. A shy girl spoke in a barely audible voice about genetic diseases
prevalent among eastern European Jews. Next we learned about a giggling young woman's trip to her uncle's Lubavitch outpost in Russia. A
studious girl who read about Jewish history in her spare time spoke
about the image of Jews as the devil common throughout Europe during the Middle Ages.

Perhaps the most entertaining presentation of all was the irrepress-
ible Dini Rockoff's talk about life as a Hasidic emissary in suburban
Pennsylvania, doing outreach to the area's secular Jews. We heard about
confused yet intrigued college students: "One guy wore an old yarmulke he had gotten when he was eight—way too small to stay on his
head now without a pin—and it kept dropping into his food throughout
dinner. You'd look up and see a plate filled with chicken, potatoes, carrots, and a black leather yarmulke." She discussed the inevitable oddballs who would show up for free food and unconditional friendship:
"This one woman, she'd always drink tons of soda and burp throughout the rest of the evening. It was so funny and so disgusting at the same
time." Just when Dini had people holding their stomachs in pain from
all the laughter, she switched to a serious mode: "But, honestly, it's the
best job anyone in the world could ask for. So many people are affected
in so many ways. They may decide just to light Shabbos candles or they
may take the whole leap and become Lubavitchers. No matter what
they do, we have touched their *neshamas* [Jewish souls]. It's great."

Such pure, innocent enthusiasm might have elicited sneering
smirks from a few dissenters, but nearly the entire class nodded in
heartfelt support. You just don't mock Dini. She had her peers laughing
one second and affirming their spiritual values the next. A lot of work
had gone into that speech; it had well-planned transitions and carefully
crafted anecdotes. Dini later explained: "If I like the teacher and the
class, I'm the best student. I'm constantly doing all the homework and
I'm so into it, whatever it is. If I don't like the teacher, then, you know,
all hell breaks loose kinda thing. Like, I'm awful." Teachers would do
well to seek her favor; she is a dynamo with the potential to define a
class's atmosphere.

For months, I had been hoping to spend some time alone with Dini and learn more about her. Her charisma and sheer strength of personality intrigued me. Dini is the sort of young woman who blasted all my preconceptions about Hasidic girls. I might have expected to find a few like her—brash, bold, intellectually agile, and quick-tongued—but I would have pegged them all as defectors-to-be. Nobody is more enthusiastically Lubavitch than Dini. Like her parents, she plans to devote her life to Lubavitch outreach work as an emissary of the Rebbe. She has no idea where she'll settle; she knows only that it will be someplace with Jews to be immersed in the ways of Hasidism. Wherever she goes, she will find unlikely supporters. The bright young instigator will surely mature into an assertive, convincing adult who will make people think: *"She is a Hasidic woman?* Maybe it's possible to be Hasidic and not give up your personality. Maybe this is worth looking into."

With many of the girls, simple friendliness was all I needed to find myself embroiled in an intense discussion. In her charming but sometimes maddening way, Dini was a bit more elusive. I invited her to my apartment several times, only to receive a vague, teasing reply: "Sometime, maybe. I'll have to think about it." When I persisted, she laughingly asked, "What's so special about me, anyway?" But after I told her that she fascinated me because she combined vivaciousness, personal independence, social popularity, and boundless commitment to Lubavitch, I received an invitation to her home. Dini has tremendous pride in her background. If talking to her would help me form a positive impression of Lubavitch, she would surely oblige.

As soon as I arrived at the Rockoff residence, Dini made one point abundantly clear: she was not about to let me get away with my role as the sole snoop. It was tit-for-tat for a while, and rightfully so. She must have been just as curious about the strange woman who had been prying around school as I was about this powerful, charismatic Hasidic girl. We met for a long talk at her Aunt Sheina and Uncle Leibel's house, her Crown Heights home; her parents and seven siblings still live in suburban Pennsylvania, where they try to impart their love for Hasidism to area Jews. "Out-of-towners" often send their children to high school in Crown Heights, to give them a taste of life in the center of Lubavitch activity. Those with Crown Heights kin set their children up with trusted family members; others pay neighborhood Lubavitchers for their children's room and board. A typical Bais Rivka class has students from all over the country and the world (although native Brook-lynites do dominate both in numbers and in tone).

Uncle Leibel is Dini's father's brother; they had grown up in the well-known Rockoff family of Crown Heights. Her mother also hails from an established Crown Heights family. Dini's parents embarked on the highest form of Lubavitch service when they left the security of Brooklyn to conquer suburban infidelities.

As we talked, Dini answered my questions with questions in classic Jewish fashion. I asked, "Was it a strange feeling moving to Crown Heights from Pennsylvania?"

"How about for you, Stephanie? It must have been strange for you, coming from Harvard University."

"Have you ever been involved in a situation where you weren't sure what was the right thing to do?"

"How about you, Stephanie? Do you feel like that now that you've been exposed to all that Lubavitch has to offer, coming from where you're coming from?"

She would grin a little after each question, enjoying my slight shock; she knew she was putting me in an unexpected position. This clearly gave her a kick. It also gave her a chance to find out about my level of Jewish observance, so she could try to win me over. "You must have come here for a deeper reason than your project," she told me. "Your *neshama* sent you here. It's no accident that you're here." She winked. Playfulness and proselytizing merged, in perfect Lubavitch fashion.

Dini's New York abode was a large, airy home on Montgomery Street right off of Kingston Avenue, arguably the ideal Crown Heights location; she was steps away from the main thoroughfare yet on a quiet block filled with caring neighbors. Her faded denim skirt, worn plaid button-down shirt, and white Keds were her typical after-school garb. She told me, laughing, "I could never get into this whole shopping thing so many of the girls love so much. With some of the girls, it's always shopping, shopping, shopping. I'm much more of a tomboy, always have been." Her build fits perfectly with this tomboy image: she is tall and muscular like a public school basketball star.

Still, Dini certainly has learned the art of cooking, that most basic of feminine chores. When I arrived at her home, I was pleasantly surprised to find that she had made lunch for both of us. Her tuna salad offered the simple pleasure of a familiar food prepared just right. She had mixed the tuna with black olives, potatoes, and a touch of creamy mayonnaise. Her lettuce, tomato, cucumber, cabbage, and carrot salad tossed with homemade lemon and oil dressing was equally tasty. Even the pita bread was an exercise in everyday perfection, toasted with the perfect edge of crispness. She prepared it all with a smile, her tongue thrust to the side of her mouth as she concentrated.

Dini ate with as much relish as she rabble-roused back at school; she took large portions and chewed slowly, as if to stretch her enjoyment for as long as possible. Guilt intermixed with her pleasure. "Boy, I sure do eat a lot," she kept saying. "I'd love to lose weight, but I guess I just love to eat too much." Her carefree exterior in the plaid shirt and denim skirt masked a fundamental layer of insecurity about her large frame and hearty appetite.

Dini's casual presentation belied the obvious wealth behind this household. The family's hired cook, a Haitian woman with lilting speech, quietly chopped vegetables throughout my afternoon in the Rockoff kitchen; a portly Russian Jewish immigrant, whose thick blonde wig gave away her newfound religious Orthodoxy, vacuumed and scrubbed throughout this home's two spacious floors. An intercom system connected people throughout the large house. When Dini's aunt (a lanky woman known for her humorous and thoughtful articles that appear regularly in Lubavitch women's publications) arrived home from food shopping, she contacted her various children around her home, checking up on their homework progress and evening plans from the kitchen speaker. Then she draped her arm around Dini and kissed her hello, giving subtle but substantial confirmation of her niece's glowing description of their relationship: "My aunt's a special person who really, really cares about me and also has this incredible ability to judge people's character."

The Rockoffs are a prestigious family, with generations of Lubavitch lineage, financial leverage, well-known and confident parents. Dini's parents both come from highly respected families who have been Hasidic for generations, and they have done marvelous work with the Jews in their Pennsylvania neighborhood, inspiring several to revamp their lives according to Orthodoxy. Dini prides herself on her *yichus,* her elite lineage. She told me, "*Yichus* is like having eight zeros after you. If you do nothing worthwhile, they're worthless. But if you live a holy life, it's like adding a one before them. The holiness of your ancestors gets added to everything good you do." In a sense, Dini is the ultimate insider, with the potential to tap not only her own gifts but also those of ancestors venerated by Lubavitch.

Yet she grew up in an area whose customs and mores differed radically from Crown Heights culture, and when she entered Bais Rivka in ninth grade, she was shocked by the cliques and the social politics; they really hadn't surfaced in the tiny yeshiva she had attended back in Pennsylvania. The social atmosphere made her uncomfortable: "The typical Crown Heights kids who always grew up here were not my style at all. Some of them were petty and they weren't very extending. They wouldn't want to let outsiders into their clique, some of them." Always an excellent social operator, Dini quickly became popular in Crown Heights, but she chafed under the social hierarchies, the snootiness she sometimes encountered, the seemingly shallow interest in fashion fads and clique identity. She was sensitive enough to resent the ostracism other girls faced, even as her own status soared. It was an old dichotomy that characterized her even now, as a high school senior—she was an outsider's insider, a questioning soul with complete faith, undying loyalty to Lubavitch, and the respect of nearly everyone in the community who knew her.

Dini is a restrained individualist. She exudes power and assertiveness, but for all her troublemaking, she never transgresses basic boundaries. In school, she continually received the highest honors and got chosen for the most competitive programs. The other girls loved her sense of humor and energy. Her personality was striking enough to win her peers' attention and mainstream enough that the attention was almost always positive; she was rambunctious and brazen, but she never breached basic codes of behavior.

Perhaps Dini's balance of character strength and religious conviction stems partially from her upbringing. Until high school, Dini lived in the small Pennsylvania suburb where her parents run a Chabad House. She was forced to shun social trends to maintain Hasidic standards. Dini went to a coed Jewish day school (there were no other options), and her classmates there were fairly secular Jews whose parents wanted them to learn a bit about their heritage. It was certainly not an ideal place by Lubavitch standards, but sacrifice is inherent to the lives of Lubavitch emissaries who move out of the Crown Heights cocoon and devote themselves to influencing the wider world.

Dini could have suffered socially. So many mainstays of suburban childhood, from movie theaters to mixed-gender games of tag, were off-limits to her. She missed parties and social events because her parents deemed them inappropriate; something as seemingly innocuous as a trip to see *Snow White* at the local movie theater was banned, for her parents, like most Lubavitchers, aimed to shield their children from the sordid atmosphere of public cinemas. Still, Dini managed to spend time with her friends in ways that harmonized with her parents' values. There were certainly no laws against sitting and chatting, playing many types of games, or inviting her pals for holiday meals. Between her charm and her parents' careful nurturing, she enjoyed her childhood social life: "I was always very popular in my class and I never felt left out or put down. And I had really, really close friends that I still keep in touch with."

Her parents rose to the daunting challenge of raising devout Hasidim in the midst of secular trappings with ease and grace; they created a safe, inviting home whose closeness and love seemed far more beautiful than the activities their children needed to avoid:

> My parents created a strong support system for us at home. When I was very young, there was absolutely no one around [beyond family], and they used to tell us a lot of stories, sing a lot of songs, you know, make Shabbos parties for us and do all that kind of stuff, and I had brothers and sisters all around me. I really grew up with them, and they were a support system.

In such an independent-spirited young woman, Dini's pure, un-qualified support for her parents' judgments and decisions may seem surprising. Throughout our long lunchtime discussion, she never of-fered even minor carping about her mother or her father. Sure, dis-agreements have surfaced, but with hindsight, Dini inevitably comes to appreciate her parents' wisdom. Her description of her father was glowing, accompanied by a bright, gleaming, thoroughly genuine smile: "I mean, first of all, he's my father, and he loves me. Second of all, he's very smart, and, in my eyes, he knows everything about every-thing. I feel that I can go home to find the truth, you know what I mean? And that's a great thing. He also has a very great understanding of peo-ple." She followed with a similarly loving, though perhaps not quite as awestruck, description of her mother:

She's also great. I just have great parents. What can I do about it? She's idealistic, which is something that I very much admire about her. She sees people in a very positive way. She's also a very dedicated, hard-working person. She's also very smart. And I guess maybe, like I trust her experiences in life. She's great to talk to. I think I would say I'm very close with my mother.

These people had a tough job: bringing up Hasidic children in suburban Pennsylvania, surrounded by people who knew nothing of their culture and whose behavior continuously violated their own standards. At least in Dini's case, they came through brilliantly. Their second-oldest daughter navigated alien surroundings with pride, confidence, and pleasure. She had a thorough understanding of the reasons behind the rules and prohibitions that applied to her and a steadfastness that hardened her against peer pressure. Her classmates sensed her strength and respected her, willing to befriend her on her own terms, even if she avoided many commonplace activities, from movies (she shunned the theaters entirely, though she did catch occasional films on friends' VCRs) to friends' parties, which were almost sure to offend Lubavitch sensibilities, with their non-Jewish music and food of, at best, questionable kosher status.

Her classmates were all Jews, and many of their parents took their religious background seriously; they were, after all, sending their children to a yeshiva, a rare choice in suburban Pennsylvania. But even those who considered themselves observant did not remotely meet Lubavitch standards. Secular music, media, and culture were ingrained in their lives. Foods that they considered kosher, like Hebrew National hot dogs or vegetarian dishes from nonkosher Chinese restaurants, did not come close to Lubavitch regulations.

Despite Lubavitch stringencies, Dini's idiosyncrasies flourished as she grew older, and she probably obliterated her friends' stereotypes of Hasidic girls: "I was a major tomboy growing up, like major, major, major. I was the best in the school in sports. I was totally into it. I wasn't into my clothing. I didn't care about that at all. I was friends with all the boys." I asked whether she found it hard to adjust to the single-sex atmosphere in Crown Heights; she said it was not at all difficult because she knew she was only in the coed school "'cause there was no other school."

Dini arrived in Crown Heights in ninth grade. She did take some time to find her niche of friends. Dini may not have missed the boys, but she had difficulty understanding these new girls. Bais Rivka was much bigger than her tiny Pennsylvania school, and the girls' attitudes and social maneuvering seemed foreign: "I remember they had like politics and cliques. I had never even heard of such things. I had come from a small school where that just didn't exist. I called my mother up like: 'I don't get it.' I didn't understand."

Since Dini is so likable and socially savvy, she had her pick of friends before long. She started out with a group of mainstream Crown Heights girls, but by eleventh grade, Dini's energy and penchant for exploration enmeshed her within a somewhat more rebellious group. These girls were hardly full-fledged rebels; they were more the fun-loving, boisterous arm of the "normal" crowd. They watched mainstream movies on VCRs (they never would have ventured to a public cinema), and they were quite rambunctious and difficult to control in school. Dini knew quite a bit about movies from her days in Pennsylvania, and she gleefully shared her knowledge with her friends. She also led the pack in school mischief: "I was very *chutzpadick*. I was very disrespectful to my teachers. I was probably the number one brat in class. I'm sure if you asked my eleventh-grade teachers, they all hated me. I was doing all this kind of stuff and totally with my friends. It was a total, total social year."

This sounds like a fond reminiscence of laughs and friendship, but Dini's active social life shielded deep-seated discontent. Immediately after telling me what a "total, total social year" she'd had, she continued: "And I was really unhappy. Like I was constantly crying to my mother on the phone. I guess in a way I could say that I sort of like hit rock bottom when I came to eleventh grade." It may seem strange that such a seemingly fun-loving year was miserable, but Dini's restless, adventuresome side was crushing her more serious intellectual and spiritual core. She squandered chances for academic and religious growth at school; stirring up trouble was an all-encompassing activity:

> I was getting into trouble and not interested in school, just that kind of stuff. I was getting kicked out of class for talking and talking and talking and answering back. And I wasted a lot of opportunities that came up that year. Instead of getting involved in all kinds of things that were happening in school, I was just like: "No. We don't need that. That's stupid; that's nerdy."

By her senior year, she had calmed down. Many people had worried about her and tried to help her. She was the sort of student whose obstreperousness inspires feverish reform efforts, for her intelligence and leadership talents could have been channeled into spiritual refinement and school service. The principal "just put her foot down. She was like: 'If you don't start behaving, you're gonna be in big trouble.'" Dini's parents and her *mashpiah* (a sort of combination spiritual mentor and confidante with whom many Lubavitchers share everything from religious dilemmas to personal insecurities) influenced her as well: "I guess with the help of a lot of people who love me, like my parents, I got out of it."

Dini still was not exactly docile, as I saw for myself every time I observed her at school: "I can't say I was like the angel of the class. I must say that one of the hardest things for me is not to be *chutzpadick* to teachers. I have a very hard time with authority in general." But she did begin to funnel some of her considerable energy into school activities. She had a key part in Bais Rivka's yearly theatrical production and galvanized the senior class gatherings held at alternating homes around town; she was often the first to try out the various skits, games, and discussions the seminary student leaders had planned.

For all her troublemaking, she was one of a handful of young women chosen to attend the most elite Lubavitch seminary in the world for the following year, an Australian school with a fearsome admissions policy. Perhaps her background helped; her family boasts prestige and money, both known to influence this school's decisions. Still, her teachers must have recommended her with unqualified enthusiasm. Dini proudly told me about her acceptance, marveling at the "truly amazing" girls she would share classes with. "Coming from Bais Rivka, it's a big competition, because it's such a big school and so many people want to go." She shrugged carelessly. Her acceptance was no surprise. Likewise, Dini was one of only two Bais Rivka students chosen to attend a prestigious conference of ultra-Orthodox girls' yeshivas during eleventh grade, her most unruly year.

I asked her about the apparent irony—unruliness and stellar high school achievement are an unusual blend—but to her the whole situation seemed natural. The very loudness that at times made her difficult to handle also attracted her teachers' attention, and academic success was always important to her, even during her most rebellious stage.

More crucial, her pride in her heritage shone: "When I say I was *chutz-padick*, I mean, I was *chutzpadick*, but I also had something my parents gave me when I was really young, like a pride in being Lubavitch and an understanding of what it means to be a Lubavitcher."

Dini is a charming amalgam of playfulness and thoughtfulness, and her rebellious stage encompassed both qualities. Beneath the clowning, fundamental questions festered. They dissipated seamlessly, though; as she delved ever more deeply into Hasidic life and thought, the Lubavitch mind-set began to meld with her own. In her words, "I had a million questions, and, thank God, I had a million answers."

Her questions spanned the gamut from women's role in Orthodox Judaism to the Hasidic notion that Judaism should drive Jews' lives and subordinate all other concerns, like career and secular interests. As she lived and grew in her community, her doubts disappeared. She equated the process to the path of a *baal teshuvah* who chooses to renounce a secular background and embrace the commandments; Lubavitch teaches that wrestling with fundamental issues and reclaiming Judaism with bolstered understanding is a crucial process for all Jews, even those who were brought up in the most religious homes:

> I think it's something that is emphasized in *chassidus* [Hasidic philosophy], that every single person has to be a *baal teshuvah*. You can't just say, "Oh, I'm born this way. Yeah, I keep Shabbos 'cause my parents keep Shabbos." It's something that *you* have to learn how to appreciate. You know, you have to also be a *baal teshuvah*, like it's something that *you've* come to.

The Rebbe and *chassidus* have impelled Dini's spiritual growth. Her profound respect for Lubavitch's particular approach to Orthodox Judaism blossomed when she attended the prestigious conference for ultra-Orthodox girls' yeshiva students. The conference draws predominantly from the non-Hasidic wing of stringently Orthodox Jews, and Dini discovered that most of her peers there lacked an understanding of what it means to have a Rebbe and to practice a Judaism enriched by Hasidic thought:

> The way I really saw it was, they had no idea of what a *tzaddick* [spiritually perfected man] is, like no concept of what it means to have a Rebbe. The ultimate for them was just not so ultimate compared to

what I had, you know what I mean? Not to put them down. These were wonderful, great people. They just didn't have the way of *chassidus* in their Torah and their *mitzvahs* [observance of Jewish law]. It was just so amazing to see how much we really have.

Her reformation did not override her playfulness and difficulty with taking orders. Teachers often reprimanded her, but with a twinkle; though she was challenging, she was never threatening. Once, in the midst of her math teacher's complaints about the girls' disappointing performance on a quiz, she interrupted with the earnestly intoned question: "But how can you speak this way to a fellow Yid [Jew]?" It was a clever play on a deeply ingrained Lubavitch theme; love of all Jews drives Lubavitchers' worldwide outreach efforts. The entire class roared, and even the teacher's attempts at an angry face soon dissolved into a grin.

Dini is emblematic of a paradox many Lubavitch girls share: they can be forceful and proud, yet completely within the boundaries of Lubavitch expectations. As I walked through the halls of the girls' school, marveling at the energy and humor, I found myself wondering what would happen when the students married. Would these delightfully loud-mouthed kids transform into meek women chained to the oven? This possibility seemed impossible to fathom in the thick of the pranks, shouts, and shoves that defined the Bais Rivka milieu. But maybe it was all a prelude, a final opportunity to revel in youth and pleasure before settling into a life of submission.

Over a year after I had returned to Cambridge, I visited Crown Heights and heard that Dini had gotten married. She had spent a year at the Australian seminary and finished school in Brooklyn (a common path, since many people want to marry during their second year of seminary, and Crown Heights offers a wide selection of potential husbands). I needed her to sign a form allowing me to write about her, so I found my way to her new apartment.

Lubavitch women must cover their hair after marriage, and I was curious to see Dini's new look. I kept trying to picture her in one of the typical thick wigs that give many Orthodox women an old-fashioned kind of glamour, but my imagination came up dry. Sure enough, Dini was wearing a snood, a cloth head covering that serves the same purpose of hiding the married woman's natural hair. Some Lubavitch women sport snoods in the house and save their wigs for the public eye.

The snood suited Dini better; it was somehow more casual, almost like a big bandanna tied over her head. She wore the same sort of clothes I remembered—a denim skirt and a long-sleeved dark blue T-shirt—but now the shirt was tucked in neatly with a belt, unlike her high school days of freely flopping shirt tails. The sight of Dini in a snood slightly jarred me; the head covering somehow clashed with my vision of the math class hellion. She did seem a bit more subdued. After all, she had no teachers to razz, no coterie of classmates to instigate. But it was Dini, sure enough, with the same lusty laugh, the same wink.

Dini's housekeeping talents were formidable; she had managed to transform her small apartment in a square concrete building into a bright, airy space, with fresh flowers on the table and a huge portrait of the Rebbe, grinning, on the wall, making me feel like I had an immediate friend in this house. Falafel balls cooked in a pan as Dini tossed a salad. "Is it okay if we have the same thing for lunch that we had yesterday?" she asked her husband, Avi, a slender, dark-haired, scraggly-bearded young man.

"Sure!" he called out from the living room. They seemed quite comfortable with each other, though they had been married for only about a month.

It was an odd query for me to hear, coming from the same young woman who had instigated small-scale coups in high school just a short time ago. The question was spontaneous, almost habitual. Dini's next words told me her old playfulness still flourished: "So you need a form signed?" she asked me. I nodded as casually as possible, but an entire chapter rode on this small interchange. If for any reason Dini decided against signing, I would have to nix all plans to write about her.

"I don't know." She chuckled. "I think I need to take a look at that introduction first, just to see what I think." I had promised Dini I'd show her the introduction to my book. She began reading and immediately tried to sniff out one girl from her class, after I had told her that everyone would remain anonymous to avoid embarrassment or unwanted disclosure. "I know she's there. I know you interviewed her," she said. "Hey, Avi! Let's see if I can find this girl from my class," she called out, giggling. She combed through the chapter and tried, unsuccessfully, to guess which quotations belonged to her classmate.

Her opinions, as always, abounded. She wanted me to present her beloved Lubavitch as positively as possible, and she bristled at my descriptions of some of the more rebellious young women. "You have to make it *clear* that they are not the typical girls," she admonished. And then, in a tone somewhere between teasing and accusatory: "You're writing so much about them because you think that's what people want to read."

As Dini perused the introduction, we laughed about it together; she said she found it fascinating to read about her peers from an outsider's perspective. She picked up her pen and made like she was about to sign my form and then suddenly asked Avi: "What do you think? Should I sign?"

"Do you know what kinds of things you told Stephanie?"

"Honestly, I can't remember."

"I think you need to know," her husband said.

Dini lapsed into a rare silence. Then she asked to see a copy of her interview before signing; I had tape-recorded in-depth conversations with most of the girls I wrote about. She smiled in her old sly way, and it was hard to say whether this was spurred by the old drive to be playfully difficult or by acquiescence to her husband's judgment (potentially an easier hurdle for Dini than obedience in school, since the husband's role as the family authority figure is prescribed in Jewish law). Each probably had its part. I promised to send a copy of the interview.

Dini brought a platter with crisp, golden falafel balls and a fresh, colorful tossed salad to the dining room table. Avi sat expectantly as his wife hurried back and forth from the kitchen with drinks, napkins, and silverware. Dini's face bore the same pleased concentration I had observed that past year when she had prepared lunch for the two of us. She enjoyed this work.

I gathered my knapsack and jacket and headed toward the door, but before I made it outside, Dini offered one final tease. She called out, "Stephanie is fascinated to see the rowdy girl with her new husband." The comment encapsulated my thoughts. I turned back to catch the eye of this impish young woman with the sensitivity to read my reaction and the guts to share her speculation. Dini thrust her tongue toward me as she served Avi his lunch. "Gotcha!" she yelled, winking.

6

Chaya Jacobson

Strip Clubs and Soul-Searching

CHAYA SKULKED THROUGH HER LIVING ROOM, head down, as if the school bully lurked about and she didn't want to catch his eye. "I'm talking about going to a strip club, and here is the Rebbe, right in my own living room, looking straight at me," she said, to nobody in particular. Rabbi Schneerson's portrait loomed above the mantel like a sentinel. Chaya shivered. That evening, she and I planned to join her friend Devorie at Hot Chix, the strip club where Devorie waitressed. Chaya was a sort of honorary member of the band of questioners at 888 Montgomery Street. She didn't show up every night, and unlike the more hard-core dissenters, she planned to settle down eventually and live an Orthodox life. But some of Chaya's closest friends hailed from that crowd, and when Devorie invited her to check out her place of business, she accepted immediately, viewing it all as a great, if guilt-inducing, adventure.

She spotted her reflection in the hallway mirror; within moments, the source of her anxiety shifted. Chaya's face bears the sort of beauty that makes people stare, despite themselves. At friends' weddings, young male photographers and caterers (the only men allowed in the women's section of the party) often inquire about her, hoping to set up a date. Strikingly fair, she has pale blue eyes, cream-colored skin, and thick white-blonde hair that frames her face with ringlets. She is chubby, though, and her weight creates endless distress for her. Sucking in her stomach, she told me: "I'm really nervous about being there with all those women with perfect bodies. I hope none of the men laugh at me."

As we walked the two short blocks to the subway station, Chaya's distress lifted. Not a mirror was in sight, and the posters of the Rebbe that hung outside many of the Lubavitch homes and stores looked somehow less real than the familiar face in Chaya's living room. An engagement party was winding down at the brownstone on the corner. The bride, a slender, pale-skinned young woman who looked more like a Bat Mitzvah girl than a wife-to-be, had migrated to the porch, where she gabbed with her final well-wishers. "Mazel Tov!" Chaya called out, offering the universal Jewish greeting during times of celebration. "Money marrying money," she whispered to me. "Perfect example." Chaya had been giving me the lowdown on Lubavitch marriage politics, an area of ever-expanding insight now that her own class had begun to date. An expert gossip who knew everyone, Chaya was an extremely reliable source in these matters.

Tonight, her knowledge of human behavior would spread into new arenas. Though we were heading to nearby Queens, the cultural jump from Hasidism to Hot Chix made our destination seem oceans away. Chaya chattered on, asking me what sort of place I thought we would discover at the end of our journey, speculating, imagining, as if we were traveling to some far-off, exotic land: "What do you think the people will be like? Are the men who go desperate, or just out for a good time? I hope we get to talk to some of the women. I really want to hear about their lives."

The subway ride to the club was a long and complex affair, with several train changes and walks down deserted tunnels that stank of urine. We started off about midnight in a car spottily populated by a sleeping homeless woman and a few middle-aged men who jostled each other roughly, sending a strong whiff of alcohol our way whenever they came close. I was scared. Scores of people had told me to avoid late-night subway rides. My Crown Heights landlord, an easygoing, adventuresome woman who has traveled to India, had warned me that "the absolute cutoff is 9 P.M., unless you want to be taking big chances."

I calmed down before long. My fellow traveler had done this countless times en route to late-night gatherings with her friends at Manhattan cafés. For Chaya, the train may as well have been an all-night playground; she spent much of the ride spinning herself from one pole to the next. When she recognized a quiet teenage boy with intricately braided dreadlocks from her neighborhood, she bounded over to meet him: "Hey, I know you. Don't you live on my block in Crown Heights?" The boy jumped for a second, probably shocked that one of his white neighbors was interested in knowing him, then introduced himself with a shy smile. "It'll be cool to see you in Crown Heights now that we've met," Chaya called to him as she walked back toward my seat. Trying to break through the entrenched Crown Heights racial barriers has always been important to Chaya; she often greets her black neighbors and tries to engage them in conversation.

At last Chaya sat down and wriggled out of her long skirt; a pair of faded jeans began to emerge. Then she whipped out a bag of carrots, which she nibbled from for the rest of the journey. Chaya had deemed this a week of dieting, with few foods other than fresh fruit and vegetables and long hours at a nearby gym. She had spent much of the previous week gorging. At several friends' engagement parties, she had hovered by the food, devouring piles of jam-filled cookies, brownies, pecan squares, and bonbons. Periodically she would rest, examine her sugar-coated fingers in horror, and observe, "I must have consumed enough calories to keep the whole neighborhood going." One evening at her home, I watched her eat brimming bowl after bowl of Frosted Flakes, after an agonizing half hour at the grocery store while she debated the relative merits and dangers of whole, low-fat, and skim milk (finally, she chose the low-fat, figuring the skim would be just too gross). Now, munching her carrots, she made amends.

From the second we spotted the mammoth former bowling alley whose roof flashed a long pair of neon legs over a now dim outline of ten bowling pins, Chaya loved Hot Chix. Devorie met us at the front door, decked out in her skintight silky black pants, white oxford shirt, and little black bow tie. She worked the tables, flirting and shaking her butt. An old pot-bellied man squeezed her breasts and passed her a crisp twenty, bestowing a pungent body odor along with his generosity. Devorie grinned mischievously. One of the many mysteries of 888—how in the world it could survive financially with so many unemployed devotees—began to unravel.

The place was wall-to-wall men, whose various scents created a stomach-turning mélange of sweat, alcohol, garlic breath, and stale cigarettes. White working-class men were in the majority, but Hot Chix transcended the class, race, and age boundaries that so starkly divide most of New York social life. Designer suits rubbed shoulders with union jackets and college sweatshirts; pale hands and brown hands competed equally to hail ten minutes with a private stripper. Everyone was ready to splurge, and men of all persuasions lapped up the extra amenities the women offered—a good groin-to-groin rub; a whirling butt in the lap; for the most adventurous and free spending, a trip downstairs to the private cubicles. Chaya gaped, grinning.

Shortly after we arrived, we were treated to the highlight of the Hot Chix experience: the lineup. All the strippers would get together and dance, topless. Chaya was hooked. The different bodies gyrating under the colored florescent lamps were an intriguing sight to a young woman who haunted art museums on the sly, fascinated above all by various artists' visions of the naked body. The women were all thin and mostly tall but from a range of ethnic and racial backgrounds and with varying body shapes. This was, after all, New York City. "Look at that woman's breasts; they're so small," Chaya commented as a petite Asian woman took center stage, savoring a whipped-cream-topped banana and throwing back her head in mock ecstasy as the men cackled and cat-called. "Ooooh. And look at hers. Can they be real? My God." It was quite an education for a girl who had never even experienced the age-old rite of passage of the high school locker room.

Soon Chaya's role as spectator came to a close, and she found herself embroiled in what Henry James would surely have dubbed a "morally interesting experience." Enchanted by the beautiful blonde in the baggy jeans, perhaps finding her a welcome diversion from the half-naked festivities surrounding them, droves of men began surrounding Chaya. "You can have any man you want, Honey. You're gorgeous," a muscular fortyish guy told her as he pinched her cheeks. "Never change those eyes. Wow," a frat-boy type in a backward Colgate University baseball cap added. Flirting and laughing, Chaya beamed. She whispered to me: "Those men are really helping my self-esteem. They make me feel beautiful."

Then Frat Boy changed the stakes and offered Chaya $200 to take off her shirt, $500 to go back to his apartment. A broad-shouldered, athletic-looking young man, the kind you'd expect to have a tennis racket slung casually over his back, he stood, ogling, licking his chops as if he were about to dig into a thick steak. Chaya knew what "going to his apartment" meant, and she was serious about maintaining her virginity until marriage. But $200 for a second's painless gesture? *That* was tempting. She stammered and stalled and finally asked the manager, who said this wasn't allowed; the Hot Chix themselves needed to make the money. She was relieved. "I probably would have done it, and then, knowing me, I would have obsessed and obsessed and made myself miserable for years," she told me later that night.

When we shared the latest tidings with Devorie, she shrugged and smiled. "Sure, I could make an extra thousand dollars a night if I wanted to," she said, "but I am a waitress here, not a stripper. For me, that's private up there."

Chaya spent the next hour or so in the dressing rooms downstairs, bonding with some of the strippers. She easily got them to joke and share their stories with her. Later she told me that was her favorite part of the evening; she spread her charm and her sincere desire to improve people's lives:

> I just love talking to people, meeting people, getting to know them as well as I can, especially when I can help them. There was one girl there, I told her, "Listen, honey, I allow you one more year working in this sleazy place, and then that's done. You're a wonderful person, and you're denying the world this beautiful person that you're hiding." I hope she listens. I like that about me, that I can make people fall in love with themselves and fall in love with me, and hopefully help them along the way.

The role of helper has been foisted on Chaya for most of her nineteen years. Her younger brother Shmuel was born with cerebral palsy. He is wheelchair-bound and unable to dress himself, use the bathroom alone, or write. Eating is a feat; the whole family celebrated when, at age twelve, he mastered the art of scooping soft food with a spoon and placing it in his mouth. Two people in the world understand Shmuel's speech: his mother and Chaya. Chaya was six when her brother was born; he boosted the Jacobson household to its final count of eleven children. As the older siblings began growing up, going away to school, and marrying, more and more responsibility for Shmuel fell on Chaya, who has a talent for handling her brother. By the time she was in high school, she spent most of her free time caring for Shmuel and helping in the house.

Chaya has cultivated a special knack for bonding with her brother. Even so, Shmuel is tough. I can still picture Chaya struggling to deposit him in the car for a doctor's appointment, a ritual repeated several times each month. He kicked and screeched. Shmuel is a lonely, angry boy who rails any way he can against his life within a body that can perform so few of the expected human duties and pleasures. Chaya cornered him and hoisted him into the backseat in a single, snapping motion somewhere between a wrestle and a hug. When she settled into the driver's seat, she looked about ready to cry.

In such circumstances, the family's emotional state is crucial; it can either soothe a seemingly insurmountable problem or cause tensions to escalate to the point of frenzy. This is a family of ballooning emotions. When you're mad, you're furious, and you let people have it with a good holler and a well-chosen barb. Periodically, Mrs. Jacobson lapses into physical abuse—pulling Chaya's hair; slapping her face; once, in a fit of fury, throwing her down the stairs and then admonishing, "We need to go to your uncle's now. You will brush yourself off and put a smile on your face for your uncle." On the other hand, love for her children can overwhelm Mrs. Jacobson to tears. Life is, in a word, overwhelming.

The Jacobsons do get by in their grueling lives without collapsing. Their marriage endures; there have been no full-blown nervous breakdowns to date; they have helped Shmuel to improve both his coordination and his social skills; their other children, despite their all too common insecurities, seem fundamentally confident and content with themselves. I would have to call them a family of hysterical survivors.

I spent a long summer Shabbos day with the Jacobsons, and they took me on a roller coaster of reactions and interactions. Shmuel was away in a special camp for the summer, and lunch that day was a small affair, with just Mr. and Mrs. Jacobson, Chaya, and me. The small brownstone, which in earlier, more crowded years must have burst with activity, seemed quiet. Life was not as hectic as it might have been. Even so, feelings exploded at times. The atmosphere heated up when Chaya accidentally sprinkled a minute amount of sugar in the soup, thinking it was salt. She was worried that she had ruined it and told her mother. Henya Jacobson, a slight woman with incredible vocal power, went on a rampage: "You *what*? You put *sugar* in the soup? Oh, talk about self-centered. That's the way you are, you're so into your own thoughts that you can't even concentrate to make the soup right?" Henya tasted the soup, and it was fine, so the incident blew over: "You got lucky this time, Chaya, but next time you'll pay for your actions, so be careful."

During the actual meal, the conversation was calm and pleasant, though people were perhaps on their best behavior because of me. Somehow, in the midst of the tension, Henya and Chaya managed to prepare a tasty spread: chicken and vegetable soup; gefilte fish; a bean, potato, and meat stew known as *cholent* (a Shabbos lunch staple because it can simmer overnight in a special pot that doesn't need to be turned on or off during the holiday); and apple cake. Only the cake bore any sign of stress; Chaya had roughly torn off a hunk to comfort herself after her mother's attack.

Chaya joked with her mother about various girls from her high school class: "She's a *mouse*! I'm so serious! Everything about her—the little chattering lips, the skinny little fidgeting body, the way she puckers her nose. . . . Have you seen her in action with that nose?" Mother and daughter united in their glee; Chaya's humor can pacify even the tightly wound Henya. Tall, dour Baruch Jacobson was silent for the most part, as he usually was, almost as if he were an interloper, not the husband and father of the people who had prepared his lunch.

Later in the afternoon, Chaya's older sister Rivky joined us with Mendy, her fiancé of three days. Ordinarily the bride and groom would not spend much time together until after the wedding, but Rivky was a tad rebellious herself. Since Rivky was a bit older (twenty-four), Henya was so relieved about the upcoming marriage that her daughter had earned herself a bit of tether. It was a good thing. Rivky was headstrong beneath her round baby blue eyes, and disagreement over Mendy's appropriate role in her life during the weeks before the wedding could have spurred emotional explosions.

Henya poured us each a small cup of vodka to make a *l'chaim*, a toast to life, a common ritual during times of celebration. Rivky toasted her mother: "I will always appreciate the love you gave me. It was so very special. It was something I could always count on, that made my days in this house beautiful." Henya was bawling; Chaya nodded a teary, emphatic affirmation. Beyond the bluster, Henya's love for Chaya was obvious even from the way she looked at her youngest daughter.

For all the love, this is very far from an ideal family arrangement. Mr. Jacobson comes across as a man on the sidelines; Mrs. Jacobson allows her tension to escalate into cruelty and even violence. A good friend of Chaya's partially attributes Henya and Baruch's problems to the circumstances of their marriage. Typical Lubavitch marriages succeed and blossom; two young people who don't know each other all that well come together and learn to accommodate and compromise as time passes and inevitable conflicts surface. Occasionally, though, a few well-spaced dates simply do not give people enough of a sense of what they will be in for over the next decades. The Jacobsons may well fall into this unfortunate category.

Baruch hails from a thoroughly secular Russian family (his given name is Mikhail), and he emigrated alone in his early twenties. He knew very little about the United States, but he had nothing keeping him in Russia. Baruch had grown up in poverty, with a deeply disturbed mother who showed him little warmth. Hungry for a new life, he circumvented strict emigration laws and managed to leave Russia for New York.

His sudden leap into American culture disoriented him, and he rejoiced when he met an incredibly friendly rabbi with a thick Russian accent who loved to reminisce about his pre-American years. Rabbi Cohn recognized Baruch's visual talents and found him a job doing graphics for a Lubavitch-run printing press in Crown Heights. Baruch was impressed with the purposeful, faith-centered people he found in the community and began studying Judaism with Rabbi Cohn and a few other concerned mentors. Before long, he decided to devote his life to Lubavitch. To ensure that his new protégé lived in the proper Jewish style, Rabbi Cohn contacted a neighborhood matchmaker to find a wife for Baruch. And so Baruch married a Lubavitch woman and settled into Hasidic life. But shell shock from his troubled childhood lingered; the poverty and the years contending with a mentally ill mother were not easily forgotten. To this day, he has difficulty expressing love and largely keeps to himself, even within his family.

Henya Jacobson (née Allison Beck) grew up in a largely Jewish neighborhood in Queens, New York. Her family was, according to her description, "traditional," meaning that they observed all the basic holidays and more or less kept kosher in their home. But she felt they lacked true commitment and belief; their observances felt like "going through the motions." On her own, she began exploring Brooklyn's Orthodox Jewish neighborhoods and developed a close feeling for Lubavitch. By the time she finished college, she was ready for the Hasidic dating scene. Female *baalei teshuvah* usually outnumber their male peers by a substantial margin, and a compatible husband can be an elusive prize. A matchmaker thought Allison and Baruch might click, since they shared an artistic sensibility (Allison is an accomplished pianist). They went on a few dates in kosher restaurants, and although they were not "in love," they accepted what their mentors had told them: that caring would grow over time in the course of the marriage. They were both very eager to get on with their duties as Hasidic adults, so they announced their engagement.

In some key ways, they could not be more different—a quiet Russian immigrant with little sense for American culture and few material desires and an outgoing native New Yorker with a submerged love of Broadway show tunes and a penchant for shopping. They seem to move onward together more out of duty than true caring.

Within this tumult, Chaya has struggled to find meaning in her own life. One savior for her has been her music. She never took lessons—her parents couldn't afford them with all the special treatments Shmuel required. Nevertheless, her music is stunning. I once heard her transform an old Hasidic melody, usually sung, on the piano. She captured the poignancy of the song and maintained the basic tune but also intermixed a bit of her own rhythm. It replayed in my mind for months, filtering in at the oddest times, giving me a subtle but clear form of instant pleasure. Chaya also has a strong, angelic singing voice and a propensity to break out in song when the mood strikes her.

This gift seems to come from her mother, who studied music at a local city college before settling into her Hasidic life, but Henya Jacobson has little interest in her daughter's talent, since Chaya uses it in ways that flout Lubavitch beliefs and sensibilities. Once Chaya performed her magnum opus for her mother—her own take on Elton John's musically complex piece "Funeral for a Friend." Chaya arose from the piano drenched in sweat, both from the physical effort and from the nagging hope that her mother would love the song. Henya just shrugged and said, "Oh, okay." Chaya was "incredibly hurt" that Henya, herself an able musician, could not appreciate her daughter's work.

When she was younger, Chaya had starred in the school musicals, sharing her sweet voice with most of female Lubavitch Crown Heights. If her mother had been any prouder, she would have exploded, but that pride has faded. Now Chaya's music has the taint of secularism; the notion that music written by a non-Jew can disturb a Hasid's soul is strong in Lubavitch, and rock music, Chaya's specialty, is considered particularly vile.

Not so long ago, Henya Jacobson would probably have accepted her daughter's interest in non-Jewish music. Like many *baalei teshuvah*, her values and lifestyle had vacillated between old and new. She was a Hasid, through and through, but with a secular twist: luxurious afternoons spent listening to her favorite Broadway sound tracks or jazz albums, an interest in secular literature, an occasional habit of taking in a movie at a Manhattan theater. She allowed her children some leeway as well—they could read a wide variety of secular books and magazines, go to the movies, even watch television openly, since a doctor's suggestion that television viewing might help Shmuel develop a sense for proper social interaction had already landed a set in the Jacobson house.

Then came the Rebbe's death. Henya underwent a psychic shift nearly as dramatic as her original path to Lubavitch. Chaya expressed it bluntly: "When the Rebbe died, my mom turned into a different woman." Out went everything from the television set to Henya's support of Chaya's college plans. It was a traumatic time for all Lubavitchers, and many resolved to step up their observance levels in line with the widespread notion that every last Jewish law carries mystical significance, the power to alter the structure of the world, and, by extension, the potential to bring the Rebbe back as the Messiah.

The idea is staggering. So were the practical effects on Chaya's life. With no parental support for her dream to enter a music school, she wound up at Touro, the ultra-Orthodox institution that enrolled several of her Lubavitch peers. Craving independence, Chaya embarked on a painful odyssey to move out of her house and into the Touro dorm—an anathema in this community, where the people who do attend college nearly always commute from home.

Chaya had spent her first semester after high school graduation in an Israeli seminary, which at first galvanized her religious commitment: "They really took my questions seriously, for the first time in my life. They cared, and they respected me. And being in Israel really brings out your *neshama* [Jewish soul]." Then her musical side—the gift that demanded exploration of nonreligious artistic realms—kicked in, along with a good boost from her alarm at the imminent weddings awaiting her observant peers. She once told me, suppressing a giggle but with an emphatic tone, "I'm nineteen now. I am *not* ready to get married. I am *not* ready for marriage. I am not ready to settle down with the same guy for the rest of my life. Also, I don't think it's necessary. I'm a little kid." As her peers began to negotiate the Lubavitch dating process, Chaya felt more and more marginal in the world of Crown Heights.

As the year progressed, she began dropping religious expectations until she found herself tasting nonkosher meat and taking in the sights at Hot Chix. She moved in steps, testing the waters of a transgression before plunging into full-fledged sin. One Shabbos she watched television when a friend flipped on the forbidden power button; the next Shabbos she guiltily changed the stations herself, generating her own verboten electrical energy on the holy day of rest. One evening she sampled nonkosher cheese with her friends; a few weeks later she tried a nonkosher burger—a much more serious breach. Late-night café-hopping and philosophizing with her friends from 888 spiced up her new post-Orthodox existence; the lives of her typical classmates seemed increasingly distant and irrelevant.

Chaya's desire to break free of Orthodox strictures combined with her mother's emotional and physical abuse began to make her Crown Heights life intolerable. She left her house and headed for Touro's dorm, only to find herself back in Crown Heights after her mother called a Touro dean and let her know that Chaya was flouting Lubavitch expectations by living away from home. But Chaya is not one to relinquish her goals. Finally she called the dean herself with a message that was impossible to ignore: "Listen, I come from an abusive family. Would you like me to go back home to my abusive family?" Before long she was settled in the Touro dorm once again.

She enjoyed the independence and the opportunity to take classes in fields ranging from classical philosophy to art history, but academics have never been her strong suit. Severe difficulty with reading has dogged her ever since she began school, and, despite her obvious intelligence, her grades have been mediocre at best. Music is her love. After a year, she joined her friends from 888 at Manhattan's Hunter College and switched her major to music. Chaya is thriving, constantly throwing herself into singing and piano projects. Since she could barely read music when she began, she needed to start with the basics. But the department took her on the strength of her obvious talent, which she is working furiously to cultivate. Her parents are dismayed but have not ostracized her, and she frequently returns to Crown Heights for some tumultuous yet oddly satisfying family togetherness.

Troubled as her family life has been, Chaya is socially confident. I remember her at a friend's engagement party during her peers' steady march toward married life. These gatherings boast an inclusiveness rarely found in other cultures; people invite their entire Bais Rivka class, and while good friends are most likely to come, others often show their support as well. Neighbors, parents' friends, family members, and business associates round out the crowd. Before long, the wedding day arrives, and the festivities reemerge on a grander scale. But even the engagement parties evoke an exuberant atmosphere. In Hasidism, marriage is the path to a holy life and the gateway to the future Jewish nation; it certainly warrants two celebrations.

Gittel's engagement party drew a particularly wide gamut of people. The passionately religious young women who had been joining Gittel in weekly discussions of Jewish texts arrived early and picked at the mouthwatering display of delicacies—peanut chews; jelly rolls; nut-filled brownies; creamy hummus with mixed vegetables; a heaping platter of bright, oversized strawberries, mangoes, kiwis, and pineapple slices. These first guests looked quiet and serious in their long woolen skirts and long-sleeved shirts buttoned to the top, but they were quick to smile and talk when I approached them. Soon another pair of friends arrived, wearing slightly shorter skirts and short-sleeved blouses that left their elbows bare. They were classmates from Stern College—the modern Orthodox girls' school Gittel attended as part of her plan to become a doctor—who were eager to enjoy their first Hasidic party. Then the relatives descended: a secular-looking American crowd from Gittel's family, olive-skinned Moroccans with melodious accents from her fiancé's. Finally, Crown Heightsers arrived en masse: young seminary students from Gittel's class, friends of her parents, a few neighbors, a former tenant who had moved up to live with the family when she ran out of money to pay her rent.

An old friend of Gittel's family commented to me: "This is really what Lubavitch is all about. Jews of all kinds—religious and non-religious—coming to wish the young people well. And different cultures of Jews coming together in the families of the young man and woman." It was a microcosm of what Lubavitch strives to do, to reach Jews all over the world and in every possible social circumstance.

Chaya made the rounds among all the guests. She laughed; she joked; she praised nearly everyone she met. A striking young Moroccan mother happily answered Chaya's earnest queries about her experiences during her first extended trip to America. Upon hearing Chaya's assessment that she looked "gorgeous," a middle-aged neighbor of hers beamed. A classmate shrieked hysterically at Chaya's apt imitation of a notorious teacher. By Lubavitch standards, the bride's family was unusually modern. Though most Lubavitchers separate men and women for these parties, here the genders mingled throughout the spacious downstairs rooms. Still, the divisive impulse took over, and most people stuck to their own: girls in one corner, neighbors in another, relatives huddled together in the kitchen. Not Chaya. For her, new people are an adventure.

Chaya's interpersonal verve has one major limitation—the crush factor. If she is infatuated with someone, nerves overtake nerve. One evening at 888, Ari showed up and squelched Chaya's personality. It was not his fault; Chaya was in love with him, a situation that invariably saps her wit and charm. She sat quietly, a tight, awkward smile plastered on her face, while Ari entertained everyone with his endearing zaniness, screeching, singing, and literally climbing the walls like an oversized spider.

Afterward, Chaya bemoaned her out-of-character shyness: "He doesn't know my real personality because I clam up when he's around. I wonder if he would like me if he really knew me." She spent the rest of the evening lamenting her fate, hoping and praying that Ari would eventually return her passion but knowing, somehow, that he never would. We sat outside her house and talked about it for hours, almost until the sun rose to greet the next day, but nothing was resolved. Ari, it seemed, was simply not interested. "I hope you don't think I'm crazy," she said forlornly as she trudged back into her house, her dreams of Ari relinquished but not forgotten.

It was not the first time. In high school, Chaya found herself mired in blissful rebellion: she had a boyfriend, for four months that she describes as the happiest time of her life. During the eleventh grade, she noticed two boys at the Crown Heights kosher ice cream shop. One was taunting a blind boy, and the other started screaming at his friend, berating him for his insensitivity. The whistle-blower intrigued Chaya, and she said a few words to him. Lubavitch social expectations sharply forbade much more than this, so they sneaked off to a hidden corner of a nearby building. Chaya told me, smiling sadly:

His name was Chaim. I was just so awed by him. He gave me special attention that I wasn't getting from my family. He was just charming, funny, sweet. My mother was taking college classes at night. He would come over my house four or five nights a week and we would just sit and talk. We were so innocent. I don't like to use the word "love." We just thought about each other a lot and cared about each other a lot.

Once, they did kiss, "but it was so innocent. I think we kissed with our mouths closed. We took turns having our mouths open. We wouldn't stick our tongue into the next person's mouth. That was too much."

Before long, the whole situation became too much for Chaim. Ambivalence plagued both of these young lovers; school was teaching them that they could not even look at or think about a member of the opposite sex. Eventually, Chaim broke off the relationship, since he felt he had grown spiritually and did not want to compromise his religious progress. Chaya was devastated: "I did not get over him for a long time. I'm breathing now, but I never thought I would. You could probably say I stalked him for months afterward; I would hang around his house for no reason." She felt guilty throughout the fling, but she loved it all the same.

Chaya's life in general has been one of push and pull, pleasure and regret, doubt and belief. We got together several months after I had left Crown Heights, and I discovered that she is now observant. Not Crown Heights observant—she is living in a dorm on Manhattan's Upper West Side, a haven for Jewish culture of all sorts save the cloistered ultra-Orthodox world of her upbringing—but observant nonetheless. She tries to follow all the basic laws and attends a synagogue that combines Hasidism and funk: Hasidic singing and dancing for a modern Jewish crowd of ranging religious affiliation. Eventually, she hopes to settle down with a more modern Lubavitcher, "someone who will respect my music, be open to secular culture, not expect me to be a slave around the house. Guys like this are rare, but they're around."

Nothing special happened to spur the change; Chaya has always planned on returning to Orthodoxy. Away from Brooklyn and content with her new life, she felt the strength to try. It has been tough ("it's like giving up smoking when you're totally addicted") but also deeply rewarding. This is where she wants to be. Looking chic and casual in her long Indian skirt and suede sandals, she could have fooled anyone who did not know her story into thinking she was just another Upper West Sider enjoying a stroll about town. But she is, fundamentally, a Lubavitcher.

I asked her if she now accepted her community's basic beliefs. She smiled, smirked, and twirled her long hair, all the while deep in thought. The question gnawed. When she finally responded with a reminiscence about the yearly Bais Rivka musical production, she managed to make me laugh for about five minutes straight and then think for many hours more:

> There were little skits about how to be a better Jew. Like, God. I couldn't deal. I was like, no way. Excuse me, but I'm not spending every evening of mine studying the lines of a play that I entirely disagree with. Because their idea of how to be a better Jew has nothing to do with how to be a better person. Like, don't work on Shabbos. Don't let your knees show. Make sure people have mezuzahs and stuff. But it doesn't matter what the person is inside. You could be a rotten fuck hole.

Her theatrical intonation all along was too much to handle. I laughed and laughed and laughed. Then she continued, in a much more somber tone:

> With it all, I do believe that the Rebbe is very, very powerful and very, very wise. The stories of his miracles are so amazing, and so many people that I know and trust had experiences with him where he did incredible things: healed sicknesses, made desperate women pregnant, you name it. I doubt. I have my big doubts. But I think I do believe.

In this sentiment, she joins most of the great sages from throughout Jewish history, whose prodigious faith was often accompanied by serious probing and doubting, all in the name of seeking the truth.

Chaya had to leave. She was meeting a friend on the other side of the city, and she would not even consider using public transportation, for it was Shabbos afternoon. The walk would take almost two hours, and she would then need to climb to the twelfth floor of an apartment building; elevators, too, are prohibited on Shabbos. She walked briskly, glancing at all the store windows she passed. At one point she stopped in front of a window, gazed in fascination, almost with longing, and continued on her way. Later, I walked by that window myself and chuckled at the sight of an attractive blue bikini.

7

Gittel Kassin

Medicine and Marriage

AT ITS BUSIEST, THE KASSINS' KITCHEN juggled several simultaneous identities: studying turf for gifted adolescents, halfway house for troubled *baalei teshuvah,* financial think tank, geriatric haven, mystical retreat. The large attached brownstone on Crown Street was a complex, always welcoming place for me to spend some time. This family of financial wizards, scientists, and physicians-to-be enjoyed spending time with a doctoral student, though my economic prospects, or lack thereof, offended their practical sensibilities. I think of a warm spring afternoon, much like many other afternoons I spent with this family. Ruth, mother and businesswoman extraordinaire (she has raised six children and has spearheaded a thriving financial consulting practice), was combing through *Forbes,* hoping to score some investment tips. "I have to say, I think I'm getting the hang of the market," she told me. "I think I may have to start my own mutual fund." Tall, blonde, and slender, she looks more Scandinavian than Jewish, but one word out of her mouth banishes all thoughts in that direction; Yiddish inflections and expressions pervade her speech.

Before long, Ruth's ninety-year-old mother shambled in from her quarters in the adjoining room. Mentally degenerating at a rapid pace, Jane Mandelbaum straddled a fragile line between wise elder and helpless child. She begged and pleaded with her daughter to drive her home to 387 Webster Avenue, her address some sixty years back. Then she looked at me and announced, in a deep, clear voice: "They don't need that. They don't need it," over and over, at least seven times.

I shuddered, reading deep meaning into her words: "they" could have been any one of a host of people I had treated harshly through the years. But Ruth just laughed and brushed the comment off: "She's teasing you. She doesn't mean anything." Ruth could have suffered continuous heartbreak at the sight of her once sharp, vibrant mother's unmistakable sinking into a senile abyss, but she reacted with her signature lighthearted, down-to-business style. Ruth giggled at Jane's confusion; she didn't have time to dwell on the situation, anyway, between carting her mother around to her various doctors' appointments and keeping track of her live-in hired nurse. The drill was familiar. A stream of elderly parents, aunts, and uncles have lived out their final frail days in the Kassin home. When Ruth sees relatives in need, she takes them in without a second's hesitation.

The old woman's mumbling soon drowned under a louder, stronger voice, for Shira, a former tenant turned temporary member of the family, had arrived home. A wavering *baal teshuvah* whose religious fervor had recently relaxed to the point where we all spotted her wearing shorts in the backyard, Shira received an invitation to join the Kassins in their own house when she lost her job and, with it, the funds to pay her rent. "Hey, everybody!" Shira called as she rushed into the kitchen to help the elderly Puerto Rican housekeeper prepare Shabbos dinner. Shira's magic touch in the kitchen, from rich, delectable chocolate cakes to fluffy matzo balls, was greatly appreciated in the Kassin house, even as everyone wondered when she would gird herself to move on. Ruth's assessment of the situation was typical of her generous spirit: "Nobody else in Crown Heights would have her, with her shorts right outside in broad daylight, but it doesn't bother me. We're open-minded in this house. And, besides, what was I supposed to do, put her out on the street?"

But Shira had perhaps an even greater friend in Gittel, Ruth's nineteen-year-old daughter. "Shira, where were you? You've been gone for a few days. I was a little worried," Gittel called out from the table where she was studying organic chemistry for a class at the modern Orthodox Stern College. As she flung back her curly dark hair and stretched her long legs, I noticed that she truly combined her parents' physical traits: tall and slim like her mother, olive-skinned and dark-haired like her father. Gittel grinned at Shira, relieved that her friend was safely back home.

Gittel's thick chemistry text lay open in front of her; an unfinished seating chart for her upcoming wedding waited on the other side of the table for her finishing touches. Shabbos would arrive in just a few hours, so all work would go on hiatus for a full day, until Saturday evening. An organic chemistry final was coming up early the next week. The following week came the dreaded MCAT, the standardized test all medical school applicants must take. One week after that, Gittel would marry Yosef, a young man she had met through a friend at Stern. Gittel's life seemed a chaotic mélange of Stanley Kaplan test preparation and hors d'oeuvre menus.

She looked frazzled. Her mother told me, half jokingly, "Gittel's having a nervous breakdown over here. I think it would be wise if she took a year off from school after the wedding."

But Gittel laughed off the suggestion: "Please. I'm fine. I like being busy." She was harried, but smiling all the while. "Oh, Mom, we haven't done your science lesson yet," she suddenly realized. Every week, just before Shabbos, Gittel gave her mother a lesson from *Science* magazine. She flipped through the latest issue. "What do you want to hear about? Genetic engineering? Recent advances in cancer research? Hybrid plants?"

"Whatever you think is interesting, honey." Ruth was slightly distracted but glad to get her lesson. She grinned at me, nodding toward Gittel. The intellectual enthusiasm and desire to share that impelled Gittel's teaching efforts made Ruth proud. Gittel launched into an explanation of recent breakthroughs in genetic engineering, her own research interest; she had spent the previous two summers working on genetic issues at a school lab.

Occasionally, Ruth's eyes would glaze. She had a lot to think about besides clones and mutations—the Shabbos meal she would serve, her clients' portfolios, her youngest son's progress on studying for his SATs. But Gittel would catch her in the act and recapture her attention: "Mom, are you *listening*?"

Gittel appeared to be the Hasidic version of the proverbial supergirl who has it all—top grades, striking good looks, impressive intelligence, a doting fiancé, plans for a long-dreamed-of medical career, social popularity despite her propensity to buck Lubavitch norms (medical school is a highly unusual choice for a Hasidic young woman). Even so, at the moment she was quite overworked between school and the wedding. "Especially," she told me later that night, "because I'm a huge perfectionist." This is a girl known throughout Crown Heights for her brilliance and diligence.

With it all, she had the energy to worry about Shira; she always set aside plenty of time to care for other people, from the college roommates she cooked for to the discombobulated former tenant who craved a little warmth. When the science lesson ended, Gittel tried to get the lowdown on Shira's whereabouts during the past few days. Shira, an energetic, strong-willed, fortyish single woman with friends throughout Crown Heights, was used to living on her own, coming and going according to her personal whim. The Kassins' concern was new for her, but her gratified smile in Gittel's direction told me that it was greatly appreciated. "Oh, I was fine. You know me. I was staying with various friends. But it's great to be back."

It was a familiar story. Friends, family, and acquaintances on the outs often find their way here, relishing the free food, lively conversation, and, most of all, the true caring that all too often had eluded them throughout their lives. The Kassins' open home is only one manifestation of their true generosity. They are no strangers to strictly financial forms of charity; neighborhood schools and floundering relatives head the list of monetary recipients. "Oh, Stephanie, if I had a billion dollars, I'd probably just give it all away," Ruth once told me, in a tone somewhere between a laugh and a sigh. In a sense, all this altruism is the true embodiment of Hasidic ideals: to funnel the rewards of financial flair into the lives of needy Jewish souls is to elevate the mundane and transform it into holiness.

For all that, this is no family of misty-eyed, impractical do-gooders. Here, the sacred intertwines with a heavy dose of realism. This house exudes a modern, this-worldly sensibility that many Hasidic homes lack. Faith in God is strong among the Kassins, but so is individual success and interest in secular affairs. Some Hasidim seem to relinquish control of their pragmatic lives; I've met people who laugh off the idea of health insurance, claiming that the necessary funds would materialize if, God forbid, a medical disaster struck. The Kassins balance their Hasidic convictions with worldly interests and values. God is everywhere, but he does not nullify the desire to plan ahead or think about intellectual arenas beyond Judaism's purview.

This balance stems largely from family history. Ruth and Daniel Kassin both hail from religious but somewhat assimilated homes. Ruth's parents had Hasidic lineage and kept a strictly Orthodox house, but they believed strongly in the modern Orthodox credo of merging secular and Jewish domains. Daniel, a talented chemist, grew up in a Jewish neighborhood in Syria. Like many Syrian Jews, his family observed all the holidays and rituals but maintained wide interests beyond Judaism. The Kassins found Lubavitch in Dallas when they were searching for a synagogue. Delighted by the warmth and vitality of the group, they joined the ranks of the Hasidim and moved to Crown Heights to build their lives around the Rebbe, but they never lost the careful balance they had cultivated during childhood between Judaism and the outside universe.

Gittel captured the Kassin way; her parents adored their clever, hardworking, quietly devout daughter with a passion for science. At Shabbos dinner that evening, Gittel had big news: she had won an award from school for a poster she had designed explaining some of her biological research. This was not an unusual event; Gittel was a star at Stern, just as she had been all through school in Crown Heights. Pictures of her raking in prizes at various awards assemblies, grinning profusely next to eminent professors, were displayed prominently throughout the dining room.

Gittel's achievements were continuous, but new ones always captivated her parents. Her black eyes sparkling, she presented her new certificate of merit to her father, a swarthy, husky man who gazed at it reverently and said, "I'm very proud of you for getting this." All Kassins and guests looked up from their heaping plates of crisp breaded chicken, green beans, rice, broccoli, and potato kugel to eye Gittel's new prize. Gittel jokingly put the certificate in front of an award her brother, also an exceptional student at Yeshiva College (the male counterpart to Stern), had won. "There's no need for that," her father laughed. "We'll buy you your own frame, and you can put it anywhere you want."

Ruth nudged me, beaming: "You see what smart kids we have in this family?" She started asking Gittel about her thoughts on applying to medical school—did she think she would apply only in the Maryland area, where she would live with her new husband after the wedding, or would she explore New York schools as well?

Gittel gave her mother a playful dig: "I'm not sure right now. Lately I've been thinking maybe I'd go into physical therapy. It's a nice field, and it doesn't take so much schooling or pressure." She giggled a little under her breath.

Ruth sank right into the trap. "No! You're gonna be a doctor. What are you talking about? This kid's gonna be a doctor, right, Stephanie?" I shrugged and looked toward Gittel, the only one capable of making this decision.

"Oh, Mom, I'm just kidding. I just get worried sometimes, with all the pressure—raising a family and everything, taking care of the house."

"Don't worry. I've got it all figured out. You'll send the kids here a lot of the time, and I'll pay for some help for you over there. It'll be fine. It'll be great." Ruth spoke rapidly, almost frantically, though with a touch of the humor her daughter had shown.

This was an ongoing family joke tinged with seriousness. Gittel's life as a Hasidic female physician would be an incredible challenge few could handle. If all goes according to plan, she will have several children, a thriving home to care for, and many patients with diverse problems requiring her medical expertise. It's a situation that demands compromises, something Gittel well realizes. Several weeks later, during a long, intense conversation, she told me:

> I want to be a doctor. I want to help people. But I don't need to be the head of the department. I don't need to be this big doctor going to conferences all over the world, you know what I'm saying? So I don't necessarily need to be the very best in my class. If you fail a course because you're giving birth or you're pregnant, they'll give you a chance to make it up.

Her eyelids fluttered from anxiety. This is a young woman who has always maintained a nearly perfect academic record. "I might not get into the best residency because I didn't do so well in such and such a course, but it's not gonna in the end make a difference." Gittel laughed nervously. Accepting less than perfection is not one of her highly developed skills. "I mean, I think having a family is very important. 'Cause when you're sixty or seventy, you're not gonna say, 'Oh, I should have spent two more hours at work.' You're gonna say, 'I should have spent two more hours with my kids.'"

Within the Crown Heights Lubavitch outlook, Gittel is a bit of a black sheep, albeit a highly respected one. "Gittel? She's a brilliant, brilliant girl. She skipped her senior year to go to Stern, and now she's gonna be a doctor," one classmate, no intellectual slouch herself, explained. But she immediately added, "You need to remember that she is not the typical girl. Very few Lubavitch girls go to Stern; it's just not seen as being *frum* [religious] enough for us. And medical school, I don't know how she'll do it. Did she happen to mention whether she wants to start having kids?" She looked at me, almost imploringly. She clearly would have been horrified if I had said Gittel had decided to wait until after she finished medical school. That sort of family manipulation is an anathema in Crown Heights; barring highly unusual circumstances (a rabbi may give permission to use birth control if he is convinced it is essential to the mother's physical or emotional health), people gladly accept whatever children come their way in the natural scheme.

In fact, Gittel planned to do it all—a growing family and medical training all at once. For her particular situation, she is not rebellious at all. She maintains her parents' ideal balancing act, with plans to build an Orthodox home undergirding her professional aspirations.

Rafi, the Kassins' youngest child at fifteen, seemed more unruly from a family perspective. Ruth laughingly called him "the rabbi of the family." Of all the Kassin children, he was the only one who really grew up in Crown Heights. Gittel came in second grade, after a few years in Texas. The Kassins' other children were older still when they moved to Brooklyn. Gittel's oldest brother, a thirty-year-old corporate attorney, was a decidedly modern Orthodox type with a knitted yarmulke and a shaved face. Her remaining siblings were more like her, balancing Lubavitch values and secular career aspirations. One brother hoped for a career in investment banking; a sister works as a podiatrist; another sister is a successful engineer. All have secular interests in areas like music and literature.

It was Rafi, a fair, angelic-looking young man, who truly toed the Crown Heights line. One morning, he lectured his mother on the spiritual dangers of getting coffee at Dunkin' Donuts. "I only do it in emergencies when I'm traveling, and the coffee itself is fine. I don't eat anything," Ruth explained; she felt that if she wasn't actually consuming anything nonkosher, she wasn't harming anyone.

No dice. "Even so, you shouldn't spend time in there. It's not right." "Oy vey," was all Ruth could say to that one.

Rafi also monitored the family's Shabbos atmosphere. In the midst of Ruth and Gittel's discussions of medical school admissions policies, he would groan, "Will you be talking about this throughout the whole Shabbos?" Ideally, Shabbos is a time for spiritual reflection, an island in time away from workaday concerns. But forgetting about work is a nearly impossible task in this home.

Rafi's teachers love his spiritual earnestness, and his parents are proud of it, too, but they worry about his financial future. Ruth confided to me:

> He wants to go on *shlichus* [become an emissary of the Rebbe and try to inspire secular Jews to become Orthodox], but a family like us, without Lubavitch *yichus* or real insider status, won't get the plum jobs. He wants to stay in Lubavitch yeshiva full-time while he should be taking college classes, too. I worry. He needs to support himself.

Rafi was within earshot; he looked up and gave a subtle scowl. Clearly, he is of the "God will provide" persuasion.

Rafi sometimes baffles his practical mother, but his father has a bit more empathy, for he has profound mystical leanings of his own. Daniel is a quiet man, not given to expounding on his opinions. Still, he has plenty of private spiritual convictions. One afternoon, I chatted with him while his wife worked on some clients' portfolios in the next room. I asked what he thought about the controversy over whether the Rebbe was the Messiah. It was several years after Rabbi Schneerson's death, and factions were strengthening, with the strong *meshichists,* those convinced the Rebbe would return to this world as the Messiah, alienated from the anti-*meshichists.* It had gotten to the point where the central Lubavitch synagogue on 770 Eastern Parkway maintained two separate offices.

Daniel smiled and answered:

> The Rebbe comes to me sometimes in dreams. He tells me things. I have always felt close to him, even now, after his death. One night after his death he came right up to me in my sleep and told me that he was not Moshiach. So, I know he's not. But other people, they can believe how they want. I have no problem with them. Everyone has their reasons.

Daniel is a humble but powerful mystic. The Kassins moved from Dallas to Crown Heights partially because Daniel had a dream in which he pictured their new Brooklyn house. Once, when Gittel was out late, the Rebbe came to Daniel in a dream and told him: "Don't worry. She's with me." Sure enough, she was at a *farbrengen,* one of the celebrations the Rebbe used to hold regularly for Lubavitchers.

Gittel has a touch of the mystical as well. Her closest friends throughout her childhood were two girls known for their intense religiosity; she remained in close touch with them even as a student at Stern. They kept up their regular study sessions whenever Gittel was back home in Crown Heights; Gittel loved to delve into Hasidic philosophy with her pals. She described her reactions to one of these friends, a young woman whose dress, diet, values, and future goals all reflected her unflagging religious commitment: "Even though she was very strong in her views, I got along with her. I mean, a lot of things I agreed with, you know? Or I really understood why and what she was doing." Gittel combined her religious conviction and her this-worldly goals easily; they were complementary, equally central parts of her psyche.

At Stern, living among young women from modern Orthodox, not at all Hasidic, backgrounds, Gittel held her ground, quietly keeping to her own standards even as she developed close friendships among the students. Many of the girls wore pants in the dorm, since there were no men around to see them anyway, but never Gittel. Inappropriate parties periodically came up, with wild music and mixed-gender dancing, and Gittel refrained, though she maintained friendships with the people who had invited her. "I keep to my guns. I like that. I want to be able to keep that. I just do what I think is right," she told me.

Of course, this is a rare talent among adolescents. The typical Lubavitch parents would not want their daughter at a modern Orthodox school; the accepted modes of behavior among the modern Orthodox, while deriving from Jewish tradition, can differ starkly from Hasidic norms. Skirts and sleeves can be shorter; dietary rules can be more lax; mixed-gender activities can crop up. Many Hasidic young people would probably lapse into peer pressure and take on some of these different standards. It's easier to stick with Lubavitch schools or, if college is necessary, the ultra-Orthodox Touro. But, then, the Kassins rarely take the easy route, least of all Gittel.

Gittel was following an unusual path for Crown Heights. She left Bais Rivka after eleventh grade for Stern College, where she had earned early admission. Unlike the overwhelming majority of Crown Heights college students (the number of Lubavitch commuters at Touro is growing, and a sizable minority of girls now attend), Gittel lived in the dorms. The high school never would have authorized this plan; the ideal for a Lubavitch girl is a full program of high school, followed by two years of seminary. The Kassins proceeded on the sly, never informing the school in Crown Heights of their intentions. At the beginning of twelfth grade, Gittel just didn't show up. The administration was miffed but simultaneously proud. The high school principal told me all about the brilliant young woman who had achieved early admission to Stern with medical school on the horizon. Gittel herself noticed the irony: "There's something interesting going on. People think it's not the best for me to be in Stern and thinking of med school, but then again, they're so, so impressed."

Now, three years after her early departure from Bais Rivka, medical school was all but inevitable. Gittel worked joyfully at her classes and at her medical research job and fretted about standardized admissions testing. She spent hours each week at the lab in school, assisting a biology professor. Stanley Kaplan sessions and practice MCATs occupied many additional hours. Number two pencil shavings had embedded themselves in the Kassins' kitchen table; Gittel's favorite spot turned grayer and grayer with the passing weeks. Of course, if she wanted a break from MCAT preparation, she had organic chemistry to round out her time.

But medical school was not all that captured her attention. She was engaged and very much in love. Most Lubavitch marriage plans are made after a few dates arranged by community matchmakers; compatibility is necessary, but love, it is assumed, will grow over time. Gittel's Stern friends had a slightly more mainstream approach to dating. Yosef, originally from a small Jewish community in Morocco, is the brother of her good friend Navah; their family discovered Lubavitch when they immigrated to Maryland. Navah sensed compatibility between these two studious, devout, even-tempered young people with Lubavitch beliefs but a modern sensibility. She introduced them directly. "We went out a few times, and Navah called to see how we were doing together, since she set us up. But then we were on our own." They continued seeing each other, and they realized within a few months that they wanted to marry.

Gittel's story seems to lend credence to the old Jewish belief that everyone has a divinely appointed mate. She went outside the Lubavitch world and there, ironically enough, found a Lubavitcher with the perfect sensibility for her, a devout Hasid whose values dovetail with hers. Yosef is an engineer who had attended Yeshiva University. Spirituality is deeply important to him; he follows Orthodox Judaism with passion and conviction. Like Gittel, he reveres the Rebbe and treasures every anecdote he has heard about Rabbi Schneerson. But he is no typical Lubavitch young man. His face is clean shaven, an ostensibly minor detail that carries a potent message in Hasidic circles, where beards are the norm, a sign of tribe membership. He enjoys reading non-Jewish philosophy, mental poison by mainstream Lubavitch standards. Yosef is no rebel. He was not raised in a Lubavitch community; his parents combine Moroccan-style Orthodoxy and a love for the Rebbe. In Gittel, he seems to have found the ideal soul mate—a true Lubavitcher with a taste for the secular world and an inspiring willingness to pursue her unusual dreams. She understands his Moroccan past; her father is Syrian, and both of these cultures have produced Jews who tend to be traditional and ritually observant but simultaneously immersed in the secular world.

Before I even met Yosef, I was very attuned to his presence in Gittel's life from my frequent evenings in the Kassin kitchen. Yosef called often from his home in Maryland, and Gittel would fly to the phone, determined not to delay the start of their conversation for a millisecond. When she talked about him, she would blush, almost as if she were embarrassed that she loved him so much. This may sound like a typical long-distance college love affair, but Yosef and Gittel never touched each other before their wedding.

I met Yosef for the first time at Shabbos lunch, not long after Gittel had introduced him to her family. He would make a great therapist, hospital chaplain, or loan officer. Mellow and sincere, he had an immediate calming effect on the bustling Kassin household. His soft voice and easy smile somehow thwarted much of the usual Kassin worry over investments and exams. Physically, he fit my stereotype of the young Orthodox scholar, with his pale skin, black hair, round glasses, and large black yarmulke.

He and Gittel were unmistakably in love. Merely catching the other's eye was a thrill; they would gaze at each other and beam. Ruth and Daniel sat sizing Yosef up, squinting and staring and trying to get his whole story. Occasionally they would glance at each other, foreheads crinkling, silently attempting to gauge the other's reactions. Their eyes must have traveled up and down Yosef's body at least twenty times. This was their Gittel, after all; they had to make sure she was ending up with a winner. Yosef passed the test. Somewhere between the gefilte fish and the soup, the parental units smiled and nodded at each other. The evening wore on comfortably, with laughter and teasing, Kassin style: "Oh, Yosef, ya got any more engineers for our other kids?"

But when Yosef left, anxiety must have blown in through the open door. Gittel's marriage was no easy proposition for anyone. Everyone in the family felt a special warmth for her. Losing her, however inviting the prospect of her new life and family seemed, would be difficult. In the weeks before the wedding, the entire Kassin family seemed a bit edgy. Daniel's asthma intensified, stopping him cold with wheezing fits that lasted for several agonizing minutes. Ruth grumbled about the cost of the wedding, a lavish affair that the Kassins would subsidize.

Gittel paced. I doubt she even realized what she was doing. One evening, her feet pounded with such force that Ruth rushed toward her, asking what was wrong. "I'll tell you later," she said, weakly.

Certainly, Gittel loved Yosef, but so much of her new life would be unfamiliar. As her family grew, which she surely hoped it would, her responsibilities would soar. Medical school applications would seem like a child's jigsaw puzzle compared with the life she would eventually face. Compounding her tension was the fact that many of her Crown Heights peers could not fathom her choice to pursue both medical school and marriage. She told me, "People are always asking me how many years of school I have left, like I shouldn't be doing anything that I can't stop doing to start a family. You know, that's the feeling I get."

Gittel was excited about her many duties in the house, lab, classroom, and hospital. Even so, it was a nerve-racking plan, especially since she knew nobody in her community who was making a similar choice. The physical therapist jokes became more abundant as the wedding drew near. Grandma Jane's gibberish would give way to Ruth's screech: "A *physical therapist*? After all that? No! You're gonna be a doctor." Mother and daughter would laugh nervously, and Ruth would switch the conversation to medical school applications, a topic that was clearly still of immense interest to Gittel.

Role juggling would not be the only new part of this marriage. Gittel had never touched a boy, not even a light tap, and soon she would be ensconced in married life. But she would not be thrown in cold; she had been taking a class at Stern, very similar to one given in Crown Heights, about the myriad and complex regulations governing Orthodox Jewish sex. She seemed slightly nervous but also quite anxious to try them out. She was, after all, in love with a young man whom she had never hugged or kissed. Despite the laws forbidding all tactile contact for about two weeks every month, physical intimacy is not only allowed but encouraged for the rest of the month, and Gittel was looking forward to honing that piece of her love for Yosef.

Most of the Lubavitch women I spoke with appreciate the opportunity to focus on conversation and verbal sharing for half of each month; they say it makes for a more well-rounded relationship. They also enjoy the special feeling that comes with the newly allowed physical contact every month. Sex can never become commonplace or taken for granted in the Orthodox scheme.

From all she has learned, Gittel finds this system challenging but ideal:

> When people go to therapists and say they're having trouble with their marriage, sometimes the therapists tell them: "Well, maybe you shouldn't have sex. You should just talk to each other for a while." And that's what we're doing every month. We don't touch each other for two weeks. Even people who live together before they get married, counselors will tell them: "Well, maybe you shouldn't live together right before you get married." And this is what we're doing every month, so it's like new, and it's something special. It definitely would only help a marriage. Of course, it's gonna be hard. After you finish your period, it's still another week we have to wait. It's hard, okay, but in the long run, I think it's gonna make a healthier marriage. I'm positively sure that it's good, you know? It really makes a lot of sense.

The classes on these laws seem to ease girls into married life and physical intimacy so they don't have to jump into their new situations blindly. As Gittel discussed these rules with me, she looked animated and joyful, with an energy I had never quite seen in her before. I don't think it was the rules per se so much as the idea of starting to explore her sexuality with Yosef.

As the weeks passed and the wedding approached, the always bustling Kassin home grew positively frenetic, and Gittel was always in motion. Characteristically, this would not be the typical Crown Heights affair. Gittel was already embarked on an unusual path; the Kassins' decision to mark the most important day of her life in an atypical way seemed completely fitting. Eschewing the local community center where virtually all of Lubavitch Crown Heights celebrates weddings,

Ruth reserved a hall in suburban New York for the party. Yosef's family found the Crown Heights building dreary (it is, but the festive spirit transcends the physical plant every time), and Brooklyn was a grueling destination for many of the out-of-town guests.

This decision necessitated extra planning. At most Crown Heights weddings, invited guests are served a catered meal, and afterward the party is opened up to absolutely anyone: classmates, acquaintances, neighbors, Jewish drifters who relish the chance to join in. People drop in, pay their respects, dance for a while, grab a chocolate or a cookie, and leave. A diverse crowd of invited guests and assorted well-wishers participates in the inevitable after-dinner dancing, which can last for hours. It is the quintessence of *heimishe*, a Yiddish word meaning homey and warm. The party is within easy walking distance for Crown Heights guests; transportation is a nonissue. People can decide at the last minute to stop by.

But Long Island may as well have been Siberia to Gittel's classmates. Most did not have a driver's license; they were young, and there was no need to drive when the subway stopped right in the neighborhood. They were used to popping in to weddings; figuring out transportation was beyond their usual scope. Ruth and Gittel organized buses for the girls so they could leave right from Crown Heights and get driven back to their doors later on. Gittel spent hours on the phone, tracking everyone down and making sure they knew where and when to catch the buses. She even planned out music for the journey, so people wouldn't be bored.

At most Crown Heights weddings, seating is a free-for-all; people claim whatever spot they find welcoming. Lone guests sneak in wherever they can, sometimes making new friends among their random companions. But this was a more formal affair, and seating charts were in order. Gittel spent hours deliberating over personality mixes and family feuds to concoct the perfect arrangement. In short, this wedding involved more work than most. But, then, so did Gittel's life.

When the big day finally arrived, hundreds of guests descended upon the synagogue nestled in a woodsy suburban enclave. Friends, neighbors, classmates, tenants, family members, business associates, and even minor acquaintances, like a woman Ruth enjoyed talking to once in a hospital waiting room, all joined Gittel and Yosef for their celebration. I, of course, was there, along with my parents, whom Ruth invited out of a feeling of vicarious closeness after spending so many evenings chatting with their daughter.

In perfect Lubavitch fashion, the Kassins opened this central day in their lives to Jews from a vast spectrum of circumstances. Among the people milling about the large, high-ceilinged hors d'oeuvres room were long beards and shaven faces, covered arms and skimpy sleeves, the large black yarmulkes of the strictly Orthodox and small shiny yarmulkes snagged from Reform temples. The Bais Rivka representation was a bit smaller than at most weddings; the traveling made it impossible for people to plan the common small stopovers so popular among the girls. But an impressive number of Crown Heights classmates did make the trek. They ranged from a few of the most observant girls to one who was frankly disillusioned with Lubavitch. Here, in their best party clothes, they were practically indistinguishable; everyone's dress was long, modest, and fit for this holiest of days in Gittel's life.

The hors d'oeuvres that greeted the guests mirrored their diversity and numbers. Many Lubavitch weddings serve just a few pickups before the main meal, maybe some knishes and some egg rolls. Others go all out. The Kassins offered up a prefeast feast. The Syrian and Moroccan elements were well represented, with shish kabobs, pita bread, hummus, and Mediterranean salad. Traditional eastern European Jewish fare was plentiful as well—chopped liver, knishes, deli platters heaped with meats and condiments. Bowls of fresh mixed fruit and crunchy vegetables rounded out the spread. Sweet kosher wine and mixed drinks flowed freely. The overwhelming majority of Crown Heights weddings separate men and women, but here, everyone remained in one room. Of course, everything was prepared by the standard Crown Heights caterer. This was the only way all the guests would feel safe indulging in these delicacies; most Hasidim are uncompromising in their dietary observance, trusting only certain brands and chefs even within the world of kosher food.

Indeed, this wedding may have been a bit eccentric by Crown Heights standards, but it was wholly Hasidic nonetheless. All the usual rituals were carried out in the new setting. I can still picture Gittel before the wedding ceremony sitting in a tall chair, looking queenly in her white satin dress with the high ruffled neck as she received a stream of admirers, who each passed by her and spoke a few words before going on. Many asked for blessings, either for themselves or for others in need; there is a notion that a bride and groom have special spiritual powers.

The marriage ceremony itself was performed outside. The bright sun and lush grass were a change from the usual evening setting in front of the Crown Heights synagogue, but the procedure was the same. Men and women sat on separate sides of the aisle for the occasion, just as in any religious service. Under the *chupah,* the traditional Jewish wedding canopy, Gittel circled Yosef seven times. As with any Jewish observance, Hasidism attaches many interpretations to this ritual; one of the most common is that it protects the groom from evil spirits.[1] Several explanations draw from the mystical significance of the number seven. One particularly intriguing idea is that the soul has seven levels, and the bride and groom are one soul lodged in two separate bodies. As the bride circles the groom, their souls intertwine and become one.[2] Yosef placed a ring on Gittel's right forefinger. It was gold, to emphasize that the groom should consider the bride as precious as gold; it was also simple and unflawed, to represent the uncomplicated, beautiful, strife-free life the bride and groom hoped for.[3] A marriage contract, known as a *ketubah,* was signed. Men whom the families had chosen recited blessings; the bride and groom took ritual sips of wine; and, finally, Yosef broke a wine glass with his foot, to remind people that they must always remember the destruction of the ancient Temple in Jerusalem, even in the midst of supreme joy.[4]

This may sound like a day's worth of activity already, but the real party had yet to begin. We all made our way back inside and settled down to a meal of tossed salad, fruit cup, and either sirloin steak or stuffed chicken. The biggest treat of all came at the end, when we discovered a breathtaking Viennese table covered with desserts—dense chocolate tortes, fruit pies, fruit bowls, chocolate-covered fruit, chocolate bonbons, nut-sprinkled cookies, jam-filled tarts, brownies, and baklava.

I was assigned to an eclectic table of single or widowed women: two young tenants from Russia, a client of Ruth's, a Bais Rivka teacher, two students at the Crown Heights yeshiva for the newly Orthodox. The vast majority of Lubavitch weddings serve the meal in gender-segregated rooms. Here the room was mixed, and there were several tables of married couples with their families, but single men and women sat separately.

A minute after I chose my seat, my parents arrived at my side: "Steph, our seating card must have gotten lost. We don't know where to go." There happened to be two empty places next to me, and my parents took them.

The two yeshiva students blanched; this was an all-female table. One of them told my father so. My mother and I looked around and spied a spot for him at a table of young Orthodox men. Normally friendly and socially fearless, my father glanced at them and then down at the floor, like we were asking him to go sit with the mean kids in the school cafeteria. The yeshiva student was adamant. "I'm sorry, but that's the way it is in Lubavitch," she announced. She was just learning all the Lubavitch regulations and customs and was determined to follow them as closely as possible. The other women were ready to accept a man's presence, but the one holdout gritted her teeth and glared at this intruder. My father stood up but clung to his seat. I chuckled to myself. Those beards and black hats intimidated him.

Before he managed to tear himself away, Ruth and Gittel appeared. They quickly surmised the problem, and Ruth pointed my father toward a seat between my mother and me: "There. Now that's fine. He's Stephanie's father; it's fine for him to sit next to her."

The yeshiva student backed off but looked uncomfortable. "This is perfect. There's no problem, Ayala," Gittel told her. Ayala brightened. She admired Gittel, and this was her wedding, after all. In a matter of minutes, the awkwardness vanished and easy conversation flowed.

Often cautious and set in their ways, my parents had been a bit worried about accepting this invitation. I assured them that I knew the Kassins well (that's why they were invited; it was all part of the trademark Kassin hospitality) and that they would almost surely enjoy themselves. Without even knowing my parents, Ruth felt a bond with them because she knew me so well; she told me several times to try to convince them to come. Sure enough, they relished this party. The rituals intrigued them. My father was in food heaven, and even my weight-conscious mother took the glorious opportunity to pile on the pastries and chocolates.

The people delighted them as well. The woman next to my mother, a Bais Rivka elementary school teacher who'd had Gittel in class years back, raved about the bride's intellectual ability and character: "She's such a great girl. So bright and responsible, the kind of person I can really respect. I'm really honored to be here today, to see her get married.

These occasions are really the best part of teaching. It's so beautiful to be with a girl like Gittel years later on her wedding day." A heavyset woman with bright blue eyes and a warm, almost loving smile, she regaled my mother with mystical explanations of various Jewish holidays and rituals. Normally, this is not my mother's idea of an enjoyable conversation; she is a practical soul with little taste for the esoteric. But her new friend spoke with such easygoing enthusiasm that my mother listened intently, with real fascination. I thought to myself: "Wow. These Lubavitchers sure are skillful; they even have my mother interested in Hasidism!"

As we ate dessert, the final, crowning activity took shape: the dancing. This is a common feature of every Lubavitch wedding I have attended. The music, like the food, spanned the Jewish cultural gamut; the band played both eastern European and Middle Eastern tunes. Most people joined in, particularly Gittel and Yosef's friends. A partition separated the men and women during the dancing; mixed dancing is strictly forbidden within Hasidic circles.

The women twisted and twirled, with Gittel in the center of it all. For about two hours, it seemed to me, she never stopped moving. She must have danced with every last woman in that room. The energy that sustained her throughout her stellar school years propelled her now on the floor. She never danced with Yosef, but perhaps the most photogenic moment of the entire affair happened when the bride and groom were raised by their friends on separate chairs above the partition. They waved to each other and laughed, before dropping down again to their respective sides. Gittel's face was radiant, but, like every Lubavitch girl I have ever seen on her wedding day (and, for that matter, every bride and groom I have known, in or out of Lubavitch), she looked a tad agitated. It was a big day. Soon, her life would transform.

Even for me, finishing up my final weeks in Crown Heights before returning to graduate school, the difference was striking. Gittel's science lesson no longer ushered in the Kassins' Shabbos; Gittel had moved to Maryland, where she would complete her last year of college at a local school and transfer her credits back to Stern. The wedding frenzy was over. While hardly somnolent, Kassin life was much calmer.

I did hear quite a bit about Gittel through her mother. "She loves married life. She's cooking lavish meals for Yosef all the time. Yosef is good to her; he's a very nice boy. It's really working out," she told me.

This was not false fluff; when Gittel came back to visit, I could see that she and Yosef had cultivated an easy, loving, caring bond.

The months rolled on, and I moved back to Cambridge, but during one of our frequent phone conversations, Ruth proudly told me that Gittel had gained acceptance into a Maryland medical school. This past year was her first as a medical student. It was hectic. She cleaned, she baked, she studied. She truly loved it all; her hands are just as nimble with pastry dough as with a scalpel. I wondered what would happen when children started coming. A calm house to clean might add a relaxing break to a domestically oriented medical student's day; a sobbing infant might just tax that same student beyond her emotional capacity; two sobbing children in the midst of medical school were quite beyond my usually vivid imagination.

Sure enough, Ruth had huge news the last time we spoke: Gittel had just given birth to identical twin boys, and she would take the year off from school. It was the summer, so the timing was perfect. I asked if Gittel thought she would return to medical school the following year. Ruth had called from Gittel's new home, and she yelled the question out to her daughter, who was too busy with her brand-new sons to come to the phone. "That's the plan!" Gittel called back, her voice crisp, clear, and confident, though slightly muffled by two distinct wails.

8

Malka (Malkie) Belfer

Miniskirts and the Messiah

MRS. BELFER WAS IN AN UPROAR. It was past midnight on the first night of Passover (Pesach in Hebrew), one of many days throughout the Jewish calendar designated as a *yontif,* a holiday with stringent regulations that help Jews focus on holy thoughts and deeds. The Hebrew name is Yom Tov, meaning "festival," but many Jewish communities use *yontif,* the Yiddish version. Answering the telephone is forbidden on a *yontif,* but the phone was ringing, every five minutes, like clockwork. The first time, people scarcely reacted. It was like a phone ringing on television; answering it was just not possible. But it kept happening, over and over—an eight-ring sequence, every five minutes, on the dot. The tone of the ring began to take on an eerie insistence and a hint of urgency.

"Maybe it's your brother," Mrs. Belfer said to her daughter Malkie, a tall, dark-haired student at the post–high school seminary. Aaron, her oldest, was in Israel; perhaps he was in danger. The phone rang again. Mrs. Belfer lunged to answer it, then caught herself. "If it happens again, I think I may answer it. There are leniencies in these situations, and I think your brother may be in trouble."

"Nooo! You can't answer the phone. It's not allowed." Malkie's voice, often light and playful with her mother, was plaintive. Mrs. Belfer figured she was right; breaking *yontif* was serious business, and this was probably just a random crank caller.

Six of the seven Belfer children had joined their parents for the holiday meal, an elaborate production commemorating the ancient Israelites' departure from Egypt. The dinner's many rituals were performed meticulously and lovingly, from dipping bits of onion in salt water to represent the Israelites' tears during their bondage to drinking four glasses of wine (the kids' portions contained mostly grape juice), symbolizing the Israelites' joy upon their Exodus. By the meal's end, it was nearly 1 A.M.

The Belfers' five-room apartment on the fringes of the Lubavitch section of Crown Heights, just past a vacant lot that serves as a convenient meeting place for area drug dealers, seemed to heave from the after-dinner bustle. Pumped up from the festive atmosphere and the sugary juice, the kids roamed from one small room to another, their pent-up energy barely contained. The apartment was quickly losing its rare state of spanking cleanliness. Lubavitchers scrupulously follow the law that every last vestige of leavened food must be purged from the house before Passover; scrubbing marathons are de rigueur. During the eight days of Passover, food with any trace of leavening is avoided to memorialize the biblical Israelites' haste upon leaving Egypt—with no time to allow their dough to rise, they ate unleavened bread. Now only very particular foods graced the apartment, so messiness was once again kosher. Dirty plates were stacked by the kitchen sink; nut shell remnants lined the floor (Mrs. Belfer and two of the children had spent a few hours shelling nuts that afternoon—they are a wonderful source of Passover starch).

Mrs. Belfer, a stocky woman who often gave the impression of rock-solid strength, looked exhausted and a bit overwhelmed. Her *sheitel,* the wig she wore in accordance with the belief that married women must cover their hair, looked matted and twisted off balance on her head; her bangs veered off toward her left ear. Little runs riddled her stockings.

Still, she seemed content and pleased with the results of her Passover preparations. I asked how she felt: "Oh, wonderful. I love this holiday. And I'm really not worried about Aaron. Things have been calm in Israel, *kenayinhorah* [no evil eye intended]." She had been telling me that she felt like her soul was truly back in biblical times, making its way from Egypt to the Promised Land: "We believe that every Jewish soul that lives today also lived through the Exodus. It's such a beautiful thought. We were all there, and now, as we celebrate Pesach, it's like we're truly back, reliving it all." Her eyes sparkled with spiritual bliss, but their dark circles and bloodshot whites betrayed another, more immediate reality—the heap of dishes to be washed and the lively children to be trundled off to bed.

Mrs. Belfer's rapture in discovering the world's divine design always buoyed her, but her secular childhood with one older brother was scant preparation for the Herculean task of raising seven Hasidic children. Usually, she did fine. She loved her Hasidic life. Still, she sometimes seemed stuck on a treadmill where one awkward step would ignite an avalanche of insurmountable expectations. Her husband, a teacher at one of the Lubavitch elementary schools for boys, dozed blissfully on the couch. Tonight's work was her responsibility. Her oldest daughter, Malkie, would help, but that clumsy friend of hers who was writing a book about Lubavitch girls would surely do more harm than good, judging from her pitiful attempt to peel potatoes and cut vegetables.

Malkie shifted in her seat on the couch, and her knees peeked out from beneath her skirt. It was a holiday, so her skirt was a bit more conservative than usual. Normally, her knees were in full view, regardless of how she sat. To the casual Lubavitch observer, this scene would seem incongruous. Malkie was clearly devout, to the point where she kept her mother in line. She looked naughty, though. It was nothing an outsider would have noticed, but most Lubavitch girls just don't wear snug skirts that leave their knees bare.

Clothes can mirror the mind, and while Malkie shared her parents' intense religious belief and craving for the Messianic age, she was a limit pusher. Her passionately devout *baal teshuvah* parents abhorred the idea of college. They wanted to keep their children completely enmeshed in the Lubavitch system, with no potentially faith-damaging outside influences. But Malkie insisted upon enrolling at Touro, a college whose ultra-Orthodox auspices do not completely erase the taint of secular studies in a non-Lubavitch atmosphere. Like many of her peers, Malkie combined her mornings at the post–high school seminary with evening classes at Touro. Most of these girls cite expanded job options as the primary motivation to pursue a college degree, but even the more career-oriented Lubavitch young women tend to want relatively low-effort positions in teaching, administrative work, and the like. Malkie aimed high. She was not sure of her career goals—she was only in her first year of college—but business and academia were clear options.

Malkie typically stirred up a bit of excitement around the house, and this Passover celebration was no exception. Her sixteen-year-old brother announced that, ideally, the laws of *negiah,* which preclude touching of any kind between members of the opposite sex, should include siblings. After dinner, Malkie spent a good twenty minutes chasing the poor young man around the apartment with outstretched arms. She then retired to the couch with a book about personality types, written by an Orthodox woman. Her father said, "I wish you'd look at a Torah book instead." He stood in the hallway, arms folded, looking stern and holy with his imposing frame and long graying beard. Malkie just giggled and returned to her reading.

She adored her parents and admired the spiritual fortitude behind their decision to devote their lives to Hasidism shortly after graduating from college, inspired by years of intense friendship with Lubavitch mentors. Malkie and her mother were great friends. The two would spend hours together, talking, laughing, bickering good-naturedly. Yet Malkie craved somewhat different circumstances for her future. "Financial security is very important to me," she told me often, as one prime explanation for her desire for a high-powered career. The Belfer children seemed happy enough frolicking around their small apartment, but the pressure of raising a large family on Mr. Belfer's elementary school teacher's salary, even with some help from Mrs. Belfer's tutoring efforts, was daunting. Malkie sensed seething undercurrents of stress from her parents' frequent groaning about bills. But the problem goes far beyond money. Stifled by her peers' "narrow view of everything, from their lack of interest in non-Jewish books to their afternoons spent gossiping about Crown Heights, Crown Heights, Crown Heights," she hopes to raise her children away from a Lubavitch enclave.

Malkie had earned financial freedom from her parents; she was footing the entire bill for college and all her living expenses from her earnings at various jobs, which ranged from a research assistantship at school to an administrative position at a Hasidic-owned jewelry store in Manhattan. Benzion and Penina Belfer do not have the common "we're paying the bills" refrain to keep their lively daughter in check. They tease Malkie constantly, and they wish she had more typical goals. Still, they must know that their stint as emissaries of the Rebbe, which lasted until Malkie started high school, has influenced her. They lived in Los Angeles, near UCLA, where they joined with other Lubavitchers in the area to share the Hasidic philosophy and lifestyle with secular Jews. Their classes and holiday celebrations attracted a diverse assortment of business owners, professors, unemployed actors, students, and drifters.

The goal is to win over the natives, but natives come complete with their own set of values and notions, which can affect impressionable young people. Malkie is technically from Crown Heights; her family has been back in town for five years. But she does not relate well to most girls who have spent their lives in Brooklyn; in her words, "They're *so* hard to talk to and very closed-minded, with very little experience outside the Crown Heights scene." The high-powered professionals, the bare-bodied beach dwellers, and the fun-loving students Malkie met in Los Angeles all insinuated themselves into her worldview.

Malkie sloughed off most of their influence, but remnants lingered. Back in Crown Heights, she carried her difference with quiet confidence. To an outside observer interested in questions of individual voice and independent sprit, Malkie was a delight. She dreamed of tackling the corporate world, or perhaps landing a tenured professorship, in a culture where both women and men typically lacked lofty career ambitions, seeing jobs as necessary but dreary tasks that should never consume much of a Hasid's central thoughts or passions. She wore her slightly too short skirts with poise, lobbing dry humor at her frequent critics (once a little girl from her building commented that her skirt made her look more like a visitor than a true Lubavitcher; Malkie told her, "Things are not always as they appear," and smiled mysteriously). She has also been known to go clubbing in Manhattan, a habit she recently discarded out of disgust that the Orthodox guys at these places took off their yarmulkes: "That just did it for me. They're *frum* [religious] guys. Why should they want to hide that?" Malkie was a rebel, but one with exquisite pride in her culture and unshakable faith in the tenets of Orthodox Judaism. She maintained her core of beliefs and personality with everyone, from hellion to religious stalwart.

Her independent spirit seems to transcend the class hierarchies that surface periodically in this community, shattering the illusion of all Lubavitchers' equality before the Rebbe and before God. The favoritism shows up in little ways—girls with elite lineage or money getting first dibs at the choice roles in the yearly theatrical production or priority for places in the more desirable summer camps. As in virtually any community in the world, it surfaces most prominently with the big issues in life: seminary admissions, job placement, marriage, an intangible but ever-looming sense of one's standing in the community.

Penina Belfer (née Carol Aronson) passionately resents these unholy but universally human intrusions of class consciousness and elitism. That Passover evening, as Malkie and I helped clear the remnants from dinner, her views came forth as part of the camaraderie of cleaning. In her second year of seminary, Malkie was hitting prime time for the dating game. She was hoping to stave off the process just a bit—she was nineteen, and anywhere up through twenty-three is an acceptable age for marriage. Her mother was eager, though: "It will calm you down and ground you," Penina told her, as Malkie rolled her eyes. And Malkie was willing to go along as Penina made the first tentative forays into marrying her daughter off.

But as Penina began mentioning her daughter to a few of the community matchmakers, she ran up against some disturbing roadblocks:

It's like we're in a caste or something. Whenever I mention someone from a "good" family, people with strong lineage or money, they immediately have a reason against it. They won't even try. And if I insist, they come back with the message that the boy's family is not interested. Unless, of course, there's something really wrong, like everyone in the family has been in a loony bin, or the boy is handicapped, or whatever. Now, I know Malkie here has not been an angel. But other girls who have done a lot worse than wear short skirts have done better than this. She's certainly cute enough. [She pinched Malkie's cheeks.] We just don't rate over here, us *baalei teshuvah* with our cramped, rented apartment and our bills up to the sky.

Of course, the choosiness went both ways. One young man seemed compatible with Malkie, but Penina had heard that his mother had suffered a nervous breakdown. "That could be a genetic thing, and I'm very inclined just to reject him. Malkie doesn't need that." In a world where random relationships, attractions, and emotions do not govern these choices, people try to foresee every eventuality, always, of course, with the notion that their child deserves the very best.

The Belfers were considered somehow less than the best in the eyes of Crown Heights society. Penina had the whole thing down to a bitter science. I mentioned a girl from a *baal teshuvah* family who had just married into a prominent old-line Lubavitch tribe. "Money marrying *yichus* [religious lineage]," she ticked off sharply.

It was not a shock; Penina had come up against this sort of thing before. Many years back, she and Benzion, fired up from their years of schooling in the ways of Hasidism, wanted to participate in the ultimate Lubavitch *mitzvah*: outreach work to influence secular Jews:

Somehow nothing ever came up. The posts were saved for the children of the families who rated. So finally we just moved to Los Angeles and did our own thing, along with a lot of helping out with other Chabad Houses. But we never got formally recognized for our work. Not that we did it for recognition, but it would have been nice to know that people noticed our efforts and considered us part of the Lubavitch team. And my oldest son, who is about as smart and *frum* as you can be, has gotten the same reception when he has looked into *shlichus* [outreach work]. It's the kids from good families with connections who get the jobs.

"*Mom,*" Malkie finally groaned, as she balanced the last of the plates en route to the sink. This sort of discussion did not much interest her. Sure, everything her mother said was true, but Malkie certainly had friends from all sorts of Lubavitch backgrounds, and teachers greatly respected her diligence in school even though her family wasn't elite. She did not feel cheated. In many ways, this community was profoundly egalitarian, with girls of all social classes in school together, becoming close friends, and sharing ultimate life goals. "I guess I'm just a more carefree person. It doesn't bother me as much. I see the humor in it, actually," Malkie told me later. Besides, she seemed strangely aloof from the Crown Heights jockeying for status and power. She went to seminary, dutifully completed her work, and in her off hours did her own thing: go to college; mull future career options; hang out with her friends, who teased her mercilessly about her short skirts and hours slaving away at college classes.

She is not all independent self-assurance, though—her insecurities about her body and her weight are obvious to anyone who spends any time with her. Eight days after our Passover seder, I was back in the Belfer apartment, trying to convince Malkie to join me at Kingston Pizza for an end-of-Passover feast. "I'd go," Malkie told me, "but I've already eaten." She'd had a half of a banana and one hard-boiled egg.

I had heard that Kingston Pizza was *the* Lubavitch hangout on that first post-Passover evening; my craving, for once in my Lubavitch life, was completely normal (I never would have invited Malkie to my occasional forays past the Lubavitch neighborhood, to the joint dismay of my arteries and my blossoming Jewish soul, for a nearby Chinese restaurant's juicy pork spareribs). Both my stomach and my sociological curiosity were calling me away, so I stood up and found my jacket. Malkie followed suit—she rarely gave up an opportunity to spend time with this strange but fascinating creature from a thoroughly secular Jewish home.

Sure enough, every imaginable stratum of Lubavitch Crown Heights jammed Kingston Pizza. A table of teenage yeshiva boys was polishing off a stack of pizzas. They bit voraciously, shoving handfuls into their mouths and barely bothering to chew. A young mother in a sporty denim jumper and a black beret cut food for her three toddlers with one hand and wolfed down a massive cheese knish with the other. Charlie Buttons, a middle-aged homeless man with Lubavitch sympathies (his name derives from the pins that cover his clothes, with messages advocating peace, love, and Jewish observance), worked the various tables, asking people about their holidays. Throngs of Lubavitchers waited on line to order, and landing a seat posed a serious challenge; this was a small storefront with about six tables. Families doubled up and crowded in, in the style of classic Lubavitch openness.

Malkie asked the mother in the beret to save seats for us, solving one major problem. It was just the sort of small but key detail she always takes care of; assertiveness and ability to plan ahead have served her well in countless situations, from landing the best jobs at school to ensuring a comfortable seat at Kingston Pizza. Then another dilemma surfaced—what to order. I knew I wanted pizza; the craving was overwhelming. Malkie was tempted, too, but she tried to overcome her desire: "Maybe I could get one piece and take off all the cheese. It would still be a lot, but that would help." She checked out the drinks in a cooler by the cash register, carefully studying the nutritional information on various fruit juices. "Two hundred calories for juice!" she exclaimed, outraged. "And so many of them have so much sugar. That is so bad for the complexion." She fondled an orange drink longingly but chose a diet Coke.

Malkie is a tall girl, about average in weight, and brimming with energy. She certainly doesn't appear to be malnourished in any way. We got our food and returned to our reserved seats, and although Malkie mopped the oil from her pizza (a definite improvement in its health profile, which made me feel a bit guilty about scarfing down my slices in all their greasy splendor), she did leave most of the cheese. In accordance with Jewish law, she washed her hands and said her prayers. After glaring at her poor plate as if it had just paid her a supreme insult, she warily dug in. She does eat, but always dogged by recrimination and fear of the damage she might be inflicting on her body.

This is a common source of anxiety for Crown Heights girls, as for so many of their secular counterparts, but Malkie takes it to an unusual degree. In her case, the problem seems connected to her heightened interest in boys. She was constantly asking me about young men I knew in secular society, about their physical preferences and prejudices in women, about how attractive I thought male friends of mine might find her.

Many girls, especially as they hit the seminary years, shared Malkie's worries, knowing that their allure for yeshiva boys would be a primary factor in landing them a good husband. Malkie had this concern, too, especially after discovering that her family background would win her no points. But her interest in the opposite sex also had some more immediate overtones. Malkie hovered precariously in this realm as in so many others: though she has never done anything explicitly condemned by black-and-white Jewish law, she has pushed the limits about as far as possible within the technically legal but practically verboten range. She has never touched a man or had anything resembling a boyfriend, but she has flirted with an aggressiveness rare even among the more rebellious set.

On a ski trip that winter (this is the impish Malkie from the ski trip described earlier, who had disrupted the boys' plans to take over the front of the bus), Malkie recognized two Lubavitch boys about her age. They had not been on Malkie's bus; they had decided on their own to try out this mysterious sport that so many in the secular world seemed to love. She approached them, brushed her long hair off her face with a flourish, and announced, giggling, "I know you guys! I'm gonna tell your principal I saw you here."

They laughed and offered the very true response that Mrs. Gorowitz of Bais Rivka would not be too pleased to discover what Malkie was doing with her afternoon. Skiing is fine with an organized group of Lubavitch girls, but never under circumstances that could inspire mingling with boys.

"But you'll never know who I am," Malkie countered; she was wearing a ski mask that covered most of her face. She was grinning and shaking slightly; this was a thrill, but it was a bit nerve-racking. Later, she used the mask as an excuse for her little fling: "It was OK, because they'll never know who I am."

Lubavitch bans mixed-gender friendships, but manning the phones at work has presented Malkie with some intriguing dilemmas. Often she will strike up a bit of a relationship with one of the men she deals with over the phone. He'll call back, continually, pretending to have work-related issues. He and Malkie will speak for hours, trading stories about their lives. This is a highlight of Malkie's life; she anticipates these calls like a secular college student might anticipate a date. "Did I tell you the *accountant* called?" she'd ask me, dreamily, and then regale me with stories about him.

College provided its own questionable pleasures. Touro maintains separate classes for men and women, with courses scheduled on separate days to eliminate coeducational mingling in the halls. But male professors, graduate students, and staff can certainly be found on campus even during the women's classes. Malkie will often spy someone out and cultivate a furtive little relationship involving nods, glances, and occasional interchanges. Before long, she will know his story. She told me about a computer science graduate student: "He's brilliant, and I just love that in men," she gushed, her cheeks flushed from excitement and a bit of embarrassment.

These flings never involve touching, never take Malkie on a full-fledged date, never amount to anything, really, beyond coy glances and conversation. I asked if she would ever consider marrying one of her phone buddies or school chums. She was horrified: "Oh no. I need a Lubavitcher. This is just harmless playing." But in a gender-segregated world, even that carries the thrill of lawlessness and the adventure of shattering boundaries.

Her behavior would probably shock many of her seminary classmates; at Bais Rivka, her responsible, bright, obedient side, the one that wins her kudos at all her jobs and schools, reigns. Malkie is a bit of an outsider at Bais Rivka. She has a few great friends, girls who get a tremendous kick out of her and love to tease her about her short skirts and rebellious adventures. But at school, Malkie's quiet, shy streak surfaces, and at Bais Rivka, loudness is what gets you noticed. A well-liked, outgoing girl in her grade confided to me that people found Malkie "a bit nerdy, though very, very nice." Little do they know.

Ostensibly, everyone is included within the Bais Rivka social scene. As engagements and weddings came around, group invitations to parties were tacked on the front door of Malkie's cohort's main classroom in a supreme message of solidarity: when the big day comes, all our classmates are a part of it. Still, they are very real girls with very real issues of popularity and social hierarchy, and in this setting, most likely because she feels so divorced from the mainstream, Malkie has difficulty finding her niche.

One spring morning I was observing Malkie's seminary classes, as I often did during that year. She sat toward the front to get a good view of the teacher and the blackboard, but never in the first row, since she did not like being called on. Her skirts were just barely long enough to avoid censure, but long enough they were, for Malkie had no desire to make a spectacle of herself at school. Her makeup was on the eye-catching side, with bright blush and thick black eyeliner, but noticeable makeup was common here, so she nearly blended in.

About fifteen students were assembled, several in designer suits, others in casual sweaters. Some wore makeup, often heavily applied, their thick foundation slathered generously and visibly. Many worked hard to give an impression of attractiveness; after all, matchmakers might ask their teachers about their physical appearance.

By far the most entertaining class that day was the 10:30 session on the biblical prophets, not for the material but for the teacher's interactions with her students. A heavyset middle-aged woman with a voice that managed to be both loud and squeaky, Morah (teacher) Greenberg evoked strong emotions in some of the girls. She even cropped up in a few of my interviews, when girls would complain about her nastiness and speculate about the reasons for it. She was an exceedingly bright woman, a point conceded by many of the girls, and some did enjoy her course. Typically, though, the class degenerated into a tug-of-war between teacher and students. Today was one of those times.

As she often did, Morah Greenberg sprung a surprise quiz. Groans permeated the room, and as the quiz circulated, people laughed and winked at each other. One girl stretched. "Sara, what was that? What is going on? Can't you sit still?" Greenberg asked.

"I was only stretching. It's natural. I'm just human. Geeeeeepers!" the girl responded, to applause and raucous laughter.

Whispers erupted. Not cheating whispers—people could not have cared less about the quiz—but editorial comments about the instructor: "Can you believe her? She's soooo strange. What is her problem?" In the midst of it all, Malkie worked away on her quiz, one of the few whose head was actually bowed in concentration. When the teacher called time, most girls just shoved their papers forward; their grade on this exercise was nearly meaningless to them.

"You girls had really better start studying more. This is very sad," Greenberg commented as she rifled through their work. Several girls were laughing so hard they needed to clutch their stomachs to dull the pain. Malkie furiously scribbled up until the last minute and then, after the teacher tapped her arm hard, forked her paper over with a grunt. She was a good but not stellar student; she worked very hard for solid grades. There were several girls with stronger native talent but few (if any) with more drive.

The next class featured a very different dynamic. This time, the teacher, Morah Firestone, was a fairly young, slender woman sporting a blonde wig; she looked both hip and unfailingly religious in her long, straight skirt and yellow cardigan sweater. Firestone knew how to work the girls, to go along when they wanted to be playful, to get them talking about their futures as Lubavitch women. The topics were of unquestionable interest to everyone: dating, marriage, and love. The seminary offers classes in this area, as well as in general women's concerns, to prepare girls for their upcoming change in status from unmarried girl to Hasidic wife and mother. Issues range from Jewish law as it relates to cooking to the mystical reasons behind the injunction that married women must cover their hair.

This session focused on dating and marriage and operated like an informal discussion, with Morah Firestone throwing out ideas and the girls responding. "Dating is the arena in which the most important decision in your life will be made," Firestone said with calm decisiveness, and the girls listened attentively, for it was true; the husbands who emerged out of the dating process would be their partners in their primary goal in life: raising a Jewish family.

Morah Firestone exhorted the girls not to divulge their dates' names in case things didn't work out, and no argument or discussion followed. This is a centerpiece of Lubavitch etiquette that few would consider breaking. Otherwise, the Crown Heights marriageable contingent would degenerate into a gossip mill of the worst sort. Things are kept confidential until engagement is certain.

"You shouldn't be dating for romance," Firestone continued, echoing a theme I heard over and over in discussions of Lubavitch marriage. "The love will grow as you start living with him." Again, no disagreement. This is a well-understood credo in Lubavitch: infatuation is ephemeral; the real test is the lifetime of caring and trust you will build.

The conversation was free-form, and Firestone quickly moved on to the actual married scene that will follow the dating game. "There is a big question here: How do you argue with your husband?"

An attractive young woman in a sleek navy blue suit was mystified: "What's so hard? Just tell him you didn't like what he said or how he acted or whatever." Other girls nodded in agreement. Indeed, wives in this community do not tend to be wilting and meek; most of the girls' mothers probably spoke their minds with ease to their fathers.

Firestone had another question that yielded an immediate response: "What if you come from a family where the men help and your husband doesn't?"

"Train him!" a bunch of girls yelled out in chorus. Here, the task may be a bit harder than the young women anticipate; exoneration from household chores seemed ingrained in many males here.

Through all this, Malkie listened attentively but offered no comment. At the "train him" comment, she glanced at me with a sly smile. She had told me many times how much she pitied women who were so swamped with housework that they lacked energy for an outside job. "Don't they want their own money?" she would ask, scornfully. But she was not one to share her views in the Bais Rivka classroom (college was another story; she was a lively handful over at Touro, constantly asking questions and challenging the professors). Here at the seminary, she seemed to have settled into the role of quiet observer.

In this free-for-all discussion of married life, Firestone moved on to the question of *shlichus*. She asked how many planned to devote their lives to this sort of work, moving far from Crown Heights and working with interested Jews. Most girls raised their hands. This is a testament to the zeal so many young Lubavitchers share; *shlichus* is a hard life marked by the inevitable alienation that comes with living far from a community of people who share your values and lifestyle. Malkie's hand shot up immediately. She has told me many times that she plans to devote much of her life to outreach work. She hopes for another job as well, to give her life balance, but she embraces with true passion the goal of teaching nonreligious Jews about Hasidism.

Firestone pointed out that this is a direct fulfillment of the Rebbe's directives—he wanted as many people as possible to devote their lives to outreach. A girl who had not raised her hand said, "It's much harder to say that we should just listen to the boss when he's not here." It was a loaded comment; many in the community believed that for all intents and purposes the Rebbe was still there, guiding them spiritually if not physically, in preparation for his return to the world as the Messiah. Others, like this girl, agreed with the biological assessment that the Rebbe had died in the old-fashioned sense and missed him terribly. Her tone was bitter and mournful.

"*Shlichus* is a business," another young woman offered, echoing Malkie's mother's observation that the wealthiest families are often given posts, since they are the ones who can handle the enormous costs associated with running a Hasidic outpost far from an Orthodox community. Many girls agreed. It was a known fact that fund-raising and financial savvy were integral to running a successful *shlichus* operation.

Firestone was right there with appropriate remarks: "The Rebbe was our life. We can't forget, not for a minute. Now, he is there in the wings, watching. It's harder that way, but that's our generation's task. When you're working for the Rebbe, you need to have a certain idealism and look beyond the practical issues sometimes."

Malkie nodded with vigorous enthusiasm. Her longing for the Messianic age and her faith that the Rebbe is the Messiah (not "was"; for her, he is still very much around, if not in a tangible sense) define her life. The same energy and organizational talent that have allowed her to attend two schools and hold down several jobs simultaneously powered her efforts at helping to organize a Moshiach Day Parade, to honor the Rebbe as the Messiah. This became an all-consuming passion, and Malkie spent hours every night on the phone coordinating tasks. Later, in various basements around town, she helped the troops she recruited design floats.

Of course, this was a politically sensitive task, given the Lubavitch community's division on whether the Rebbe is Moshiach, and, if so, whether to publicize his kingship. Among the girls, politics generally remain in the background. I'm told that the boys typically have become much more embroiled in the controversy, with the different sides slugging it out in frequent arguments. Malkie never tried to take on her dissenting peers in discussion, but she did have a strong and unshakable faith that the Rebbe was Moshiach and that we should be doing everything possible to disseminate this message.

With this conviction Malkie was completely in line with her parents: the Belfer household carried the constant expectation that the Rebbe would return right then and there to spearhead the Messianic age. "We're always ready," Mrs. Belfer told me, and her entire family nodded their assent with absolute assurance. They just knew the Rebbe's return was imminent, and in their home, this faith had the ring of an acknowledged fact; even I would find myself speculating as to when he would come and how the world would change.

One evening Malkie invited me to a parade preparation meeting, held in the large finished basement of a supporter of the cause. These basement gatherings are typical of Crown Heights; high school production tryouts, parties, and assorted gatherings of all sorts take place in basements around town. Malkie had six other young women assembled—all seemingly fastidious in their religious observance even by Crown Heights standards—from the high school and seminary. They wore long, formless skirts and shirts that covered their necks, and they spoke mostly of spiritual concerns: their love for the Rebbe, their delight in studying his ideas, their excitement about this Moshiach Day Parade. Of course, other concerns crept in as well, like the deplorable state of Bais Rivka lunches these days and the incredible air of snootiness a certain clique was developing.

Malkie frisked about, motivating her troops and adding her artistic sense. "Make that float bigger. We want it to really stand out in the crowd," she exhorted a chubby redhead working on a cardboard model of Jewish children from all over the world—a blonde Russian, a swarthy Moroccan, a freckled American, a curly haired Israeli—grinning broadly under the banner: "Moshiach is coming. Be a part of it!" "You should use bright or dark colors. People will be looking from long distances," she warned a serious girl who was painstakingly drawing a group of long-skirted women shaking tambourines to herald the coming of the Messiah. Malkie dressed the part, with a long wool skirt and a gray long-sleeved sweater, for she wanted nothing to stifle her credibility with her charges. To her, this was the most important business imaginable: honoring the Messianic age.

Malkie's relationship with me epitomized her seesaw-like alternation between pushing boundaries and spiritual conviction. We met at a small birthday party for one of her friends. I noticed her immediately. At school she received little attention, but within her small circle of friends, she was a real character who reaped constant good-natured teasing. "Hey, Malkie, where's the flood?" a blonde young woman called out, eyeing Malkie's green satiny skirt that left her knees bare.

"Malkie, are you using that men's deodorant today?" an olive-skinned girl asked, giggling. A few weeks before, she had found the deodorant in Malkie's room and was stunned and oddly delighted. It was a very Malkie-like form of rebellion—on the cusp of the unacceptable. I asked the group if Jewish law prohibited women from using men's deodorant.

"Oh, I *knew* you were going to ask that," Malkie laughed. She never did answer the question. People are not supposed to wear clothing meant for the opposite gender, but deodorant, after all, is not clothing. As always, Malkie verged on the forbidden but did not quite cross over.

She was fascinated to hear about my project, my years at secular universities, and my life. Her questions abounded: What were my career goals? Did I have a boyfriend? What was my family like? What did I do with my spare time? All of a sudden, my pedestrian old life as a graduate student had glitz and allure. A representative of secular youth, I provided a glimpse into another world. We exchanged numbers, and in a novel experience for me in Crown Heights, she called me first. For a young woman feeling claustrophobic in this community, friendship with me was exciting.

With many of the girls, I had to be a bit pesky. I was the one seeking insight and knowledge, and I had to tag along, hoping people didn't mind too much. I'm sure my note-taking, tape-recorder-wielding presence was a nuisance at times. Malkie's invitations were bountiful—to join her at her family's holiday celebrations; to shop with her; to spend the evening at her home, just chatting. Every nuance of my life intrigued her, and she treasured my advice on everything from future goals to fashion choices. I never did tell her that her new confidante was a confused graduate student whose nickname in high school had been "Space Cadet." Often, Malkie seemed envious of my freedom. She would ask, almost wistfully, how it felt to go to college far from home, or where I thought I'd end up working after I finished my Ph.D.

But my newfound stardom was shaky, for while Malkie found certain aspects of my life enthralling, she knew that, at bottom, I had it all wrong. She asked me when I planned to get married; marriage was not one of my plans. I looked at the floor. Malkie frowned. "I think it's about time you found someone. Raising Jewish children is the most important thing you can do."

She looked straight into my eyes and gazed, like she was trying to climb inside the mind of this strange friend whose life diverged radically from the rhythms of Orthodox Judaism. I laughed, to break the tension, but Malkie stared me down and shut me up. This was serious business. Perhaps my behavior could spur the coming of the Messiah; Lubavitch teaches that every Jewish law followed, no matter how seemingly trivial, has profound mystical power. One more Jewish wedding could catapult the universe into the Messianic age. Miniskirts and mysterious phone pals notwithstanding, this was Malkie's most fundamental craving.

9

Leah Ratner

Mystic and Maverick

THE RATNERS HAD ME CORNERED. I was spending Shabbos dinner at their modest brick house with the poster hailing the Rebbe as the Messiah prominently tacked on the front door. My aspirations for the evening were simple: intriguing conversation, delicious food, and a deeper sense of the passionate spirituality that imbued this family. Without question, I got what I came for. Nosy writers aren't the only ones with agendas, though. I was eyeing a copious spread of baked chicken, beef brisket, steamed broccoli, and rice pilaf, about to spear a crisp, juicy chicken thigh, when Simon Ratner turned my thoughts from my stomach to my soul: "Sara, do you know why my daughter has been so nice to you?" This entire family called me "Sara," since Lubavitch teaches that Jewish souls are intimately connected to their Hebrew names. I glanced over at Leah, a dark-haired, delicately built Bais Rivka junior, wishing she would wink, or something, as if to say, "Oh, that crazy father of mine, up to another one of his jokes." She looked dead serious.

I cringed. "Why, does she want something?"

"Absolutely," he said, and then hesitated just a bit, enjoying my suspense. He stroked his long beard and shot me a playful grin. "She wants you to become *frum.*" I was insider enough that he used the Yiddish word for "observant" but a spiritual failure nonetheless unless I became Orthodox. This was not news; Leah had made countless attempts to win me over to Hasidic life. Her bountiful gifts to me included a prayer book, pamphlets about all the major Jewish holidays, and written instructions for lighting Shabbos candles. She had given me her solemn promise to answer any question I might have about Judaism, as long as it fell within her vast scope of knowledge. I was silent. Finally, Simon laughed and nodded toward my plate; even infidels need to eat.

Leah was not laughing at all. My silence betrayed my unwillingness to take the final plunge and follow Jewish law. Throughout the rest
of the meal, Leah would glance at me from time to time, her furrowed
brow conveying a mixture of sadness and curiosity. She had developed
a religious fire—a potent, unshakable faith in God, the Rebbe's Messianic role, and the power of Jewish law to reveal holiness throughout
the world. A grave question hung unanswered: After all my experiences
in Crown Heights, learning, meeting people, developing friendships
with families like the Ratners, how could I abandon the Hasidic world
for pleasures like jeans and shrimp?

We cleared the plates to make room for the final course of jelly rolls,
and Leah offered her prediction for my future: "When you get back to
Cambridge, Massachusetts, and you see how empty life is over there,
you'll be coming right back here. Crown Heights is your home, Sara."
It was the only way she could make sense of the situation—a Jewish
woman she respected who immersed herself in Lubavitch life and left.

As I sat in the Ratners' dining room, with the big portrait of the
Rebbe smiling in a way that made me feel like he was thinking about
me, Hasidism did tempt me; the simple, clear joy this family felt at the
imminent coming of the Messiah was a persuasive advertisement to
anyone who craved a more optimistic life philosophy. Perhaps some
other Stephanie Levine, one who was a bit more adept at housework,
child care, and swearing off nonkosher restaurants, would have become
observant.

The guests around the table were a testimony to this family's spiritual influence. Shoshana, a twenty-five-year-old kindergarten teacher,
attributed her newfound Orthodoxy to the Ratner mom, Fruma, who
more or less adopted her when she began studying at the yeshiva for
baal teshuvah women; she had an open invitation to stop by the house
any time for a meal, a chat, or intensive spiritual advice. Simcha, a
plump, middle-aged Israeli who immigrated to New York after her husband died, had thought all ultra-Orthodox Jews were "big, big hyp-
ocrites" until she discovered Fruma, the first person she ever knew who
seemed to embody Orthodoxy's highest ethical and spiritual ideals, at
a weekend program meant to expose secular Jews to Hasidism.

Fruma nearly shines with kindness and sincerity. Unlike many of
her style-conscious peers, she is plain and pure, with utilitarian clothes,
no makeup, and a slightly rumpled look. She greets all her holiday
guests with a warm smile that makes them instantly glad they've come.

There is much more to her than surface sweetness; she is a learned woman who tutors her friends in Jewish texts. My own mother's attempts to convince me of the importance of chic and high fashion fall apart at the sight of Fruma Ratner; her almost disheveled appearance creates a holy glow, as if she is beyond the typical concerns of this world. Fruma's slight Dutch accent (both Ratner parents were born in Amsterdam, to entrenched Hasidic families) gives her speech an old-world tinge that adds to her otherworldly air.

The oldest Ratner child, Shterna, was visiting with her husband and newborn son from Oregon, where they had recently set up a Chabad House to teach interested Jews about Hasidic life. "The Jews out there are pretty secular for the most part, but so many of them really, really want to learn. I love it. Some are really coming around to *frumkeit* [Orthodox observance]. It's hard, but it's fun," she told us when Shoshana asked how she was enjoying her new home. The self-sacrifice is profound—no Lubavitch community, a tremendous distance from her family and friends in Crown Heights, no appropriate entertainment or social activities, no kosher restaurants, and a starkly limited variety of kosher food. But the chance to win devotees to Orthodox life makes it well worth the struggle.

Ordinarily, financial stress makes these emissary jobs all the more arduous; central Lubavitch funds are limited, and Lubavitchers must raise their own money to support their activities. You would never know it from exploring his small, spartanly furnished house, but Simon Ratner runs an enormously successful electronics business, and he fully supports the upkeep of his daughter's Chabad House (one envious Crown Heights neighbor dubbed the Ratners' lifestyle "conspicuous nonconsumption"). With only two other children, Leah and a son studying in England, Simon could well afford to set all his kids up in Chabad Houses and provide the practical underpinnings behind the highest spiritual practice in Lubavitch.

Leah herself has already done her share of bringing Jewish souls around to their rightful place. She spends many afternoons traveling with like-minded Bais Rivka girls to various areas of Brooklyn and Manhattan, passing out information and encouraging non-Orthodox Jewish women to try out various observances (men are off-limits for reasons of modesty). Leah's obvious sincerity has inspired a few people to visit Crown Heights for themselves; one woman went so far as to call Leah a saint. Many of her classmates envision the perfect afternoon as haunting the Gap with lots of cash, but, like her mother, Leah has little interest in fashion. Her clothes are plain and sturdy, with the main function of covering her up in all the proper places. She is happiest when she's either teaching Judaism to others or studying Jewish philosophy herself.

Leah has cultivated a mystical sensibility unusual even among Lubavitchers, and she often seems to transcend this world, as if she is just stopping by for a bit of fuel or a light snack on her way to someplace more ethereal. A slender young woman with dreamy eyes, she is often startled by the mundane interests and picayune concerns that surround her. Most girls have difficulty nurturing constant spiritual striving in the midst of their social schedules and personal desires, but Leah's religious quest infuses her life and mind.

One spring afternoon, Leah invited me to a Hasidic philosophy discussion group she led for eighth-grade girls—one small slice of her tremendous dedication to community service, which compelled her to help out all around town: tutoring, baby-sitting, volunteering at hospitals, organizing religious events.

She mentioned a rarely practiced custom of drinking the water that had surrounded the Rebbe during a ritual immersion, a remnant of an old Hasidic belief that everything the Rebbe touches acquires mystical power. One young woman shouted, "Eeew!"

Leah flinched, amazed at the giggles and the faces contorted in disgust. "But it's from the Rebbe," she said softly. She composed herself and continued her discussion, but the laughing, munching, and kicking that surrounded her as she talked about a letter the Rebbe had written to a Hasid unnerved her. She was not angry; the noisemakers were, after all, just students unwinding after a school day. But these girls mystified her. She blinked as they tramped out of her house, shoving each other and planning shopping excursions. "It's so beautiful. The Rebbe wrote that letter years ago and it seems like he's speaking directly to us," she explained to me amid the clatter.

Among her peers as well, Leah seems like a stranded vessel of pure spirituality. Many of the high school girls sport designer suits on holidays and stylish sweaters and skirts after school, but Leah's clothes border on the dowdy: sturdy skirts in dull tones; shirts to match, buttoned all the way up to the top. Despite her family's wealth, she has little use for material goods and is visibly distinct from her grade's mainstream girls, with their funky shoes and snazzy sweaters.

Leah's eleventh-grade class relishes pranks and laughter. During her classmates' antics, her dark eyes widen and her forehead wrinkles; her expression juggles fascination and bewilderment. Once, on a typical day in her English class, Leah's teacher was engaged in a valiant battle. Trim and neat, with sharp, angular features, Morah Kadish looked almost like a drill sergeant as she tried to stamp out an ever-growing offender: bubble gum. Sara Esther Eisenberg, a mischievous redhead, had blown a bulbous pink bubble, then popped it, adding a huge *whack* to Kadish's discussion of *Lord of the Flies*, a perennial Bais Rivka choice because it provokes thought about substantial moral issues without any overt mention of sexuality. Kadish jumped. "Sara *Esther*, what *was* that?" Sara Esther rolled her eyes in mock confusion and brought the house down.

"Girls, you have your Regents exam next week, and I'd hate to see anyone fail. We really need to concentrate here," Kadish warned. She was referring to yearly standardized testing, administered by New York State, that even marginal schools like Bais Rivka must sit for. The girls quieted down for a few minutes, but soon more bubbles surfaced around the room, followed by pops and giggles. At first glance, the students all looked similar, in their identical green skirts and white shirts, but a moment's additional observation, especially at a rollicking time like this, showed the same diversity of behavior you'd find in public school. A slender blonde was howling with laughter; two pals toward the back took the opportunity to pass some notes; a few students blew bubbles of their own; Leah, sitting quietly near the front of the classroom, looked uncomfortable and bewildered. She tried to smile. These were her Lubavitch peers, after all. But she appeared as though she longed to be almost anywhere other than in that classroom, watching the shenanigans around her.

Throughout the time I have known Leah, a question has nagged at me: Is she happy? The issue is truly complex. Myself a spiritual seeker who craves faith in the very notions that undergird Leah's life—divinity, transcendent meaning, survival of the soul beyond death—I might expect her to be downright blissful. She is, in a way. But the sensitivity that has sparked such exquisite religious understanding can turn against her and drag her into depression. Leah also feels the inevitable loneliness that comes with bucking social norms, for she is unusually spiritual, even among Lubavitchers.

Leah has cultivated a poignant, almost poetic sense of godliness. She is certain that the era of Moshiach (a Messianic eternity of pure, unconcealed holiness) is imminent, and she tries to siphon off and savor every drop of divinity in her workaday life, from housework to shopping. In this sense, she is a model Hasid. Since its inception, Hasidism has striven to elevate the sparks of holiness within the physical world. When Leah explains mystical concepts to me, her eyes shine; she seems to be touching some realm of rapture I have never known.

For Leah, the Rebbe's influence is not only real but palpable. She answers the phone with "Yechi HaMelech. Hello." Literally, *yechi HaMelech* means "long live the king." Among Lubavitchers, the phrase has come to signify a sense of welcoming the Rebbe as King Moshiach, the Messiah himself. Clearly, it also suggests that the Rebbe is—spiritually, anyway—alive. The phrase is contentious in these politically volatile times; Lubavitchers who do not agree that the Rebbe was the Messiah or who disagree with publicizing this belief speak scornfully of the "*yechi* people," who often chant about the Rebbe's Messianic role after every community function. But for Leah, the issue far transcends politics; it is a matter of expressing her soul in every possible manner as she goes about her daily life. The way she answers the phone captures her attempt to fill her entire existence with divinity.

Her supreme goal is to do whatever she can to help bring Moshiach. As we have seen, Lubavitchers believe that every act of kindness and every Jewish ritual serve—in some unfathomable metaphysical sphere—to hasten Moshiach's arrival. So Leah follows all Judaic laws precisely. Like a true Hasid, she keeps her mind and soul ensconced in the Orthodox world, avoiding all music, reading material, art, and movies that do not have direct bearing on her religious life. She tries, in all her thoughts and actions, to be caring and considerate. And she packs her life with community service: leading activities for younger girls, sharing information about religious holidays with nonobservant Jews, teaching at the Crown Heights school for newly religious women, volunteering in hospitals.

One afternoon, I joined Leah and several other Bais Rivka girls on a trip to a nearby hospital. It was during Hanukkah, and the young women were toting boxes of jelly doughnuts. As the girls explained to the gleeful patients, it is customary to eat oily foods during the eight days of Hanukkah to commemorate Jewish warriors' triumph in 165 B.C. over Greek oppressors who had captured the Holy Temple. After the victory, the Jews entered the Temple and lit the tiny amount of oil available, enough for one day. Miraculously, it lasted for eight.

Of course, oil- and sugar-saturated doughnuts were against doctors' orders for many patients, who had to focus on the young women's cheer, which was rich and sweet in its own way. One man was not about to settle. Frail as he was, he came hobbling after us, yelling, "They don't know what's good for me! I want a doughnut!" I looked and inwardly shuddered. His skin had a yellowish cast; he was so thin that I felt I could effortlessly crack his arms in two. He seemed to be dying. But he and Leah hit it off joyfully, without a touch of sadness or worry. She told him the story of Hanukkah, and he nodded and smiled. As we turned to walk toward the van that would take us back to Crown Heights, Leah looked content. I, on the other hand, was agitated, my submerged fear of death and disease yanked to the surface by the hospital.

I asked her how she could remain peaceful in the face of ravaging illness, and she said, "It's very, very hard to watch. But Moshiach will be here soon, and all the sick will be healed, and all the dead will be brought to life." She sensed my doubt. "You'll see," she promised me, and she touched my arm in an attempt to pass some of her equanimity to me.

For all this, happiness does not always come easily to her. The intensity of feeling that allows Leah her exquisite appreciation of spirituality can also plague her with anxiety and gloom. She told me, "Sometimes I like the fact that I feel deeply, but sometimes it's also hard. I try to be positive. So sometimes I wish I could just, you know, do it naturally. Just *be* happy. But it's a struggle sometimes. It's hard."

Leah hopes to extract the spiritual essence from all experience. She seems most content in mystical contemplation and in performing activities with explicit religious significance. Sometimes, daily existence overshadows her spiritual mission. At times life is just plain tough. One Friday afternoon, I called Leah and found her sounding dejected. Scraping and beating sounds filled the background. She said she was preparing Shabbos dinner for her family because her mother was away. I asked, "Do you like to cook?"

A long hesitation followed. "I get tired of it," she finally admitted. She asked me what I had been doing.

"Nothing much, really," I told her. "Just reading and listening to music."

"Oh, that's *nice*," she said, wistfully. Of course, anyone could tire of cooking after a while, but Leah's soft, slow speech, long hesitations, and desire to talk with me for over an hour in this languid fashion suggested something deeper than casual boredom, perhaps a bout of depression. Often when I saw her at school she looked pensive. She could have been enmeshed in religious speculation, or she could have been brooding. Probably it was a bit of each. "I am a person who really cares," she told me. Really caring carries great capacity for all emotions, from exultation to pain.

Characteristically, Leah has used spiritual grappling to help her overcome her melancholy periods. She believes that if she could experience true *bitul,* a transcendence of self-consciousness and personal longing that paves the way for becoming a channel for godliness, she could achieve permanent happiness. In her words:

> There's nothing personal. The only thing is to serve Hashem [God].
> You become so much more when you're not thinking about yourself.
> You don't get pulled down by yourself. And how can you be one with
> Hashem? When you have *bitul.* When you don't feel yourself and you
> can connect with Hashem, then you get the confidence from Hashem,
> that he'll help me no matter what. If a person trusts in Hashem, he
> won't worry. And all this happiness comes along.

In her sensitive, understated style, Leah captures the fundamental tensions and contradictions of exploring independent voice in this community, particularly among the most religiously passionate. The ideal is self-nullification. But the self is hardy; it cannot be numbed. Leah extols the experience of not feeling herself and merging with God because it gives her the confidence that God will help *her.* She has not overcome herself. She is, ineluctably, concerned with personal gain, contentment, and pleasure. Her personality, subtle and refined yet tough and uncompromising, endures. Leah's battle to overcome the psyche is unwinnable. In a peculiar sort of irony, her own strength of character impels her single-minded mission to fuse with God, ignoring her peers' more mundane concerns.

In fact, the spiritual passion that shapes Leah's sense of godliness has bred ambivalence about her basic identity and place in her community. Orthodox Judaism offers women the realm of the practical, the material, the quotidian. A true scholar by temperament, Leah relishes theological speculation and debate. Lubavitch ideology emphasizes that women's job of caring for the home and children is holier than study, but Leah naturally gravitates toward pure intellect. Her lack of enthusiasm for cooking and housework partially signifies a general discomfort with her role as a Lubavitch woman.

I joined Leah during yet another afternoon at a hospital as she watched over a sick Lubavitch baby whose mother needed some time for the rest of her family. Leah's commitment to community service finds her quite often in hospitals and other places with people in need. The child was suffering from an infection—not terribly serious, but because she was so young, just enough to put her in the hospital for a few days as a safety precaution. The hours grew long, my conversation with Leah became intimate, and I found myself posing personal questions and getting heartfelt answers. At one point I asked Leah if she had ever wondered what her life would have been like as a boy. It was a straightforward question, one I had asked many girls. Most had not thought about it much.

In Leah's case, this topic touched the heart of her uneasiness within her community. She laughed silently and looked up at the ceiling, contemplating, perhaps praying. Then she told me:

> It seems like the boys learn more. They have a longer learning day, so they cover more. I feel like they know more. The girls are probably more involved in shopping for things and clothing and cooking, different things, I think, than the boys. Like, a boy quickly buys a suit—there's not as much to buying your clothes as girls' clothing. The boys' life sounds very nice—learning and doing *mivtzoim* [community outreach work that involves passing out information and encouraging secular Jews to perform religious rituals]. They don't have as many responsibilities at home. Sometimes I want to have a taste of that kind of life. It seems more spiritual in a way than the girls'. But it's different I guess, you know? When I was younger I wanted to be a boy. And sometimes still now I think: "Oh, it would have been nice."

Even our time at the hospital seemed to confirm Leah's sense of alienation from Lubavitch womanhood. I had proposed that we get together at some point, for I wanted to get to know this thoughtful, sensitive, deeply religious young woman better. She immediately suggested that I meet her at the hospital. I arrived and found her sitting, perplexed, in front of the baby; she didn't know quite what to do with her. When she saw me, she grinned and visibly calmed. She was much more comfortable talking with me, even about touchy subjects like her desire to be a boy, than she was trying to occupy the baby. Certainly, she cared for the little girl and did her best to keep her comfortable, but with a sort of awkward stiffness. After I joined her, she zestfully engaged me in a conversation about the power of Jewish law, relishing the intellectual give-and-take.

I remembered my experiences with the Lubavitch outreach center in Boston. Leah hopes to run one of these centers somewhere around the world with her future husband. Rabbi Posner took on the role of teacher and intellectual partner, often debating and discussing issues for hours with the many interested Jews who visited his home. Chani, his wife, spent most of her time cooking and caring for the ever-growing brood of Posner children, though she did teach some classes as well. Both appeared content. Leah would adore the rabbi's job but might tire quickly of Chani's.

Leah has searched Jewish tradition to help her cope, her trademark technique for combating difficulties. She discovered that in the ancient Temple, the Kohanim, the priestly caste of men, had the job of cleaning the floors and pots. This made her feel a bit better about her predicament, since "to be a Kohain was a very special thing. They were the ones that got a chance to do it. And that's the job of the woman. It's a holy job."

Holy or not, the traditional woman's function doesn't appeal to Leah nearly as much as the life of the male scholar. Regardless of the place of the female role in the spiritual hierarchy, it does not easily mesh with Leah's innate inclinations. Housework tires and bores her; clothes give her little pleasure. Her greatest love is study. She is striving to accept that she will never be a man, but she's having difficulty. As we left the hospital, Leah offered her final word on the subject with a sigh of resignation:

I'm trying to accept that Hashem made me this way. Obviously, that's what he wants from me. It's not a matter of what I would have liked. Even now, I really think that I would have liked the boys' life, but it's not a matter of what I want to do. Obviously, Hashem wanted me to be this way and deal with myself and work it out. So it would have been nice to be another way, but obviously it wasn't meant to be like that.

"That's hard," I said, for lack of anything helpful to suggest. Leah nodded silently. It seems clear that some of her fundamental desires will always be submerged. On one level, she will probably always long for the life of the male scholar who devotes hours each day to intensive study, secure in the knowledge that his wife is caring for his children. She does not express much joy when she envisions herself in the role of the Lubavitch woman. She is resigned, like a person who realizes that she will never fully overcome a disability and figures that something positive may come from her lifelong struggle. That's the way it is, so Leah will deal with it.

Her predicament struck me as insurmountable, but I underestimated her. Leah does have fairly standard goals for a Lubavitch woman. She plans to marry a Lubavitch man. She hopes he will be "dedicated to the Rebbe's ideal of spreading Yiddishkeit [Judaism]. And someone I feel comfortable with, understanding, caring." She wants to have children as well: "I want to give my parents *nachas* [pride] from their grandchildren." Ostensibly, she seems willing to eclipse her own desires. But in her own unassuming yet determined way, Leah will most likely cultivate her intellect within this context. Leah's personal voice is firm at the core, though gentle and easily modulated. Lubavitch does not ban women from learning; it simply expects them to make running a home their first priority.

Slowly, Leah is mastering the art of cultivating her own idiosyncratic personality within the framework of Hasidic womanhood. It's harder for her than for most, since her basic desires seem to conflict with her fundamental role, but it is not impossible. Lubavitch allows for a surprising amount of latitude within the basic structure of Hasidism. All sorts of characters call themselves Lubavitchers—eccentrics, nonconformists, *baalei teshuvah* who wear tie-dyed shirts and sing odes to the Rebbe set to Bob Dylan tunes.

Leah may well carve a niche for herself as a female Hasidic scholar and mystic—not an oxymoron, as long as she manages her family responsibilities. It will be a tremendous challenge; deep contemplation is not exactly a spontaneous reaction to daily housecleaning, diaper changing, and large-scale cooking. But I can picture Leah with a vacuum cleaner in one hand and a book in the other, meditating on the spiritual power of domestic tasks as she works.

She has already begun the complex tightrope walk between her unusual interests and Lubavitch expectations. A few weeks before the school year ended, the juniors had a gathering in a classmate's house, an event that happens several times each year to give girls a chance to socialize as a grade in a homey atmosphere. Perhaps because it was so close to the end of the year and people worried about missing their friends over the summer, well over half of the grade showed up. Girls milled about the spacious first floor, eating sour cream and onion potato chips and homemade chocolate chip cookies.

My trained eye picked out all the major strata of Bais Rivka society. Throughout the room, I saw mainstream, popular girls—the bulwark of these gatherings—sporting stylish sweaters and sweatshirts, in many cases along with the newly fashionable thick-soled shoes that had been spreading throughout Bais Rivka culture. They excitedly planned afternoon outings to walk in a nearby park, shop for summer clothes, and chat with friends at the pizza shop. A game of charades sprung up, and after each attempt to imitate a biblical figure, the most outgoing, popular girls would lead the way in a chant to celebrate the actress of the moment ("Rivky! Rivky! Gooo, Rivky!").

In one little corner were some rebellious types, who sneered a bit about the game. "Why, oh why, did I come to this *nebby* thing?" one young woman asked, laughing, and soon her friends were roaring hysterically. Some looked indistinguishable from their mainstream peers, but an attractive, long-haired girl wore a skirt so tight I could see the outline of her hips, and a tall, skinny comedian was decked out in all black, with silver rings and a touch of pasty face powder—nothing overt to the average American observer, who would see a typical teenager with a long black skirt and a few innocuous rings, but in the Lubavitch world, a strong hint of countercultural leanings.

Sitting in a calm corner at the edge of the festivities were a few quiet, studious, *chassidishe* girls, including Leah and her friend Feigie. They clapped and cheered throughout the charades game, though not as loudly as many of the girls. Feigie did a fair imitation of Moses, playfully separating two classmates with her hands to represent the parting of the Red Sea, and Leah giggled for several minutes. Leah and Feigie were dressed similarly, with long-sleeved white-collared shirts buttoned to the top and long, straight cotton skirts.

People were sharing plans for the summer. Most would counsel at Lubavitch camps throughout the world. There is a sort of unwritten rule that girls Leah's age will spend their summers at camps, helping to imbue their younger peers with spiritual energy and spreading the word about Hasidism to secular Jews (Lubavitch camps welcome both insiders and less religious children interested in exploring Orthodox Judaism).

Leah said, a bit apologetically, that she would work at a camp for just one session and spend the rest of the summer at home, studying Torah. She'd attend classes for women at the synagogue and read on her own. So she would go to camp like the other girls but would not let it stop her from using some of the summer to focus solely on study. Many of her classmates found this desire for summer learning unfathomable. They rolled their eyes. The girl in the tight skirt whispered loudly to her friend, "You see? I think Leah wins the prize," referring, presumably, to a prior argument about who was the *nebbiest* girl in the grade.

"Well, I would have gladly gone to summer school if it was offered," commented Miri, a popular girl sporting a funky pair of green Keds. This shut down the peanut gallery; ragging a bit on Leah was one thing, but Miri was practically beyond reproach in this class.

Summer school was not offered, but Leah would organize it for herself. She conforms meticulously and absolutely to religious doctrine, but she's willing to defy her peers' expectations. She does not dress like them or join in their antics at school, and she may well carry this nonconformist strain with her into the future.

I saw Leah a few times that summer in the women's section of the synagogue, either reading on her own or discussing Hasidic philosophy with a study partner. Often, her partner was a new *baal teshuvah* hungry for guidance. Leah was perfect with these women; her spiritual energy and impressive Jewish learning made her the ideal teacher for someone fired with the recent discovery of Lubavitch who craves deeper Hasidic insights and broader Jewish knowledge. From Jill Reich (who now goes by Rivka), the fifty-two-year-old psychologist who spent the summer in Crown Heights to solidify the studies she had completed through her local Chabad House in Philadelphia, to Susan (now Sara) Kaufman, a twenty-year-old Cornell University philosophy major who commuted from her parents' Manhattan home to pray at the synagogue in Crown Heights (to the never-ending irritation of her parents, who wanted her to spend the summer working at her father's law firm), all the *baalei teshuvah* who met Leah raved about her sincerity and spiritual purity. Jill went so far as to call her a *tzaddekess* (a female *tzaddick,* a spiritually perfected, wholly righteous person).

Discussing ideas with bright women who have decided to devote their lives to Judaism fits Leah's personality much more naturally than entertaining younger girls. She looked calm in the synagogue, like it was an extension of her home. The nervousness that she so thinly disguised while working with eighth-grade girls was absent. On her own, bucking the expectation that she spend the entire summer at camp trying to attract secular Jewish girls to Orthodoxy, Leah found a way to combine the community's hope that she use the vacation for outreach with her love for scholarly thinking and debate. Nobody could quarrel with her summer arrangement—she did spend one session at camp, and she influenced several newly religious women to observe Jewish law with more devotion and to think more deeply about their faith. She is a maverick of sorts, but one who remains staunchly within the framework of Lubavitch ideals.

Lubavitch extols humor, laughter, and joy along with holiness and prayer. It took a while for me to realize it, but Leah is certainly not all seriousness and study. She jokes; she laughs; she teases her family and friends. Her lighter side surfaces most endearingly with her best friend, Doba, a wiry young woman whose religious passion matches Leah's. Doba's playful nature has balanced Leah and kept her smiling throughout much of her spiritual quest. The girls grew up together, right next door, and though Doba was a few years older, Leah's maturity closed the gap.

Their pleasure is quiet and underplayed but no less real than the raucous banter of some of their peers. It consists mostly of small, untranslatable situations, like the time Leah offered Doba and me honey cake when neither of us was hungry. "Oh, I'm the only one eating? Is that what this is all about? Huh? Tell me, please," Leah demanded with a twinkle. The words on a page don't elicit much of a reaction, but we were all chuckling and enjoying some simple, lighthearted friendship.

At times, the joy goes much deeper, like at Doba's wedding, which happened shortly before my year in Crown Heights ended. Like virtually all Crown Heights weddings, the celebration included a sit-down dinner for invited guests, followed by hours of traditional dancing, when all community members are welcome. Most of Doba's Bais Rivka class showed up for the dancing. Several newlyweds donned new *shei-*

tels, the wigs they would wear after marriage, though about half of her class was still bareheaded. The young women were the center of the dancing activity—they formed a whirling ring, with people constantly breaking in to join them.

Doba, looking both flushed and radiant in her white gown, spent much of her time in the center, dancing with ever-changing partners. Lubavitch teaches that your soul is connected to everyone who dances with you at your wedding, and Doba gazed thoughtfully into the eyes of everyone she danced with, as if she were wondering just how her particular connection to her partner of the moment manifested itself. One minute it was a Bais Rivka friend with a long, curly *sheitel*; next came her jovial, round-faced mother, beaming with pride for her fifth daughter (the bride's father and brothers were with all the other men on the opposite side of the partition, celebrating with the groom).

Leah and Doba went wild together on the dance floor. They twirled and leaped at a pace far quicker than the band's lively rhythm; they seemed to career into a realm of their own. The young women's faces bore the most curious, complex expressions I have ever seen. Their smiles nearly touched their ears, tears rolled down their cheeks, and their brows were deeply furrowed. They were ecstatic. According to Hasidic thought, weddings carry supreme holiness. The two friends were also deeply pensive, probably wondering about critical issues: how Doba's life with this young man whom she had met only three times would turn out, how their own bond would evolve after the marriage, what the circumstances of Leah's wedding would be, what sort of children would come into the world from this union and, later, from Leah's.

A partial answer to that last question came about a year after the wedding. I was visiting Crown Heights a month after Doba's son Menachem was born, and while I was chatting with Leah in her living room, Doba arrived with her new child. He was adorable, with round blue eyes and soft pudgy cheeks. Of course, he was also a tremendous challenge, crying and squirming as only babies can. At one point, Menachem became supremely uncomfortable and began yelping. Doba looked confused and overwhelmed. "I think I might just call my mother," she joked, with a tone of real worry.

Leah grabbed Menachem. She had been in the midst of an intense discussion with me about the fate of the soul after death, but she broke it off for a minute as she patted her new friend's back and calmed him down. She looked at him with love; he was, after all, Doba's son. Still patting, she resumed her thought, recommending books and articles I should read. Menachem spit up a bit on Leah's shoulder. She nearly gagged, then smiled and wiped the bubbling droplets with the back of her hand as she passed the now content baby back to Doba. With no prompting at all, Leah began laughing, subtly at first, but eventually so hard she shook, relishing some private absurdity she herself could probably never explain.

10

Into the Future

Adulthood and Insights from the Hasidim

MONTHS AFTER MY LAST VISIT to Crown Heights, I find myself thinking again about all the charismatic, surprisingly confident young Hasidim who inspired my life's richest year. I begin to consider the girls on their own terms, to ponder their theology, to marvel at the spiritual weight their faith attaches to every thread of thought, speech, and action. Once more I wonder: What drives their assurance and vitality? The ideas that imbue Lubavitch lives provide a crucial clue to the girls' sense of power. To the average reader, what follows may sound like mythology, but for Lubavitchers, these notions are as real as the sun.

In the beginning, God infused the world with his holy light. This light has fueled the universe since creation—our silent, all-powerful lifeblood. If it faltered for even a millisecond, everything would vanish. The highest mountain; the most delicate flower; the desire, anger, virtue, and love within every human being would instantly collapse into the black void of nonexistence.

The newly created physical world was unable to absorb the pure radiance of God, so he concealed his holy light in vessels that dimmed its brightness. Even these mystical urns were too weak for God's light. They shattered, releasing tiny sparks of the divine illumination throughout the globe. But shards of the broken vessels hid these sparks from earthly eyes, and human beings could no longer discern the holy glow. Thus, godliness was concealed in our world.

Humankind now had the power to turn against the Lord, to scoff at his laws and indulge in evil, for his light was no longer apparent. It sounds like a cosmic accident, but God is omnipotent. Free will and the potential for evil are essential in his master plan. The pain, hatred, and confusion that can propel human lives give us a certain majesty. We are free to love God but also to deny him. We are not puppets. God has stepped aside and given us room to explore.

Our power extends far beyond our individual selves. God has made us his partners in the world's survival, development, and eventual fulfillment—when the Messiah will usher in a new millennium bathed in the Lord's unveiled light. We have the potential to restore God's radiance to the world and also to bury it ever deeper beneath a shroud of human misery. Every action each one of us performs has a role in the mystical drama of the universe.

Within this worldview, a typical moment in an average Hasidic girl's life carries stunning metaphysical implications. According to Lubavitch philosophy, Sheva Rosen, a Bais Rivka sophomore, has just saved the world—and altered its spiritual fabric in magnificent and horrifying ways. Let's visit her Crown Heights brownstone on this seemingly uneventful Friday afternoon, where she has just ushered in the Shabbos by lighting candles in accordance with Lubavitch custom. Only the mother of a family is obligated to light Shabbos candles, but, as in so many realms, Lubavitch goes beyond the letter of Judaic law and encourages girls to light as well. Observant Jewish women around the world perform this ritual before sundown on Friday afternoons; each releases powerful spiritual forces. As Sheva said the required blessing, she smiled. She has always loved candle lighting. It makes her feel close to God. Indeed, she unleashed intricate godly forces when she performed her weekly lighting ritual:

A holy spark has just emerged from the shard that had concealed it since the world began and the vessels filled with God's light shattered. Feelings of peace, love, and contentment spread throughout the world as the godly point of light dispersed its energy and shot into the realm of holiness. We are now measurably closer to the Messianic era, which will dawn when all the original sparks are liberated from their shells.

An angel was created, not a creature with wings but an intangible concentration of goodness, a sacred spirit born of a human being's earnest attempt to cleave to God. This mystical being will serve as an emissary from the physical world to the spiritual; it will carry Sheva's love for God into the metaphysical realms. Our new angel's influence on the highest mystical spheres will never cease.

For one barely discernible moment, Sheva was the only person throughout the globe engaged in a holy act. The saints were all asleep; the rest of us were wreaking havoc in large and small ways. Sheva lit her candle a bit early this afternoon, so nobody in her time zone coincided with her. Of course, there are millions of other ways to express goodness. Yet, for the slimmest fraction of a second, there were no kind words, no noble gestures, no Judaic rites anywhere—except for Sheva's candle lighting. It is extraordinarily rare for one person to be the lone holy actor throughout the universe, but it can happen. If at any instant no display of human goodness graced our world, God's radiance would vanish, and the universe would shrivel. The divine light that sustains everything needs some small sign of humanity's merit at all times to remain on earth. A split-second absence of virtuous deeds would signify the end of all creation. Sheva's simple ritual on a Friday afternoon has saved the world.

After Sheva lit her candle, her father came into the dining room, settled into a chair, and proceeded to pick his nose. She was mortified. Her friend from camp was visiting, and Bassy stared at Mr. Rosen, barely stifling a laugh. Bassy's father would never do such a thing; Sheva could picture that charming, well-mannered restaurateur all too well. Sheva glared at her father, seething with anger and resentment. He looked up, hurt, oblivious to the reason for his daughter's wrath. An essential commandment, to honor one's father, was breached. Sheva's fury reverberated in the mystical realms:

A holy spark retreated further within the shard that had concealed it since the vessels broke. Its shell grew thicker and darker, making the spark's dim light even harder to discern. Sensations of loneliness, strife, and family discord spread throughout the globe. The Messianic era will now be harder to activate, for Sheva must repent before the spark can extricate itself and merge with its divine source. Every buried spark of God's holy light makes the Messiah less likely to come.

A demon was born, a subversive angel powered by Sheva's pernicious impulses—not a horned devil but an impalpable infusion of malignancy. This destructive angel will act as a conduit between our world and the lower planes, funneling the anger that spawned it down into the realms of deepest spiritual corruption, tempting its young creator with the special knowledge of sin it brings from the sphere of malevolence, and spreading its influence wherever it senses an evil inclination among humankind.

Sheva's alleged powers are not unusual; all Lubavitch young women believe they unleash mystical dramas with every move. What amazes me most about these girls is their confidence and spirit within

Orthodox Judaism's unabashedly patriarchal structure. Considering them within the depths of their theology, I realize that it's not a paradox so much as a multidimensional view of the universe. In the spiritual spheres, women command every bit as much influence as men. They can bring the Messianic era; they can create angels and demons; they can bury sparks of God's infinite light; they can save the universe from extinction. Of course, vexing problems remain—why, for instance, does the literature generally present God as male?—but to focus on such questions is to lose the thread of typical Lubavitch girls' lives. They make their way through each day, wielding the spiritual swords within their souls to produce good and evil at every turn.

Such cosmic leverage linked to stringent regulation—Hasidic rituals drive behavior from morning to night—could produce withdrawn, anemic lives. I can imagine measuring each action with obsessive solicitude, paralyzed by a constant fear of damaging the world's spiritual foundation. But most girls find freedom and expansiveness within this structure. They matter, deeply. And they have a framework that shapes and guides them so they can channel their mystical might in concrete, attainable ways.

As for the nonprogrammed parts of their lives, the relationships and activities that provide a personal context for all the rituals, they do the best they can. They realize they have buried their share of holy sparks and mothered a host of demons. But they also know they're human, that sin tempts the overwhelming majority of us, and that there is time to mend their ways.

Lubavitch girls are buoyed by the grandeur of their mystical beliefs. Still, their ardor derives from more than pure religious thought. Their particular mode of traveling in the wider world but with a spiritual shield around them is an ideal breeding ground for religious passion. They live according to the rhythms of Jewish law; their families and schools build their schedules around it. School teaches Hasidic philosophy in ever greater complexity each year, with the overarching message that these are ideas to be lived, breathed, and wrestled, for abstract intellectual understanding is only one small step along the path to a holy life. Friends come from the ranks of the faithful. Even social trips to buy summer clothes reinforce spiritual messages, with everyone juggling strict modesty standards along with personal taste.

These young women do not live in a Hasidic bubble, though. As we have seen, they glimpse their share of magazine covers; hear at least snippets of secular music on the radio; in many cases, see a fair number of the tamer secular movies and television shows. Most have met scores of Jews whose beliefs differ radically from Lubavitch practice. Outreach work brings these strange characters to holiday tables throughout Crown Heights, where they may attack basic Lubavitch tenets with zest.

Religious commitment is built into the girls' lives. And their carefully controlled exposure to the ideas and practices of the outside world gives them something to push against, a sort of anti-Judaism that makes Judaism itself seem all the more majestic. It's hard to develop passion for something that simply is. True ideological momentum most often builds when your convictions run up against challenge, when there is some *other* belief out there that you heartily reject. I have never spent time with the more cloistered Hasidic sects that have little contact with secular trends and ideas. I know many of these groups believe that Lubavitch taints itself with outside exposure, but I would speculate that the Lubavitch girls' inspiration has grown at least in part out of their engagement with the outside world. These young women come alive when they explain their ideas to someone like me, trying to empathize with my point of view as they strive to win me over to the truth.

The very process of mental struggle compels us to assimilate our assumptions more fully. A calm understanding becomes an impassioned defense and finally settles into a deeply considered, life-enriching conviction. It happens daily in Lubavitch. The girls' religious conceptions are so engrained in their lives that they are nearly indestructible; their regular contact with alternate visions can escalate their faith into fervor and give them a sense of mission as they try to spread their worldview to the wider Jewish universe. Their beliefs take on a fire that undergirds their conceptions of themselves and their lives; they view themselves with confident passion, for their purpose in life is to follow the mandates and spread the word of this tradition that touches them with such force.

For nonconformists, though, the beauty and mystery of Lubavitch philosophy—the intricate tapestry of human soul, physical world, spiritual realms, and God that implants a sense of true power in most girls' hearts—can only intensify their dilemmas and erect a straitjacket around their innermost desires. They are not merely bucking social trends, a profound enough move in a tight social system; they risk shifting the world order in unholy ways.

I have been wrestling with a pivotal question: What is good about Lubavitch theology's effects on the girls' lives, and what is bad? The simple answer is clear. It gives most girls a combination of comfort, direction, and sense of strength that eases their lives and cultivates a deep-seated confidence in their ability to influence the wider world. But, because of the spiritual potency it assigns to the ideas and actions of every Jew, it can crush those who fall outside basic boundaries with the force of infinite horror. It embraces only people whose thoughts, desires, and life visions can adapt to its path. Rebels allegedly leave a trail of spiritual damage every day. Even those who lose faith often retain a haunting speck of openness to the Lubavitch worldview. Their doubts are strong enough to alienate them but not to transcend the framework of their upbringing. For people with some quirk of belief, personality, or desire that excludes them from core expectations, guilt and despair are nearly inevitable.

That, as I've said, is the simple answer. But I think of the young women who left Crown Heights and realize I must delve further. They had a level of faith in their own unique talents that is rare in mainstream America. Their goals had a certain purity that typical Americans tend to lose early on. In short, they exuded passion for themselves and for their unfolding lives.

Self-doubt did plague them at times, but it rarely touched their central, abiding confidence. This was not arrogance. It was a simple knowledge that they had gifts, and that with these gifts they could enhance their world. The Lubavitch conviction that all Jews pack a tremendous mystical punch with each move bestowed a sense of splendor and urgency on life, even for the questioners. They would sit and discuss their ideas—hanging on every word, probing, analyzing, imagining—as if every thought that entered their minds and each bit of insight they shared had profound implications. I haven't seen anything like it before or since.

I do not mean to glamorize their suffering. They clearly do not enjoy the pain they feel every day, the psychic demon of their forsaken beliefs and rituals never budging from their shoulders. All of them would ask wistful questions about my secular childhood in suburban New Jersey, and while I saw little charm in the Short Hills Mall or the Mountainside Pool, they might well have traded life histories with me. My admiration is selfish; I, personally, was inspired by the fervor I sensed among all the Lubavitch girls I met, and I include the questioners with unbridled enthusiasm. I think not merely of religious beliefs, but of an overall orientation toward life that lingers even when faith disappears. As I wound down and prepared to move out of Brooklyn, I felt an odd yearning to stay, for my new life could never reproduce this intensity.

I cried when I left Crown Heights. Partly, it was the joyful outpouring of my squelched desires—Pants! Oysters! Showers on Shabbos! Much of it was sadness about all the friends I'd be leaving behind, these wonderful people who had opened up their minds, hearts, and lives to me. But I also felt that I was cutting my ties to an essential insight, that I would never re-create the mystical depth I had come to treasure in Brooklyn. Why? I had spent time with scores of spiritual groups and intended to explore many more. Most religions have profound mystical traditions that will alter a believer's core sense of meaning. I know this will hurt my Lubavitch friends, but I have no reason to believe that Hasidism captures the absolute "truth" with more accuracy than other cherished worldviews.

So what, exactly, was I renouncing as I piled my worldly goods into the station wagon and headed back to Cambridge? I am finally arriving at an answer: it has something to do with the interwoven tapestry of Lubavitchers' lives. Their never-ending prohibitions and rituals were grueling, but every second fit within the overarching scheme of godly devotion. When you say the required blessing before eating your cookie, a divine spark is released; an angel appears on high. Teach a benighted Jewish soul about lighting Shabbos candles, and you have inspired a new spiritual actor with the potential to save the world. Sisters in the divine struggle surround you at home, in school, in the streets. It is life at a fevered pitch, suffused with meaning. I would mourn it.

I confided my sadness to Ruth Kassin, mother of doctor-to-be Gittel. I knew what was coming: "You're almost there, Stephanie! You're on the right track now. Just start small; start with lighting Shabbos candles. The rest will come, eventually. You'll be back here before you know it." Before I left, Ruth gave me a month's supply of candles to start me on my way.

The candles sit, unopened, on my bookshelf. Candle lighting is so basic, so easy; it requires no willpower and induces no discomfort. But I perceive my life in terms of my future. I hesitate to begin a course that could take me somewhere I'd never want to be. Hasidic womanhood would clash with nearly all my preferences and dreams. Raising a large family—the tension, the financial burden, the nitty-gritty chores—would make me crumble.

I wonder about the actual Lubavitchers, whose backgrounds and beliefs differ so dramatically from mine that I mustn't allow my own desires to color my interpretations. What happens to the young women's inspiring confidence and energy when they marry and give birth? After all, their spiritual—and physical—mandate grows larger and more complex as each child arrives. I picture the girls' lives, their all-female social world combined with their family niches, and ask myself what will remain and what will disappear.

Lubavitch girlhood offered a sense of strength and serenity for the overwhelming majority but left a few feeling estranged, adrift, and distraught. The die-hard questioners will never enter into Lubavitch womanhood unless they undergo a profound change of heart. The girls who moved out of Crown Heights have begun lives that veer radically from Hasidic wifehood, with casual boyfriends, a few explorations within the lesbian world, all-night parties, intense work and school schedules that leave little time for outside obligations.

But what becomes of the overwhelming majority who remain in the fold and enter into the crowning stage of Lubavitch womanhood? While the girls have surprising leeway to express their individual personalities, their main responsibility is themselves, hefty household chores notwithstanding. What happens to this flexibility when a girl becomes a woman and her expected domain widens to include a spouse and children? Do some who found a comfortable niche within Hasidic girlhood languish in their role as women?

On a structural level, women's social worlds are somewhat similar to the girls' lives, though of course children preclude the spur-of-the-moment shopping and pizza gatherings so important in teenage friendships. Public socializing is nearly always single-sex. The rare exceptions include occasional celebrations hosted by the most modern families, who sometimes prefer to entertain men and women in the same room. Families do invite both men and women to join them for smaller holiday meals.

Crown Heights Lubavitch women enjoy an array of all-female or gender-segregated social activities: engagement parties, weddings, speakers, musical performances, discussion groups on Jewish mystical themes. At their gatherings, they don't express the youthful exuberance

I found at Bais Rivka; I saw no pranks or women galloping down the halls. But the basic camaraderie and energy do endure. Crown Heights women from diverse backgrounds attend these functions, often enlisting the help of well-trained older daughters to care for the youngest children. Lubavitch women analyze, laugh, argue, and kid each other at discussion groups on religious themes; sing away at spiritual rallies; spin arm in arm at weddings; perform and cheer each other on at community shows. A certain good-hearted rowdiness develops, an adult version of the Bais Rivka ebullience, that makes the typical couples' activities Americans tend to plan at restaurants or the theater seem rather staid.

Of course, not all women fit into the social scene. I can still picture a middle-aged mother eyeing a pair of sneakers before choosing dress shoes. While the girls have more leeway in clothing choice, married women are expected to look mature and stately, though they often enjoy showcasing their fashion sense within these bounds. This woman told me:

> It's a terrible thing for me to be saying, but this community isn't very forgiving. They hold it against you if you wear tennis shoes, if you leave the house in a hat and not a *sheitel* [wig], even if you wear a denim skirt. I'm not so concerned for me, but it would really hurt my children's marriage chances. And you know what? I have no friends here. I don't like the classes and gatherings so well. I get sick of just the women all the time. You know what I would love? A night out with another couple. But that just doesn't happen here.

The frustrated mother was brought up in a strictly Orthodox community whose interpretations of Jewish law were a bit more lenient than Lubavitch mores. She craves some mild backsliding, but she loves her children too much to hurt their marriage prospects—inevitable if word got around that her standards were slack:

> I used to watch the TV occasionally in the kitchen, just harmless things to keep up with the world, but my daughter made me hide it in the bedroom. She's a really *frum* girl and she's probably right—the kind of boy she wants to marry would want nothing to do with her if he heard I watched the television right out in the open.

A woman must consider not only her own name but also her children's future.

And then there are the husbands. They, too, need care, both culinary and romantic. The girls I have known are just beginning married life; I do not know how their marriages will develop. I have seen a few of them with their new husbands. New Lubavitch couples always make me marvel. These young people who might have met four times are now life partners, sharing a bathroom, a bed, and every major decision.

Often, the matchmakers seem to have triumphed. Two intensely spiritual young Hasidim whose ex-hippie parents gave them an unusual knowledge of secular affairs invited me for dinner shortly after their marriage. They acted like old friends, kidding, laughing, and alluding to each other's childhoods. They didn't fit my notion of young lovers, but only because Lubavitchers never display physical affection in public.

On the other hand, it's frequently obvious that the pair will need some time before they fuse. I paid a short visit to Yehudis, a studious young woman I had known from Bais Rivka. She had been married about two weeks. Her new husband hovered awkwardly as we chatted; at times he and Yehudis would exchange uneasy glances. They acted more like two kids on a blind date than husband and wife. But they do have an entire lifetime to grow on each other.

The crucial question is how Lubavitch marriages develop as they mature. My holiday rounds throughout Crown Heights can offer clues, though a festive meal with guests is not always an accurate indicator of daily life. The stereotype is that Hasidic husbands become tyrants. I did find two women among the scores I got to know whose husbands appeared emotionally abusive. They looked at their wives with faint disgust. On Shabbos these women would wait far longer than necessary for their husbands to return from synagogue and then endure insults to their cooking. "This is bland," one man would say, making faces. His wife would stare at her hands. I did not know any women who treated their husbands with similar disrespect in front of company.

In most other cases, women seemed forceful and secure within their marriages. They would tease their husbands, joke, express their opinions. A fair minority were rather quiet during holiday discussions, possibly in deference to the belief that women should be modest in mixed-gender public settings (guests, both male and female, were the norm at holiday meals). A handful stole the show, regaling the table with stories while their husbands sat in the background. The men rarely entered the kitchen, but their wives did not appear to mind; the kitchen was their domain.

The sexual side remains a mystery to me. Physical affection is reserved for the bedroom; I have never witnessed even a quick caress between a Lubavitch husband and wife. I do know that sex within marriage is considered holy as long as it conforms to Jewish law. As I have discussed, several women raved to me that, because of "family purity" laws barring all tactile contact between spouses during menstruation and the following week, each month carries an exciting new opportunity for physical intimacy. It does make sense that forbidding something pleasant for a time makes it all the more enticing when the craving can finally be indulged. What's more, limiting physical contact can, with the right mix of personalities, encourage deeper intellectual sharing, rounding out the relationship between husband and wife—another explanation many women shared.

Not all wives have such sunny views, though. A handful of couples appeared to avoid conversation, let alone romance, and while the laws did not cause their problems, they did not seem to assuage them either. According to an ultra-Orthodox volunteer at New York's Shalom Task Force hot line, which helps Orthodox victims of domestic abuse (about as prevalent among Hasidim as in America at large),[1] the family purity laws can intensify the strain in embattled relationships. A woman's body is not always predictable, and a husband can feel frustrated if his wife's period lasts a bit longer than normal or if it comes sooner than expected. Men with autocratic personalities might blame their wives for their bodily cycles, escalating patterns of anger and discord.

These laws cannot be considered abstractly; they interact with complex relationships, and here lies a key divide between Lubavitch women and girls. The fabled iron cage that might have squelched Lubavitch girls into limp submission never materialized. Their own independent voices always found a way to dialogue with the tradition, and their relative freedom allowed them to find space for their own needs and desires. Many married Lubavitch women do likewise. But in marriage, tradition interacts not with one independent voice but with two entwined personalities. The cleverness and flexible thinking that allowed some of the quirkier girls to adapt themselves to Lubavitch life will not always work in a marriage. Successful relationships depend on two people, and if one tends toward physical or verbal cruelty, the other is often powerless to rectify the damage.

If a marriage becomes unbearable, divorce is an option, but Orthodoxy's patriarchal underpinnings are stark in this arena. A woman can receive a valid Jewish divorce only if her husband willingly issues a *get* (divorce document). Nobody other than the husband can issue a *get*, and recalcitrant men occasionally wield this power over disgruntled wives. Some husbands simply refuse to grant a divorce; others extort fortunes of money or wrest child custody in exchange for the desperately longed-for *get*.

Thankfully, these problems are uncommon in Lubavitch. In the cases I've heard about, women obtained the *get* easily, though at great cost to their community status. Men, too, lose status upon divorce, as do their marriageable children, whose desirability can plummet. In Lubavitch, every marriage is sacred and must endure unless extraordinary circumstances prevail. Some feel pressure to remain in problematic marriages. A divorced mother of three poignantly captured the dilemma: "It is said that the *mizbeach* [the altar in the Temple] cries whenever a divorce happens. But what about me? What about my life?" The fervent hope is that husband and wife can work together, compromising their individual desires to help the family as a whole.

The fundamental shift that comes with a girl's marriage is simple; her time and space are now intricately interwoven with her new family's needs. This is a huge shift from adolescence. Even in the best marriages, large families overwhelm mothers' personal preferences and whims; someone is always hungry, or missing, or creating a colossal pigsty. At times, women buckle under the tension, screaming at their children for minor infractions or letting the mess in the house pile to epic proportions. A few never adjust to the daunting demands of Hasidic motherhood, but, in general, women handle the transition quite well and grow to enjoy their new challenges.

Make no mistake: the community does prize originality and personal flair among women. The situation dovetails with the girls' lives—personal spark is applauded as long as it fits within the confines of cultural and religious expectation. I remember a religiously zealous mother with heartfelt unusual views on medicine; she believes antibiotics are dangerous and does not allow her children to take them. She is also an editor at a Lubavitch women's magazine, where she shares her formidable intelligence and wit with hundreds of devoted readers.

I think of another woman, brilliant and charismatic, who spends much of her time befriending adolescent questioners, challenging them to reconsider Judaism and return to the fold. She invites these kids to Shabbos dinner, showing them concern and pushing them to see the intellectual integrity within Hasidism. Crown Heights boasts a devoted artist who shares her creativity in regular workshops for women. And then there is Ruth Kassin, Gittel's mother, who runs a thriving financial consulting business, encourages her children to develop highly atypical aspirations (Ruth was the driving force behind Gittel's medical ambitions), and defines the atmosphere in the Kassin home with her spark and humor. All these women have received profuse praise from community leaders; people admire their intelligence, motivation, and vision.

For a few unlucky souls, though, the structure of Lubavitch womanhood seems to clash with their psychic core. I think back to the girls and ask myself just what qualities pushed them beyond the pale. In almost all cases, if their beliefs remained strong, they could create a satisfying place for themselves within Lubavitch. Take Leah, whose distaste for her female role joined a rich, electrifying faith. She found ways to indulge in her beloved Torah study; she avoided spending a whole summer as a camp counselor since she would much rather teach older women than care for younger girls.

Leah did seem rather depressed at times. Some may say she would have been better off in a mainstream American family where gender was not so rigidly defined. But when I envision Leah in a typical coeducational high school, I cringe. The social jockeying, the sexual games, the crass materialism without any underlying spiritual vision to place it all in perspective might have crushed this sensitive young woman. I believe she carved out as enjoyable a life in Lubavitch as she could have anywhere, given her melancholy strain.

How she will fare as a wife and mother remains to be seen. Marriage and motherhood are gigantic pieces of a life; they cannot be skirted or reworked like a summer camp session. Leah's distaste for household tasks intermixed with her burning faith reminds me of a Lubavitch woman who clashes on a fundamental level with her daily existence. Shimona's ten children are everywhere and nowhere, materializing and disappearing at the most inopportune times. They find their way into neighbors' bushes and occasionally even slip into random houses. Come dinnertime, you can bet that at least three are at large, and Shimona comes tearing out of her home like a madwoman, hollering their names. Her face reddens, she sweats, and by the time she rounds up the errant trio, she looks ready to explode. Back in the house, children are racing up and down the hall, breaking their mother's concentration so that cooking a simple dinner becomes almost too much for her to bear. Perhaps if fate had granted her two quiet children she would have been fine, but her current load is suffocating her.

Of course, mainstream ideals for middle-class American women are hardly simple. They may have fewer children, but they feel more pressure to carve out a career (many Lubavitch women do work part-time, but they rarely seek acclaim or high-status positions). Some of my married friends are frazzled by the various expectations they juggle: to succeed at demanding jobs; to raise perhaps two children; to complete innumerable housework and cooking chores, which their ostensibly egalitarian husbands never seem to tackle without abundant prodding. Choices can overpower them: How do I balance my career ambitions and my children's growing needs? Just how hard should I push to save a marriage that seems to have lost its romantic pull?

Lubavitch women's lives are deeply complex, but their priorities are clear. Their central mission is to create the best possible Jewish home. Barring extreme circumstances, they will have the same husband for life and will occupy a well-defined position within the family. For the fortunate majority who enjoy their marriages, this security brings comfort. Crown Heights women often enjoyed a sense of calm and assurance about their lives that eludes many of my female friends. They know where they're headed and what their role should be, though of course issues do arise within these boundaries.

Choice can be a lifeline, though. Women in mainstream America can fashion alternative lives with much more ease than Lubavitch allows. This is the Hasidic system's primary weakness; there is little place for the person who falls beyond basic assumptions about belief, desire, or personality. For many, a limited band of choices can offer a measure of safety, but for others, it walls off the only satisfying options.

For those whose sexuality deviates from the orthodox, Hasidic norms are intransigent. Marriage is an ironclad expectation. I wonder about wives who cringe at the thought of sex with their husbands: lesbians, asexual women, anyone for whom the holy procreative act inspires more horror than bliss. They certainly exist; the rebels on Montgomery Street were a font of information about these matters. I find myself thinking about one girl who had mastered the tricky art of looking thoroughly masculine in a long skirt. She sported a buzz cut; oxford shirts; straight, severe skirts; and thick, manly shoes. This young woman was popular among her peers and known to nurture a deep faith, though she did love secular reading. I did not know her well; I have no idea about her actual sexual desires. One of her friends described her as being "very butch," but I do not know if she understood the implications of this label.

Regardless of her sexuality, Lubavitch adolescence had a place for this girl as an eccentric but valued peer, and she seemed quite content at social gatherings. As a wife, if she is not heterosexual, she is likely to suffer. Shlomo Ashkinazy, a social worker whom Lis Harris interviewed for her book *Holy Days*, discussed Lubavitch gays and lesbians who squelched their desires for many years before succumbing to depression and breaking down.[2]

For a budding Hasidic woman, traditional marriage and motherhood feel like the only viable options. Indeed, this life carries so many nitty-gritty tasks, expectations, intricate rituals, and responsibilities that it begins to take on a life of its own, apart from the belief system undergirding it. The myriad tasks and rituals of Hasidic womanhood may protect a few from brewing existential doubt. I think of Rishe, a Crown Heights neighbor of mine whose mother had recently died. I commented that her faith would probably boost her now, that she must feel better knowing that her mother's soul would live on; this belief is intrinsic to Hasidic thought. A long silence followed before Rishe replied, "Stephanie, I don't know what I believe." Then this busy mother moved on with her daily life. She had carrots to peel, a Shabbos table to prepare. Closing her eyes to soak in the holiness of the ritual, Rishe lit her Shabbos candles. She probably had no idea whether their glow forecast a change in the divine spheres, but with her ravenous family about to descend on her for the holiday meal, it did not occur to her to wonder.

The marvelous interweaving of mind, heart, and ritual had come full circle. It can take tremendous faith to maintain this life, but its expansiveness can save a wavering mind from full-blown questioning—there is no time for luxuries like disbelief. Perhaps this is one reason unruly girls tend to calm down as adults; rebellion wouldn't fit on their agenda. Rishe had enjoyed an almost symbiotic closeness with her mother for many decades, and they had spent the past several years in the same house. Had Rishe not been a Lubavitcher, she could have fallen much further. But the reason is not the obvious one; the beliefs that might have buoyed her were tenuous. The rituals themselves, coupled with her countless responsibilities, gave her life purpose in difficult times and prevented obsessive grief. I do not think just any packed schedule would have had the same effect. This system is so cohesive and so suggestive of meaning at every turn that, if properly followed, it can carry even a doubter toward peace.

Lubavitch would say that this peace is metaphysical, that when you abide by the Lord's holy decrees, your soul scales the divine spheres. I am not convinced that these laws are from God. But I profoundly respect the *baalei teshuvah* who have found within Hasidism a philosophy to guide their lives. I wish my own life had the discipline and assurance they have developed. While faith is an unlikely prize for a skeptic like me, I plan to continue my search for spiritual mooring within Judaism and far beyond.

Many Americans fancy themselves independent journeyers among the world's ideologies; they hope to move far beyond the confines of the messages they imbibed as children. Certainly, bearded or long-skirted Hasidim are nothing like the people mainstream Jews may remember from their Hebrew schools or synagogue youth groups. Lubavitchers' appearance, mystical beliefs, and spiritual intensity contain a certain exoticism that many find appealing. The Jewish seeker feels that she has found the Lubavitchers on her own, as part of her unique quest, for she is in the presence of something far different from the reading group at Temple Emanuel.

Yet if her search has brought her far, it has also brought her home. That, at least, is what the Lubavitchers stress to a potential *baal teshuvah*. Observant Judaism may seem foreign, but it is the path of her ancestors. It touches the essence of her soul. A key doctrine of Lubavitch theology, that Jewish souls differ fundamentally from gentile souls, dovetails with the larger American tendency to view our cultural backgrounds as essential shapers of our personalities and identities. Ethnically oriented social groups and academic departments (e.g., Hillel House, African American studies) are centerpieces of U.S. university life, touted as necessary and fundamental to embrace a diverse student body. Lubavitchers' unabashed group narcissism mirrors the peculiar sort of ethnic pride that has developed in our heterogeneous modern world. They exploit their various levels of appeal with skill; their flyers emphasize the exoticism of a class on Jewish mystical texts along with the allure of gefilte fish like Grandma's.

At the dawn of a new millennium, two strains collide in the United States: a drive to explore among the world's vast wisdom and a yearning for the comfort of our cultural homes. Far from outdated relics, Lubavitchers mesh beautifully with these trends. Although their outreach efforts are aimed at Jews, anyone can learn from the lives I shared. All the Hasidim I met had a sense of wonder, mystery, and far-reaching personal potency. Each tiny angle of their lives had meaning, both for themselves and for the unfolding world. Their entire existence cohered around a core set of values; every move they made formed a piece of the divine puzzle that would be revealed when the Messianic era arrived.

Many of us in mainstream America lead compartmentalized lives. We work. We spend time with our friends and family. When time permits, we indulge in our hobbies. And, as exhausting as all this seems, an ever-growing number of us maintain another project on the side, a search for the meaning of life.

Often, these facets of our lives do not intersect. A car trip with your children has nothing to do with the office, and the book you're reading on the lives of ancient mystics will not enter your mind when you play your weekly tennis game. We have become schedule-happy, toting our organizers and date books; a business meeting at one-thirty, a talk at the synagogue at eight, and never the twain shall meet.

Lubavitch takes a different view: that everything we do, in all aspects of our existence, is bound together within our mandate to bring holiness into the world. No piece of your life is unrelated to any other; it is all part of your godly mission.

When I moved from Crown Heights back to Cambridge, I missed living among people on a quest that encompassed every breath. My new companions were like me. We relegated some of our lives to the refuse pile, with no relevance to our larger plans and dreams: all those hours in the shower, in front of the television, on the subway, or falling asleep. And our various goals—to perfect our writing projects, to improve our relationships, to savor sensual pleasures, to earn a living, to maximize our health—were disparate and often downright antagonistic.

Perhaps a shift in outlook would help us all to achieve some of the Hasidic sense of purpose: a simple awareness, consciously nurtured throughout the day, that our lives are one—that the same person who teaches an organic chemistry class at ten-thirty will take his daughter to soccer practice at four, and that something he learns in class just may have some relevance to his deteriorating relationship with his oldest child. We could take a panoramic view of our lives, realize the themes that steer us in all our roles, and alter our overall course if we feel dismayed at what we have become. In short, we could attempt to perfect ourselves with an overarching perspective of everything we are and hope to be, bound together in the unifying sheaths of our souls.

It is a daunting ideal that requires enormous self-understanding, emotional energy, and confidence in the importance of our lives. Lubavitch tends to cultivate these traits. The reformer in me wonders whether we can rework Lubavitch philosophy to enrich people far beyond the Hasidic world. Lubavitchers' faith in small actions, sense of personal power, and desire for large-scale self-perfection are nothing short of sublime.

Whenever I compare my adolescence with the Lubavitch girls' lives, two issues dominate my thoughts: their nonfamily activities are single-sex, and they view the world and themselves through the lens of overarching values and beliefs. My supreme respect for their principle-driven universe must be evident by now. I found considerable benefit in their all-girl social system as well. They are not allowed to socialize or attend school with boys, a key reason they so often maintain the rambunctious, lively spirit that boys typically claim in mainstream America. Entire orbits of behavior open up out of this restriction, from spearheading the pranks in school to skipping flamboyantly down the hall with no fear that hormone-driven young men will razz them. Sexuality is staunchly forbidden, perhaps one reason Lubavitch girls (and boys) can focus with clear heads on spiritual concerns.

A sticky question arises: What can we in mainstream America do with these observations? I would not want to spread Lubavitch's ultimate goals for girls beyond Hasidic borders. For all its strengths, this culture is miserable for some of the most creative, passionate people: the trailblazers whose needs and visions are not contained within their world. Hasidism, with its circumscribed worldview and restricted notion of the worthy life path, could never serve as a universal human vision. But I do believe that we can extract certain core Lubavitch strengths and shape them to suit a broader universe, that this intriguing brand of traditionalism can be a source of progress if we view it with the right balance of skepticism and openness.

There is enormous beauty in Lubavitchers' opportunity to explore the most rarefied notions of life purpose without sexual jockeying and with the freedom to take roles often reserved for the opposite gender. Some small-scale sex segregation early in life just may help mainstream America transcend gender constraints. Without the other sex, young people may try out behavior that otherwise seems inappropriate (Lubavitch girls were the jokesters, the loudmouths, the aggressive attention-getters).

I recently attended a roundtable discussion with Harvard undergraduate women, and most of them craved single-sex forums, both social and academic. They lamented that social gatherings too often degenerated into heterosexual meat markets, and the few who had experienced all-female classes fondly remembered the sense of intellectual and emotional support they fostered. Yet even these gifted, strong young women were unsure how to create all-female spaces for themselves. Many wished Harvard itself would step in and institutionalize them.

To my readers who have power in schools, camps, youth groups, and other places where teenagers spend their time, I present this challenge: create a space for adolescents to explore life-driving philosophies without heterosexual tension. The experience should be intense and far-reaching; a once-per-year seminar probably won't influence people enough to change their lives. Summer programs may offer retreats where discussion leaders encourage single-sex groups to share their passions, explore ethical issues, and study ideas with an eye toward refining their own assumptions and beliefs. Schools may incorporate these suggestions into a regular, yearlong class. I mention possibilities to spark youth leaders' imaginations; there are hundreds of ways to proceed. Appropriate options will differ depending on the institution and the actual adolescents involved. Participants will almost certainly question the single-sex forum, but this is just one activity, one small facet of an otherwise coeducational existence.

The supreme goal is to encourage teenagers to focus, for once in their chaotic, hormone-infused lives, on overarching questions—morality, deep-seated motivations, our core conceptions of ourselves and our world. I don't mean religion per se. There are many places to look for inspiration: literature, movies, art, music, philosophy, other people's lives, our own experiences. . . . The possibilities are nearly infinite.

Many adolescents desperately need perspective. Recent work on girls' concerns portrays hermetically sealed worlds where the value of a young woman's life can depend on the whims of a certain clique. We should open teenagers' minds to a wider universe that heralds ideals and faith in unseen glory—a universe that reaches far beyond the domain of conservative theology.

Why must these activities be single-sex? I saw firsthand the power of all-female groups exploring life's fundamental questions together. The other gender was not there to distract, inhibit, or usurp key social roles. I would imagine the same could be said about the boys. I witnessed marvelous intellectual and emotional energy. A communal bond developed, a sense of comradeship that my high school activities never approached. If possible, I would love to see secularized versions crop up, programs that might help mainstream American adolescents enjoy some small piece of Lubavitch strength.

Participants may even incorporate some of their experiences into their larger lives. Like Malkie and Brocha, the Lubavitch girls who refused to let the boys take over when they found themselves on a coeducational bus, mainstream Americans may want to retain their role flexibility in the mixed-gender world. Some small-scale gender separation may help combat sex-typed behavior when boys and girls come back together. The girl who becomes the queen rabble-rouser in her all-female group may not want to relinquish her influence in coeducational settings.

Of course, gender segregation is already in place at single-sex schools. Studies comparing single-sex and coeducational schools' impact on girls are equivocal; there is no consensus about which atmosphere is better. The evidence does suggest that all-female environments bolster girls' initiative and confidence in subtle, often nonquantifiable ways. Myra Sadker and David Sadker observed an all-female private academy and found that the girls were much more assertive in class than most young women at the coeducational schools they studied; girls in mixed-gender institutions were often drowned out by the more aggressive boys.[3] In a nationwide survey sponsored by the National Coalition of Girls' Schools, alumnae reported that their schools' single-sex environment helped them develop confidence and a sense of identity.[4] Carole B. Shmurak, who has taught and studied girls at both coeducational and single-sex private schools, has noticed that "there is a particular atmosphere at [girls'] schools that is very distinct. . . . I think it may be a playfulness that adolescent girls have when there are no boys around to inhibit them."[5] I discovered this same playfulness at the Hasidic girls' school, where the young women joke and tease with a verve rare among girls at coeducational institutions. And Karen Stabiner's *All Girls* is an inspiring account of two very different girls' schools: one an elite private academy, the other an East Harlem public school for gifted inner-city teens. At both, she describes young women who blossomed in their new settings, developing newfound academic and social confidence.

Even so, Lyn Mikel Brown and Carol Gilligan base their evidence for adolescent girls' newfound inhibitions and insecurities on research at an all-female private school; their book *Meeting at the Crossroads*, which inspired nationwide discussion about these problems, was set in an all-girls' academy. Rachel Simmons's heartrending account of girls' meanness among themselves also draws partially from all-female schools. Single-sex education is a wonderful option for some young women (and, I've heard from alumni, some young men). My year among Hasidic girls suggests that single-sex schools may offer profound benefits to some who languish in coeducational settings. But girls' schools are hardly a panacea.

Gender segregation in Lubavitch goes far beyond school. Outside the Hasidic world, even young women at single-sex residential academies have plenty of social contact with boys; these places often have "brother schools" that join them for parties, dances, and the like. Their vacations offer still more opportunities. There is something profound in Lubavitch's added layer of separation. Open flirting, dating, and sexuality are not a part of Lubavitch girls' lives (except among the most ardent rebels, and even they can be extraordinarily tame by mainstream standards, like Chaya, who could not imagine putting her tongue in her boyfriend's mouth).

This seems fundamental. As concerned as Lubavitch girls are about their looks, as much as they crave pleasure and adventure, as much as they can sound like girls everywhere, they stand apart from mainstream America in a most basic way. Ilana, a sixteen-year-old girl interviewed by Rosalind Wiseman for *Queen Bees and Wannabes*, her book about girls braving their teen years, puts the matter bluntly: "It's weird when you have a friend who has had sex and you haven't. Definitely weird. They have entered a whole new realm of being."[6] I would make a further distinction: in America at large, all teenage girls, regardless of their sexual experience, have been initiated into a social world saturated with erotic energy, a realm of being fundamentally different from a child's world. Not all adolescents are ready for the change. For all its potential beauty, this energy has enormous destructive power as well. It alters self-conception at the core of personality. The overwhelming majority of Lubavitch girls stand apart from this sphere—they have natural human desires, but sexuality does not surface actively in their daily lives, perhaps an essential reason they maintain their playful, uninhibited spirit.

Let me explain with a personal story. Between seventh and eighth grade, I attended a summer program at Pennsylvania's Dickinson College. A young man named Jason had a crush on me, and at a campwide party, he asked me if I wanted to go outside with him. I liked Jason and wasn't especially enjoying the party, so I agreed. He led us to a tree, and we sat there for a while, talking. It was a wonderful conversation; we both shared feelings and ideas that to us, at that time, were deep and important. And then he moved closer, nudged his face up to mine, and began kissing. I was shocked. Nothing like this had ever happened before; nobody had ever seen me in this way. He moved his lips forcefully against mine and then pressed his tongue into my mouth. I remember that his breath smelled like stale egg, and that he seemed to be releasing a forceful desire that had been brewing inside of him for years. It was, frankly, unpleasant, but I did not stop him because I was flattered. He was an attractive, sweet young man, and this was something other girls would covet. So I went along. We sat kissing for a good twenty minutes, and then he hugged me good-bye.

By the next day, our writing class buzzed with the story of Stephanie and Jason. Ben, another boy in our class, would monitor my behavior and say things like "Oh, Jason *loves* it when you do that," if I made an unusual comment or rubbed my nose. I wasn't even attracted to Jason, not in that way, but the idea of influencing someone so profoundly was intoxicating, and I did not want my power to end. I developed a self-consciousness I had never before known. My contributions to our class were no longer spontaneous; I thought about every move I made in Jason's presence. I wondered if he noticed my greasy skin or my soft stomach, and whether he wished I were taller. I wore my red shirt over and over because Jason thought it looked good against my face.

To most minds, this is an innocent story. Jason was a lovely boy; he treated me with the utmost respect. But something inside of me died that evening under the tree: my child's spirit. I couldn't just yell out my ideas in class anymore, couldn't be so careless about my behavior, for I had a newfound power that I needed to coax—a paradoxical power that squelched my freedom.

The next year in school, I felt like something had shifted; sexual desire seemed omnipresent as air. Boys pinched girls' butts and shouted about who was hot and who was a dog; girls giggled and flirted to win the boys' affection. My old means of gaining attention and an odd strain of popularity had become outmoded. No longer did people get a kick out of my goofy questions in class or my refusal to wear a dress for the school production. Sexual prowess had become the prime criterion for social prestige, and it seemed to involve coyness, subtlety, and restraint, none of which appealed to me. It was all so puzzling, like I had been thrust into a new country with foreign rules and expectations. I longed for the old days, when life seemed so much simpler, when I could be myself.

And I was far from the only girl who suffered during the emergence of public sexual energy. Rosalind Wiseman offers parents chilling insights on the subject; I have excerpted a few:

> At some point, a girl will pretend to be not as smart, strong, or capable around a boy she likes. She may be embarrassed by her behavior but not know how to stop.[7] Girls understand that their social status and identity are tied to relationships with boys. Even when [a girl] knows better, she may sacrifice her personal boundaries to please a boy. . . . At some point, most girls will lie, connive, or backstab to get the boy they want. . . . Girls, just like everyone else, have trouble defining the difference between acceptable flirting and sexual harassment. . . . Your daughter can be trapped in an abusive relationship even if she's confident and self-assured.[8]

According to Wiseman, fully one out of four girls endures an abusive boyfriend at some point.[9] Recent surveys at American high schools and colleges corroborate this claim: apparently, 40 percent of boys condone coerced sex when the guy treats the girl to an expensive date, and 32 percent of young women think it's all right for a boy to force sex upon his girlfriend if the couple has been together for a long time.[10] If that sounds implausible, consider this observation by a seventeen-year-old girl: "For most teenage girls, guys are everything. Boys validate their existence; they define who they are and where they stand in the world."[11] Many girls would not relate to this insight, but, when I consider adolescents I have known, I am dismayed to observe that young women often do see their sexual appeal among the boys as a primary gauge of self-worth.

Here's the irony: Lubavitch girls, ensconced in their patriarchal system, validate their own existence and define their own standing in the world—at least until the marriage search. Spirited personality, not the ability to inspire male desire, is the key to popularity in their circles. In the more egalitarian precincts of mainstream America, many girls will endure hell to maintain the status a popular boyfriend can offer. And many others jeopardize female friendships, expression of their thoughts and talents, and personal preferences to land a desirable young man. These themes run throughout Wiseman's book based on intensive research among teenage girls. It starts in junior high and lasts into adulthood.

This is a world fraught with danger and the potential for psychological meltdown. And let me be perfectly clear: it's the world that most American girls, regardless of race, ethnic background, or social class, inhabit. Even if they've never had a romantic encounter, they sense that their sexual caliber is under constant appraisal (recall the boy on the coed bus who loudly assessed each young woman's looks as she boarded).

For months, I have been pacing my apartment, trying to corner the most essential reason for the Lubavitch teens' surprising disinhibition. Then it dawned on me: they're like elementary school girls, who run and scream and say it like it is,[12] with no fear that their behavior will hurt them in the realm of sexuality. Sure, some Lubavitch girls suffered with crushes that would have sparked no guilt in mainstream America, but they rarely inspired misery. People had such busy lives that these desires tended to recede into the background. In America at large, early sexual experimentation pushes many girls (and boys) into bewilderingly complex and emotionally charged relationships that they are too young to handle. Those who haven't entered this terrain can feel estranged from the prevailing social atmosphere. And youngsters with problems or issues that make them targets for sexually charged taunting (e.g., "You can have *her*!" Steve yells to Dave whenever the girl with the misshapen head comes within earshot) can endure emotional trauma that haunts them for life.

Even girls who maintain their voice and confidence on many fronts can freeze when problems arise in the tricky terrain of sexuality. In high school, a girl named Ellen intrigued me. She was brilliant in every academic area and knew it. When arguments arose in class, she would pummel her opponent with the cool, calm composure of someone who knew, instinctively, that her mind could handle any challenger.

She inspired little envy, though, for she was obese. A few boys had an inspiration that haunted her school days: Ellenphant! They would shout it, regularly, often after catching her eye and making little kissing motions. Ellen would stand, silent and dumbfounded, her confidence quashed. I would love to say that I stood up for her, delivered an impassioned speech on the evils of their ways. But I'd had my own problems with other boys, and I knew that a clumsy, short person like myself might turn the tide of their humor in a direction I could never bear. Both Ellen's voice and mine were drowned within our own bodies' failure to offer the right kind of power.

Lubavitch girls had all the typical concerns about their appearance, but that sense of physical vulnerability—of knowing that your peers are publicly sizing you up and finding you either desirable or defective—was not there. And while the usual correlation between attractiveness and popularity held somewhat, I noticed a much broader range of physical types among the best-liked girls. As I discussed in the introduction, most people felt that the "loud girls" had the best chance at social prestige; they did not even mention beauty. I found fearlessly loud girls whose physical appearance spanned the widest gamut. The Lubavitch system is far from perfect in this sphere. The girls' looks will have an enormous impact on the husbands they land, which can cause great consternation and intense preoccupation with body-centered concerns. Still, there is power in two Lubavitch teens' shock when they heard a boy from another community yelling out his assessments of various girls' attractiveness, in their incredulousness that such a thing could exist in our world.

It is no accident that researchers date girls' common loss of confidence, energy, and spirit to early adolescence, precisely when sexuality blooms in their social universe. I have described Lubavitch teenage girls' playful, uninhibited quality, and I believe abstinence, not just from intercourse but from the entire domain of public sexuality, has influenced these strengths. This absence gives them leeway to hold on to their childhoods a bit longer, to work on their friendships, their spiritual growth, and their intellectual development without the shock that can come with peer pressure to plunge into sexual behavior or the pain that can come from erotically tinged ridicule. Even when they begin the marriage search, the atmosphere among their friends is unchanged. Lubavitch girls' dates are private and divorced from their social life; they would never dream of bringing a prospective husband to meet their friends.

Lubavitch is in no way an ascetic culture, and sexual enjoyment is perfectly kosher within a marriage. Limiting sexual pleasure to heterosexual marriage is deeply alienating to people whose desires fall outside that boundary. But the basic idea of controlled sexuality—of keeping it at bay through adolescence and then limiting it to the private realm, with no spillover into the worlds of work or public socializing—acknowledges what we in mainstream America too often forget: public sexuality can overwhelm, even devastate. For some, it's a damaging ingredient in the already heady mix of adolescent anxieties.

Again I ask: What can we non-Hasidim learn? I am well aware that, for many, sexual relationships (which I am defining as all relationships with an overt erotic element) are the high point of teenage life. Young women often flourish in our current system, handling the sexual undertones wonderfully, enjoying their newfound powers. For many girls, sexuality is a key avenue for social exploration that brings tremendous pleasure. But perhaps alternative options could help some of the girls who now struggle. There are so many reasons a young woman might benefit from waiting a bit before entering the world of sexuality. An immature girl would have several more years to find herself in other realms; students confused about sexual orientation or identity would escape the punishing combination of adolescent conformity and heterosexual assumptions; a sexually precocious but emotionally childish teen would avoid difficulties like teen pregnancy or abusive partners—possibilities that all sexually active girls face.

I have always believed in choices geared to individual needs. Not every student does well with the same academic expectations; not all teenagers will find social success in the same atmosphere. Ironically, by studying a group that expects lockstep behavior in so many ways,

I discovered an option I never would have imagined on my own. Mainstream America has an unwritten assumption that all teenagers should live in a world infused with erotic maneuvering, though perhaps not full-blown sexual contact. I disagree. Surely other environments should exist. In the past several decades, we have moved toward greater sexual openness and freedom, but freedom *from* sexuality has vanished from most public places catering to teens. Even my friend from a predominantly Mormon town tells me that, while most of her peers followed strict rules about sexual behavior, she was keenly aware of being noticed and judged as a potential partner.

Perhaps single-gender boarding schools with strict guidelines about sexual behavior would help some girls. They could eschew coed dances and mixers and focus on nonerotic concerns. Of course, they would need considerable funding to open their doors to less affluent students. This would not duplicate the Lubavitch experience (for instance, students would have ample exposure to other modes of life during school vacations), but it might offer a sufficient change to help some young women. For others, extended breaks from the sexual realm might be the best option. Maybe residential summer camps along these lines could fill a need for young women who attend more typical schools. For six or eight weeks, girls could enter into a world with no contact from males on the outside. They may discover interests, talents, or personality traits that had been overpowered by adolescent eroticism; they may find this respite refreshing.

I am not advocating repression of sexual feelings; this system would encourage students to talk with staff about their developing needs and desires and how they fit within the program. Eventually, some participants may well discover that this vision no longer suits them, in which case they should leave. Students in these programs would have exposure to the world of open sexuality in their off months and in the media, so rejoining the wider world should not bring shock. Still, counselors could meet intensively with students before they move on to discuss worries and concerns. After all, young people who find themselves in this environment are likely to have had difficulties or traumas related to sexual expression. My argument is not that teen sexuality in itself is dangerous or immoral, but that the constant onslaught of overt eroticism that overtakes adolescent life can be harrowing. I have offered mere suggestions; others may take these insights in other directions.

For lesbian and bisexual girls, eliminating heterosexual contact would in no way preclude erotic relationships. I have no autocratic motive here; schools and programs would have differing reactions depending on their goals. Ideally, some programs would serve as a refuge for gay and lesbian students; others would offer a nonerotic option for anyone who wants it, regardless of sexual orientation.

Here I call not merely for single-sex enclaves but for a different mode of life—not for all girls, but for some whose sense of self-worth is ravaged by the pervasive sexuality they face and, perhaps, for some others who may miss the ease and honesty of childhood, who may see in the Lubavitch girls' spirit the promise of another way.

Certainly, these suggestions would not create a social utopia—girls can be every bit as heartless as boys. But I am struck by how often girls' most virulent conflicts are spurred by sex-related jealousy: two girls liking the same young man, one young woman stealing (or even flirting with) another's boyfriend. Hundreds of other sources of conflict arise, but sexuality figures prominently in many of these social horror stories. Adolescent self-doubt coupled with sexual pressure can create bitter rivalry among friends.

As I make these observations, I feel saddened. I do believe my suggestions are feasible and that they would help some girls maintain psychological health. But the Lubavitch life path is quite unusual. Lubavitch teens are headed for single-sex adulthoods beyond the family and, perhaps, the workplace—a possibility that is neither practical nor wise for America at large. I never propose complete gender separation, only breaks for certain specified periods, an academic year or a summer. Within this time frame some may develop confidence that would help them engage the coeducational world more powerfully. Still, I would much prefer to see boys and girls treat each other with respect and civility, transcending erotic energy and hierarchies of sexual desirability, in preparation for an adulthood of similar strength.

There is much to be learned from the commingling of the sexes in adolescence, both to prepare for adulthood and to broaden relational perspective. Ideally, we would surpass our black-and-white conceptions of gender and understand people in all their complexity; the presence or absence of one chromosome would not drive our interpersonal universe. The trouble is this: life as we know it is far from ideal.

The social traumas girls—and boys—face stem, in essence, not from a failure of gender relations but from stunted empathy. I see no difficulty with two teens who let mutual caring, physical desire, and maturity guide their sexual exploration—wherever it takes them. The problems arise when one human being belittles another using the potent mix of eroticism and adolescent insecurity: when a boy pushes himself on a girl, or loudly turns her into a sex object, or makes her feel repulsive. Or when sexual immaturity ostracizes teens. Or when boys' hormonal drives and vested powers combine to make girls feel that their agency depends on their ability to fit narrow molds of appearance and behavior, regardless of their interior gifts. Or, for that matter, when girls and boys unleash their cruelty for reasons having nothing to do with sexual expression.

Perhaps I am naively sanguine about human nature, but I wonder whether adolescents might build a more humane social world if they understood the damage they can inflict on each other. I think back to my year in Crown Heights and the level of empathy I felt for the girls, all of them, even the ones whose personalities seemed radically different from my own. I find myself wondering whether my experience in Crown Heights, using a research method that captures inner lives to study a group who revered the human soul, might help us transfer some of the Lubavitch strength to the wider world.

I explained in the introduction that I derived my interview technique from Lyn Mikel Brown and Carol Gilligan's *Meeting at the Crossroads*. Their book's power derives largely from its method. This is no typical psychological study, with standardized tests and neat statistics. Brown and Gilligan threw out their fixed interview schedules and let the girls steer their conversations; the researchers' findings were based on real sharing between two human beings. They wanted to know these girls deeply, to touch the root of their personalities, to coax their psyches into expression.

Mainstream psychology is not directly concerned with the psyche, with subjects' underlying spirits or souls. Most psychological researchers focus on concrete questions. Indeed, the *Crossroads* girls, students at the selective Laurel School, were well-adjusted according to all the standard measures. Academically, they were strong, and they fit all the common conceptions of healthy psychological development. The girls scored higher on standard tests of "sociomoral reflection" and "ego development" than similar groups from other studies.[13] Brown and Gilligan explain:

> Our study provides clear evidence that as these girls grow older they become less dependent on external authorities, less egocentric or locked in their own experience or point of view, more differentiated from others in the sense of being able to distinguish their feelings and thoughts from those of other people, more autonomous in the sense of being able to rely on or take responsibility for themselves, more appreciative of the complex interplay of voices and perspectives in any relationship, more aware of the diversity of human experience and the differences between cultural and societal groups.[14]

In many studies, the story would end now, but Brown and Gilligan went beyond the standard measures and discovered issues that could surface only through in-depth conversation. Their research subjects seemed to lack intangible but deeply important qualities like self-knowledge and psychological flexibility, and they often shrank back when conflicts developed to preserve the illusion of goodwill among everyone involved. In the authors' words:

> If we consider responding to oneself, knowing one's feelings and thoughts, clarity, courage, openness, and free-flowing connections with others and the world as a sign of psychological health, then these girls are in fact not developing, but are showing evidence of loss and struggle and signs of an impasse in their ability to act in the face of conflict.[15]

Thus, a complex dichotomy emerges: girls who, according to all the usual gauges, are developing beautifully, yet who struck the researchers as being profoundly troubled.

How could such a contradictory picture arise? At bottom, the question comes down to a definition of identity. Who are these girls? How would one capture their essence, their most central traits? Most psychologists would choose some important intellectual and social issues and try to measure them objectively. Brown and Gilligan found this approach incomplete. They wanted a sense of the young women's inner worlds, their personalities in motion. They wanted to *know* these girls by talking to them in a serious way. And when they sought this level of knowledge, their ostensibly ideal adolescent specimens seemed distressed indeed.

Struck by this more interpersonal research vision, I brought it into the Crown Heights Hasidic community. My results were striking. According to the criteria Brown and Gilligan cite as being crucial in mainstream psychological evaluations, many psychologists would probably find typical Lubavitch girls lacking. They are dependent on external authorities, both human and divine. They are aware of different cultures but from a seemingly closed-minded vantage point; they believe their system is unequivocally the best, and the only path toward the truth. However, when I consider the criteria Brown and Gilligan use to explain why the Laurel School girls unsettled them, the Hasidic adolescents seem, on the whole, splendidly well-adjusted. From ardent questioner to popular kid to brooding scholar, these young women have an exquisitely refined sense of their feelings and thoughts. They are open about their insights and willing to share them with a trusted outsider. Often, they handle intense conflict with poise, grit, self-understanding, and courage, whether they be questioners struggling with desires that flout Hasidic values or religious stalwarts aching for like-minded peers and a more pious community.

In other words, when it comes to the strength, development, and expression of the psyche—an internal awareness of their ideas and feelings and an ability to share this knowledge with others—these young women thrive. Again, the big question looms: Why? How do Lubavitch girls develop an apparent advantage over others in this sphere?

Conflicting conceptions of identity, of the building blocks of our unique selves, may well provide clues. Lubavitch maintains an unwavering belief that Jews are, at bottom, souls: intricate, God-infused beings who cannot be reduced to numerical models or understood in purely cultural terms. Personality development and self-understanding are crucial within this scheme, for what could be more holy than honing instruments of godliness? The notions most Americans learn are more concrete and one-dimensional. Their schools explore their genetic underpinnings, their country's history, their society's place in world events. Many do attend religious school, where a spiritual sense of self is broached, but few assimilate that understanding with nearly the depth Lubavitch students reach.

What makes us who we are, intellectually, ideologically, emotionally? The question has universal resonance. In psychology—and in the popular American mind—the issue often comes down to one conflict: nature versus nurture. Is our intelligence determined primarily by genes or by environmental opportunity? Is violence spurred by innate drives or by a history of trauma? Is temperament inborn or forged by life experience?

In Brown and Gilligan's work, the currently vogue nature-nurture debate does not appear, for their central research entity, the psyche, transcends that conversation. These scholars explore their subjects' slippery, ever-evolving inner worlds, self-conceptions, and life visions. They focus not on one dimension, like temperament or intellectual capacity, but on their interviewees' global minds and hearts, their selves, in the truest sense of the word. Those with a religious bent might read: souls. The girls' stories cannot be reduced to neurology, physiology, culture, the sum of their life experiences, or even some interaction among them all. There is more—the speech patterns they used, the relationships they cultivated with their interviewers, their body language, their expressions of joy and pain. Attention to these considerations rounds out the girls' characters and adds depth to the insights they provide. An uncomfortable silence, a response of "I don't know," or a wary expression can speak volumes. Brown and Gilligan's unusual research philosophy allows them to pick up an emotional sickness that may well have remained covered over with traditional techniques, for their subjects were bright, articulate, and successful by all the standard measures.

I went into a Lubavitch community armed with the same psyche-based research method and uncovered striking psychological health beneath the all-too-common adolescent agonies: a surprise and a puzzle when placed against Brown and Gilligan's disconcerting findings in a secular elite girls' school. One explanation is that Lubavitch explicitly cultivates the psyche. The centerpiece of the *Tanya*, Lubavitch's defining philosophical text, is a discussion of the Jewish soul's complexities and mysteries. It enumerates psychic conflicts, physical urges, evil impulses, ethical dilemmas, struggles toward self-improvement. In the words of Lubavitch writer Nissan Mindel, "The philosophy of the *Tanya* begins with the self and ends with the self."[16] The *Tanya*'s central conflict, the relationship between Jews' "animal souls" (the seat of their natural desires and instincts) and their "divine souls" (the aspect of their consciousness that transcends their physical natures and allows them to strive toward holiness), begins unfolding in elementary school and continues, in ever-expanding complexity, through seminary and into adulthood. Lubavitchers refer to this book throughout their lives. *They* are key players. The *Tanya* illuminates the Jewish soul's pitfalls, gifts, and extraordinary potential for growth. A mystical, God-driven philosophy impels Lubavitch, but each individual Jewish soul is crucial and worthy of intense scrutiny, for every Jew is central to the unfolding of divinity within the world.

In keeping with this emphasis on self-awareness, Lubavitchers encourage everyone to have a *mashpiah*, a confidante and spiritual leader, a wise role model who acts as a combination rabbi-therapist. Ideally, each girl will have an older woman with whom she can share her deepest fears and most mortifying thoughts, with the ultimate goal of personal and spiritual growth. Of course, it doesn't always work this way, but the emphasis on self-exploration the *mashpiah* ideal represents seeps into all Lubavitch girls' minds.

In I waltzed—a pseudo-*mashpiah* with abundant curiosity but no spiritual wisdom to dispense—hoping the girls would be willing to share their inner worlds and self-conceptions with me. The beginning was hard. I needed to earn precious trust. Once I broke that barrier, I was amazed at the openness and exquisite self-insight I discovered, qualities that surely influenced the girls' boldness and confidence. By directly encouraging self-exploration and personal development, Lubavitch helps to stave off much of the emotional confusion that plagues many secular girls, leaving them vulnerable to fearfulness, psychological insecurity, and difficulty asserting their opinions and needs. Perhaps self-knowledge gives Lubavitch girls a strength of personal vision, a consciously developed emotional resilience. These young women are survivors, from the questioner who harnessed the will to move from Crown Heights and fashion a new life at a secular college to the intense mystic who bucked peer scorn and developed her intellectual talents.

From an outsider's perspective, Hasidic beliefs and culture seem to dwarf the individual. The weight of history is immense. The palpable world intermixes past and present—as each holiday approaches, Lubavitchers believe their souls relive the event it commemorates, that a whiff of the past filters into their current consciousness and shares the spotlight with their own affairs. Within the Hasidic worldview, many Jews are reincarnations of deceased Jews;[17] their spiritual lives began long before their most recent birth, making their current concerns seem minuscule in the grand scheme of their own existence.

Even if a Hasid limits her vision to *this* lifetime, she finds herself part of a complex and interconnected psychological and spiritual world. Most likely, she comes from a large family; her daily life involves sharing her parents' attention and resources with several equally needy people. Her connection to all Jews throughout the world is mentioned continually; she is one cog in a vast network of brothers and sisters. A Hasidic girl's life trajectory is inextricably bound with other people. She will marry, bear as many children as possible, and devote her life to theirs. Her very identity is not complete until she finds her mate; Jewish mystical tradition stresses that we are all unfinished souls who must merge with our opposite-sex counterparts to attain spiritual wholeness. Autonomy as perceived by a secular mind does not exist in this culture. Obedience to God drives Hasidic lives, controlling dress, diet, public demeanor, and daily schedules along with ultimate beliefs and visions of life. Hasidism is a seemingly all-encompassing system.

Yet, as we have seen, "seemingly" is the critical word here. If nothing else, I hope my profiles show the tremendous variety among these young women and the individual vitality each one has cultivated. Part of the girls' strength derives from their understanding of their own unique characters, their clear visions of who they are and what they represent, even if certain parts of their lives confuse them. Their psychological clarity develops not in spite of their Hasidism but because of it.

The Lubavitch system presents an intriguing paradox. Each Jew is one of millions of souls that have existed throughout history, one small part of an omnipotent God's master plan. However, every Jewish soul has a substantial role in the world's unfolding. Each one of a Jew's deeds carries immense metaphysical implications. One holy act by any Jew in the world might spur the coming of the Messiah. No Lubavitch girl could make any mistake about the matter: she is important; her actions carry stunning significance; she is eminently worthy of intense self-scrutiny.

This project focused on the girls' independent voices and spirits. Before I started researching, I wondered whether Hasidism's stringent rules and all-encompassing spiritual vision would stunt individual voice. Perhaps the psyche—the desires, dreams, and thoughts of the innermost self—would be squelched. As I have already explained, the psyche clearly emerges within the Hasidic framework. Now, with the benefit of hindsight, I will take my argument one step further: Lubavitch philosophy allows self-understanding and independent personality to flourish beyond the levels many Americans reach. This community's reverence for the soul pushes the faithful to develop their psyches with the care of an artist.

Lubavitch girls grow up in a culture that emphasizes internal scrutiny. They are constantly examining their desires, their drives, their difficulties, their triumphs—it is all part of their effort to refine their spirituality and to ensure that their mystical effects on the universe are positive and powerful. Their careful study of the *Tanya* gives them a rich vocabulary for considering their personalities; the book abounds with descriptive words for the nuances of our souls. Eventually, these concepts become permanent fixtures in their minds, forming an arena for them to explore their motivations, conflicts, goals, and dreams. Even if they question their faith, their philosophical training continues to guide them; they must wrestle a refined system of thought that provides sensitive explanations for many of their struggles. They may choose to renounce this system, but they must engage with it first.

In other words, Lubavitch provides intensive training in self-examination, a rare phenomenon in our fast-moving, visually centered society. The United States at large certainly values individuality and independent spirit, but typical Americans seem to trust that the psyche will develop on its own, with no conscious effort at nourishment. Lubavitchers study their individual, unique souls the way an ambitious mainstream American might pursue a sport or a musical instrument, with passion, determination, and unstinting discipline.

When I think back on my year in Crown Heights, I marvel at my good fortune. This project unfolded magnificently. Interview after interview provided splendid material; the girls' voices were strong, forceful, insightful, and deeply compelling. In my more spiritual moments, I attribute my success to divine intervention. But a more earthly explanation could suffice, for there was a wonderful harmony between the girls' religious training and my goals. I was using an unusual research method, an interview technique based on the intriguing assumption that our psyches are worthy of rigorous intellectual analysis. These girls believed this already; it is a central dogma of their faith. The questions I posed—about self-perceptions, life goals, and philosophical dilemmas—were questions they continually ask themselves. Once they realized they could trust me, their thoughts flowed naturally.

The profiles in *Meeting at the Crossroads*, which used the same psyche-based method, often reveal tentative, muted voices. Brown and

Gilligan argue that mainstream America can wall adolescent girls off from their own thoughts and feelings. The expectation that young women be "good," "kind," and "nice" sometimes steers girls away from sharing their honest opinions with other people. In time, the silence entraps their own sensibilities; they become confused about their place in the world, their relationships with others, and their ability to tackle their problems, leading, in all too many cases, to anxiety, depression, and loss of the vibrancy that had flourished in earlier childhood. At bottom, they seem pained in spirit, hurting on the core level of the inner self.

Lubavitchers believe that Jews and non-Jews differ in one fundamental way: only Jews have a godly soul, the piece of the self that yearns for holiness. Non-Jews can be ethical, benevolent, and compassionate, but they lack the divine spark, the aspect of the Jew that transcends her physical nature and seeks communion with God. This doctrine confused my secular, egalitarian mind. Constantly, I asked my Lubavitch friends for evidence, for the practical ramifications of this profound disparity. "You can just tell," they would explain. "We are more . . . refined. It's subtle but unmistakable."

Indeed, this group *does* encourage refinement of the soul, which has an unmistakable impact on personality, self-understanding, and psychological health. However, to take the nature-nurture debate to a metaphysical level, I do not believe that the disparity is innate. Most human beings carry the seeds of a cultivated, secure inner world—a strong, confident psyche—whether we want to perceive it in religious terms or in terms of the natural wonders of the human mind. But, unlike most of America, Lubavitch eases the psyche into full-blown expression with its rigorous self-analysis and veneration of Jews' sacred aspirations.

The Lubavitch version goes something like this: At Mount Sinai, Israel accepted the laws of the Torah, and with the yoke came a gift from God—a piece of the Divine Soul, the cherished birthright of all future Jews. My version goes as follows: The Lubavitchers' faith in the Divine Soul leads them to an indispensable insight, that our human makeup transcends most current discussions about identity. We are more than our genetics, more than our life histories, more than our cultural baggage. These are all important, but the human psyche, the underlying seat of our minds and hearts, contains an independent power we must respect and master if we want any real hope for a vital life.

Within this worldview, to savage the confidence of a classmate would carry profound implications, for every human being is a fragile balance of drives, desires, and a potential for goodness struggling to triumph. Lubavitchers develop this mutual respect through their theological study, but I wonder if there's a way of broadening this notion, of spreading an insight so simple it aches: the human spirit is a delicate instrument that needs care to flourish. Most American high schools are not amoral places. Classes decry racism, laud the day when women gained suffrage, debate the ethics of war. But nearly always, the focus is on large-scale movements and historical moments. People are examined only as aggregates—blacks during slavery, the underclass, Vietnam War protesters. English courses may explore literary characters, but they are nearly always fictional and divorced from teenage life. A student may come away from history class inspired by the civil rights movement but unaware that mocking the kid with homemade clothes is a terrorizing form of prejudice.

I propose that our schools embrace the individual within their curricula. Perhaps psychology should become a standard discipline long before college. Students could study the effects of teasing and social alienation along with chemistry and trigonometry. They could unpack the factors that drive some young people to depression, violence—or success against the odds. Students might also keep formal track of their own inner lives through journals, discussions with teachers, and group projects. Armed with this self-knowledge, they could interview classmates intensively and then analyze the conversations, really communing with peers who have thoughts and difficulties they never would have imagined. When I went through that process as I researched this book, I found that I had climbed inside the minds of people I could not have understood otherwise: popular teenagers, religious conservatives, unabashed believers in Jews' innate superiority. I felt so close to each interviewee that I couldn't imagine deliberately hurting her—and I am no saint.

The major courses of study in the precollege years are entrenched: English, math, science, history and social studies, foreign language. Psychology is at best a watered-down elective. But what could be more fundamental than the study of the human mind? What could have more potential to shape ethical, thoughtful, powerful women and men? Here I don't necessarily mean psychology as it's perceived in the academic world. I mean the study of individual people, their drives, motivations, insecurities, triumphs, and pains, whether the focus is an interview, journalistic article, film, religious text, personal essay, psychological study, or some other form. Lubavitchers' respect for the strength and fragility of the human spirit is rare, but it is easily secularized.

For all its emphasis on the human psyche, Lubavitch does not view the individual in isolation. Crown Heights is a close-knit community, a place where people feel responsibility for one another, if not always affection. This, too, offers profound advantages. When a community member needs help, scores of people typically jump in. Psychotic single *baalei teshuvah*, disabled students from out of town, ill children from overwhelmed families, or any other needy people who reach community awareness inspire heated conversations about the best approach to the problem, followed by action. At times the discussions turn more gossipy than salutary, but the desire to help is real.

Sadly, this surprised me. I had certainly known struggling people before, but they rarely received support beyond their immediate friends and family. If they lacked caring family or friends, they languished. I am embarrassed to think of conversations I've had through the years about people I knew in graduate school or in buildings where I have lived. Several of us knew they were in trouble, had a sense they had nobody who cared, and yet did nothing. They fell outside our domain.

A culture that places stark emphasis on the nuclear family also introduced me to a wider, broader form of family that can embrace an entire neighborhood, all fellow believers, unacquainted souls with a common bond. Even I, a temporary interloper among Lubavitchers, knew that if I fell into distress, the Jews of Crown Heights would help me. It was a feeling both wonderful and strange. Every other place I've lived (various suburbs and cities in the northeastern United States) had a notion that personal responsibility ends with our families and closest friends. The simple idea that others in their community fall within the realm of their intimate care undoubtedly improves the Lubavitch girls' treatment of one another. In a sense, a fellow Bais Rivka student is family.

That American society lacks a satisfying sense of community is hardly a new idea. Indeed, Robert D. Putnam, author of the widely discussed book *Bowling Alone: The Collapse and Revival of American Community*, cites recent surveys suggesting that over 80 percent of Americans believe we need more emphasis on community ties.[18] The call for community seems particularly relevant to our adolescent girls. Typical American high schools certainly try to forge common bonds, but they reach few students. I remember biting my cheeks to squelch laughter during my high school's mandatory celebrations of the football team, the cheerleaders, and the homecoming royalty. This had nothing to do with me or the overwhelming majority of my peers.

It is tragic that so many American girls feel they must claw their way into acceptance by backstabbing, mockery, and sexual games. A terror of abandonment, of isolation, lurks in every story I have read or heard about young women's interpersonal machinations. The Lubavitch girls' social lives involve plenty of tension and exclusion, but at least an underlying vision of communal bonds assuages the problem. For school administrators, teachers, and others who influence teenagers' lives, I have one final request—search for ways to increase communal ties among teens. There is no universal solution; schools differ immensely in the populations they serve. But the drive to fit in, to feel important, and to trust that others would care in dismal times *is* nearly universal. We must help more of our adolescents meet these needs. Respect, concern, and a certain level of caring based on community bonds are possible without religious doctrine.

Even the mystical grandeur of Lubavitch can speak in some form to outsiders. The spiritual passion that drove Lubavitch girls' lives stunned me. This is, of course, the underlying fabric of Lubavitch, the energy that defines the Hasidic way. Lubavitch intensity derives partially from a paradoxical belief: Life is complex beyond our wildest imaginings; it is crafted and powered by metaphysical forces that no mundane experience could hope to capture. Yet, mundane experiences are crucial to the unfolding of divinity within the world.

I began this chapter with a description of the mystical power Lubavitch attaches to every move. Few secularists will warm to the notion that our behavior is linked to godly sparks and angels, but it doesn't take a mystic to realize that we are constantly affecting other people and the world at large, just by moving through our lives. Even shorn of the metaphysical, the notion is both glorious and terrifying.

Say you're riding in a cab. You think the driver is deliberately taking a long route to jack up the price. It's a final annoyance in a grueling day, and you explode: "Where the hell are you taking me? What kind of idiot would take such a long route?" The driver, meanwhile, truly does not know of a shorter way. It's his first day on the job, and he's nervous.

His previous boss insulted his intelligence before firing him; your comment unearths painful memories of past humiliations. After dropping you off, he is so worked up that he causes an accident, leaving a young woman with unsightly scars that destroy her self-esteem and affect her dealings with thousands of people. Needless to say, he loses his job. The man's family slips into poverty and turmoil. . . .

Now imagine yourself on the same cab ride. Your driver is nervous, and you want to calm him down. You start a conversation and enjoy talking to him; he has brilliant insights into friendship dynamics. Before leaving, you tell him so as you hand him a generous tip. He feels invigorated. It was his first day working after a string of bad luck with bosses who fired him, and this last passenger has given him confidence in his ability to handle the job. He remains a cabby for thirty years, which allows his family some measure of financial stability. His daughter blossoms and becomes a physician, helping hundreds of people maintain their health. . . .

At times small deeds carry immense ramifications, an issue we in mainstream America rarely consider. Indeed, I hadn't considered it myself until Lubavitch theology spurred me to think deeply about the power we all wield as we go about our lives. Every action carries tremendous responsibility. We should proceed with care to reduce the damage we inflict and cultivate our incredible potential to generate good. Our influence is so delicate, so complex, and so far-reaching, with such mystery surrounding how it will take root in the world, that it's almost mystical even if we throw out the supernatural.

I think of the girls I've described in this book. So many variables will shape their lives: their husbands' temperaments, the number of children they must care for, each child's unique personality, financial situation, health, the developing course of their own psyches through everything fate delivers. I want to fast-forward, to see where they'll be at, say, forty-five. But I am no Cabalist. And to really understand, I'd need to watch things unfold. Hasidism, after all, preaches the importance of every move. I can only hope that their extraordinary faith in the power of their minds, hearts, and deeds is borne out, and that my own small role in sharing their stories will add to their vision.

Notes

NOTES TO THE INTRODUCTION

1. See David Berger's *The Rebbe, the Messiah, and the Scandal of Orthodox Indifference* (Portland, Ore.: Littman Library of Jewish Civilization, 2001).
2. Peggy Orenstein, *Schoolgirls: Young Women, Self-Esteem, and the Confidence Gap* (New York: Doubleday, 1994), pp. 92–93.
3. Jill McLean Taylor, Carol Gilligan, and Amy M. Sullivan, *Between Voice and Silence: Women and Girls, Race and Relationship* (Cambridge: Harvard University Press, 1995), pp. 19–21.
4. Lyn Mikel Brown and Carol Gilligan, *Meeting at the Crossroads: Women's Psychology and Girls' Development* (New York: Ballantine Books, 1992), p. 19.
5. Ibid., p. 20.
6. See ibid., pp. 25–31, for a more thorough explanation of this method of analyzing interviews, known as the "Listener's Guide."
7. Hyo-Jung Kim, "Do You Have Eyelashes?" in *Women, Girls, and Psychotherapy: Reframing Resistance*, ed. Carol Gilligan, Annie G. Rogers, and Deborah L. Tolman. (New York: Harrington Park Press, 1991), pp. 201–211.
8. Mary Pipher, *Reviving Ophelia: Saving the Selves of Adolescent Girls* (New York: Ballantine Books, 1995), p. 18.
9. Brown and Gilligan, *Meeting at the Crossroads*, p. 217.
10. Taylor, Gilligan, and Sullivan, *Between Voice and Silence*, p. 40.
11. Ibid., p. 43.
12. Janie Victoria Ward, "Raising Resisters: The Role of Truth Telling in the Psychological Development of African American Girls," in *Urban Girls: Resisting Stereotypes, Creating Identities*, ed. Bonnie J. Ross Leadbeater and Niobe Way (New York: New York University Press, 1996), p. 88.
13. Lyn Mikel Brown, *Raising Their Voices: The Politics of Girls' Anger* (Cambridge: Harvard University Press, 1998), p. 69.
14. Mary Jane Rotheram-Borus, Steve Dopkins, Nuria Sabate, and Marguerita Lightfoot, "Personal and Ethnic Identity, Values, and Self-Esteem among Black and Latino Adolescent Girls," in *Urban Girls: Resisting Stereotypes, Creating Identities*, ed. Bonnie J. Ross Leadbeater and Niobe Way (New York: New York University Press, 1996), p. 45.
15. Naomi Wolf, *Promiscuities: The Secret Struggle for Womanhood* (New York: Random House, 1997), p. 25.
16. Bonnie Morris, "Agents or Victims of Religious Ideology? Approaches to Locating Hasidic Women in Feminist Studies," in *New World Hasidism: Ethnographic Studies of Hasidic Jews in America*, ed. Janet S. Belcove-Shalin (Albany: State University of New York Press, 1995), p. 170.

NOTES TO CHAPTER I

1. Edward Hoffman, *Despite All Odds: The Story of Lubavitch* (New York: Simon and Schuster, 1991), p. 17.
2. Lis Harris, *Holy Days: The World of a Hasidic Family* (New York: Macmillan, 1986), p. 48.
3. Hoffman, *Despite All Odds*, p. 17.
4. Ibid.

5. Unless otherwise noted, population statistics about the Hasidim come from Robert Eisenberg's *Boychiks in the Hood: Travels in the Hasidic Underground* (San Francisco: HarperSanFrancisco, 1995), pp. 1–7.

6. Simon Jacobson, *Toward a Meaningful Life: The Wisdom of the Rebbe, Menachem Mendel Schneerson* (New York: William Morrow, 1995), p. ix.

7. Samuel Heilman, *Portrait of American Jews: The Last Half of the Twentieth Century* (Seattle: University of Washington Press, 1995), p. 148.

8. Riv-Ellen Prell, *Prayer and Community: The Havurah in American Judaism* (Detroit: Wayne State University Press, 1989), p. 97.

9. For inspiring and eloquent book-length explorations of Jewish Renewal, see Arthur Waskow's *Godwrestling—Round 2: Ancient Wisdom, Future Paths* (Woodstock, Vt.: Jewish Lights Publishing, 1996); and Michael Lerner's *Jewish Renewal: A Path to Healing and Transformation* (New York: Putnam, 1994).

10. "Frequently Asked Questions about Jewish Renewal," p. 1, http://www.aleph.org /html/faq.html [3 June 2002].

11. Harris, *Holy Days*, p. 22.

12. Menachem Mendel Schneerson, *Beautiful Within: Modesty in Conduct and Dress as Taught by the Lubavitcher Rebbe Menachem Mendel Schneerson* (Brooklyn, N.Y.: Sichos in English, 1995), p. vii.

13. Ibid., p. 25.

14. Ps. 45:14 (standard traditional Jewish version).

15. Moshe Meiselman, *Jewish Woman in Jewish Law* (New York: Ktav Publishing House, 1978), p. 14.

16. Note that this spelling differs from the version I have used: "Hasidic." I have chosen to use the "H" versions (e.g., "Hasidim," "Hasidic") because this spelling is most familiar in mainstream America. But, among insiders, "Ch" spellings (e.g., "Chassidic") are the norm.

17. Harris, *Holy Days*, pp. 233–37.

18. Jewish law prohibits kindling a fire or burning on Shabbos and eating pork. Driving on Shabbos is forbidden largely because driving creates sparks and burns gas.

NOTES TO CHAPTER 7

1. Harris, *Holy Days*, p. 247.

2. Chana Feiga Siegel, "A Wedding Guide" (unpublished document passed out at Siegel's wedding), p. 10.

3. Ibid., p. 12.

4. Ibid., p. 13.

NOTES TO CHAPTER 10

1. She did not have specific information on Crown Heights Lubavitchers, but she surmised that Lubavitch would more or less fit the overall trends.

2. Harris, *Holy Days*, pp. 235–37.

3. Myra Sadker and David Sadker, *Failing at Fairness: How Our Schools Cheat Girls* (New York: Simon and Schuster, 1995), pp. 234–37.

4. Shulman Yankelovich, *Girls' School Alumnae: Accomplished, Distinguished, Community Minded* (Concord, Mass.: National Coalition of Girls' Schools, 1990).

5. Carole B. Shmurak, *Voices of Hope: Adolescent Girls at Single Sex and Coeducational Schools* (New York: Peter Lang, 1998), p. 174.

6. Rosalind Wiseman, *Queen Bees and Wannabes: Helping Your Daughter Survive Cliques, Gossip, Boyfriends, and Other Realities of Adolescence* (New York: Crown, 2002), p. 255.

7. Ibid., p. 202.

8. Ibid., p. 235.

9. Ibid., p. 269.

10. Joan Jacobs Brumberg, *The Body Project: An Intimate History of American Girls* (New York: Vintage Books, 1997), p. 190.

11. Wiseman, *Queen Bees and Wannabes*, p. 236.

12. For an in-depth discussion of girls' honesty and openness at this stage, see Brown and Gilligan, *Meeting at the Crossroads*, pp. 42–88. Within these pages, and later in Brown and Gilli-

gan's book, is discussion of the fragility of this openness and how it so often goes underground as girls move into their adolescent years.

13. See ibid., p. 236 n. 14, for more information on these results.

14. Ibid., pp. 5–6.

15. Ibid., p. 6.

16. Nissan Mindel, *The Philosophy of Chabad: Rabbi Schneur Zalman of Liadi,* vol. 2 (Brooklyn, N.Y.: Kehot Publication Society, 1973), p. 13.

17. Gershon Winkler, *The Soul of the Matter: A Jewish-Kabbalistic Perspective on the Human Soul before, during, and after "Life"* (New York: Judaica Press, 1992), pp. 17–19.

18. Robert D. Putnam, *Bowling Alone: The Collapse and Revival of American Community* (New York: Simon and Schuster, 2000), p. 25.

Selected Bibliography

Alperowitz, Yosef Y. *I Believe: Jewish Teachings on Faith in and Anticipation for the Coming of Moshiach*. London: Lubavitch Foundation UK, 1993.

American Institutes for Research. *Gender Gaps: Where Schools Still Fail Our Children*. Washington, D.C.: American Association of University Women Educational Foundation, 1998.

Behar, Ruth. *The Vulnerable Observer: Anthropology That Breaks Your Heart*. Boston: Beacon Press, 1996.

Berger, David. *The Rebbe, the Messiah, and the Scandal of Orthodox Indifference*. Portland, Ore.: Littman Library of Jewish Civilization, 2001.

Berger-Sofer, Rhonda. "Pious Women: A Study of the Women's Roles in a Hasidic and Pious Community, Meah She'arim." Ph.D. diss., Rutgers University, 1979.

Boteach, Shmuel. *The Wolf Shall Lie with the Lamb: The Messiah in Hasidic Thought*. Northvale, N.J.: Jason Aronson, 1993.

Brod, Menachem. *The Days of Moshiach: The Redemption and the Coming of Moshiach in Jewish Sources*. Kfar-Chabad, Israel: Chabad Youth Organization, 1993.

Brown, Karen McCarthy. *Mama Lola: A Vodou Priestess in Brooklyn*. Berkeley and Los Angeles: University of California Press, 1991.

Brown, Lyn Mikel. *Raising Their Voices: The Politics of Girls' Anger*. Cambridge: Harvard University Press, 1998.

Brown, Lyn Mikel, and Carol Gilligan. *Meeting at the Crossroads: Women's Psychology and Girls' Development*. New York: Ballantine Books, 1992.

Brumberg, Joan Jacobs. *The Body Project: An Intimate History of American Girls*. New York: Vintage Books, 1997.

Brussel, Sylvia Ginsburg. "Continuity and Change: A Study of the Hasidic Community of Boston." Ph.D. diss., Boston University, 1975.

Coles, Robert. *The Spiritual Life of Children*. Boston: Houghton Mifflin, 1990.

Cruz, Barbara C. *Separate Sexes, Separate Schools: A Pro/Con Issue*. Berkeley Heights, N.J.: Enslow Publishers, 2000.

Davidman, Lynn. *Tradition in a Rootless World: Women Turn to Orthodox Judaism*. Berkeley and Los Angeles: University of California Press, 1991.

Davis, Natalie Zemon. *Women on the Margins: Three Seventeenth-Century Lives.* Cambridge: Harvard University Press, 1995.

Donin, Rabbi Hayim Halevy. *To Be a Jew: A Guide to Jewish Observance in Contemporary Life.* New York: Basic Books, 1972.

Eisenberg, Robert. *Boychiks in the Hood: Travels in the Hasidic Underground.* San Francisco: HarperSanFrancisco, 1995.

Feldman, S. Shirley, and Glen R. Elliott. *At the Threshold: The Developing Adolescent.* Cambridge: Harvard University Press, 1990.

Garrod, Andrew, Lisa Smulyan, Sally I. Powers, and Robert Kilkenny, eds. *Adolescent Portraits: Identity, Relationships and Challenges.* Boston: Allyn and Bacon, 1992.

Gilligan, Carol, Nona P. Lyons, and Trudy J. Hanmer, eds. *Making Connections: The Relational World of Adolescent Girls at Emma Willard School.* Cambridge: Harvard University Press, 1990.

Goldberg, Robin. "Imagining the Feminine: Storying and Re-storying Womanhood among Lubavitch Hasidic Women." Ph.D. diss., Northwestern University, 1991.

Harris, Lis. *Holy Days: The World of a Hasidic Family.* New York: Macmillan, 1986.

Heilman, Samuel. *Defenders of the Faith: Inside Ultra-Orthodox Jewry.* New York: Schocken Books, 1992.

———. *Portrait of American Jews: The Last Half of the Twentieth Century.* Seattle: University of Washington Press, 1995.

Heilman, Samuel C., and Steven M. Cohen. *Cosmopolitans and Parochials: Modern Orthodox Jews in America.* Chicago: University of Chicago Press, 1989.

Helmreich, William B. *The World of the Yeshiva: An Intimate Portrait of Orthodox Jewry.* New York: Free Press, 1982.

Hoffman, Edward. *Despite All Odds: The Story of Lubavitch.* New York: Simon and Schuster, 1991.

Jacobson, Simon. *Toward a Meaningful Life: The Wisdom of the Rebbe, Menachem Mendel Schneerson.* New York: William Morrow, 1995.

Johnson, Norine G., Michael C. Roberts, and Judith Worell, eds. *Beyond Appearance: A New Look at Adolescent Girls.* Washington, D.C.: American Psychological Association, 1999.

Kagan, Jerome. *Galen's Prophecy: Temperament in Human Nature.* New York: Basic Books, 1994.

Kaploun, Uri, ed. *Lessons in Tanya: The Tanya of R. Shneur Zalman of Liadi.* 5 vols. Brooklyn: Kehot, 1987–1993.

Kaufman, Debra Renee. *Rachel's Daughters: Newly Orthodox Jewish Women.* New Brunswick, N.J.: Rutgers University Press, 1991.

Kim, Hyo-Jung. "Do You Have Eyelashes?" In *Women, Girls, and Psychotherapy: Reframing Resistance,* edited by Carol Gilligan, Annie G. Rogers, and Deborah L. Tolman, 201–211 New York: Harrington Park Press, 1991.

Kranzler, George. *The Face of Faith: An American Hasidic Community.* Baltimore: Baltimore Hebrew College Press, 1972.

———. *Williamsburg: A Contemporary American Hasidic Community.* Northvale, N.J.: Jason Aronson, 1995.

———. *Williamsburg: A Jewish Community in Transition.* New York: P. Feldheim, 1961.

Landau, David. *Piety and Power: The World of Jewish Fundamentalism.* London: Secker and Warburg, 1993.

Lavi, Nadine. "Why Many Religious Girls Are Dying to Be Thin." *Forward,* 7 November 1997, 16.

Lerner, Michael. *Jewish Renewal: A Path to Healing and Transformation.* New York: Putnam, 1994.

Loewenthal, Naftali. *Communicating the Infinite: The Emergence of Habad School.* Chicago: University of Chicago Press, 1990.

Meiselman, Moshe. *Jewish Woman in Jewish Law.* New York: Ktav Publishing House, 1978.

Mindel, Nissan. *The Philosophy of Chabad: Rabbi Schneur Zalman of Liadi.* Vol. 2. Brooklyn, N.Y.: Kehot Publication Society, 1973.

Mintz, Jerome R. *Hasidic People: A Place in the New World.* Cambridge: Harvard University Press, 1992.

The Modern Jewish Woman: A Unique Perspective. Brooklyn, N.Y.: Lubavitch Educational Foundation for Jewish Marriage Enrichment, 1981.

Morris, Bonnie. "Agents or Victims of Religious Ideology? Approaches to Locating Hasidic Women in Feminist Studies." In *New World Hasidism: Ethnographic Studies of Hasidic Jews in America,* edited by Janet S. Belcove-Shalin, 161–180. Albany: State University of New York Press, 1995.

———. "Women of Valor: Female Religious Activism and Identity in the Lubavitcher Community of Brooklyn, 1955–1987." Ph.D. diss., State University of New York at Binghamton, 1990.

Morse, Susan, ed. *Separated by Sex: A Critical Look at Single-Sex Education for Girls.* Washington, D.C.: American Association of University Women Educational Foundation, 1998.

Orenstein, Peggy. *Schoolgirls: Young Women, Self-Esteem, and the Confidence Gap.* New York: Doubleday, 1994.

Pipher, Mary. *Reviving Ophelia: Saving the Selves of Adolescent Girls.* New York: Ballantine Books, 1995.

Poll, Solomon. *The Hasidic Community of Williamsburg.* New York: Schocken Books, 1969.

Prell, Riv-Ellen. *Prayer and Community: The Havurah in American Judaism.* Detroit: Wayne State University Press, 1989.

Putnam, Robert D. *Bowling Alone: The Collapse and Revival of American Community.* New York: Simon and Schuster, 2000.

Rotheram-Borus, Mary Jane, Steve Dopkins, Nuria Sabate, and Marguerita Lightfoot. "Personal and Ethnic Identity, Values, and Self-Esteem among Black and Latino Adolescent Girls." In *Urban Girls: Resisting Stereotypes, Creating Identities,* edited by Bonnie J. Ross Leadbeater and Niobe Way, 35–52. New York: New York University Press, 1996.

Sadker, Myra, and David Sadker. *Failing at Fairness: How Our Schools Cheat Girls.* New York: Simon and Schuster, 1995.

Schneerson, Menachem Mendel. *Beautiful Within: Modesty in Conduct and Dress as Taught by the Lubavitcher Rebbe Menachem Mendel Schneerson.* Brooklyn, N.Y.: Sichos in English, 1995.

———. *The Chassidic Dimension: Interpretations of the Weekly Torah Readings and the Festivals.* Brooklyn, N.Y.: Kehot, 1990.

———. *Letters.* Brooklyn, N.Y.: Kehot, 1979.

———. *On the Essence of Chassidus.* Brooklyn, N.Y.: Kehot, 1978.

———. *Timeless Patterns in Time: Chassidic Insights into the Cycle of the Jewish Year.* 2 vols. Brooklyn, N.Y.: Kehot Publication Society, 1993–1994.

Schochet, Jacob Immanuel. *Chassidic Dimensions: Themes in Chassidic Thought and Practice.* Brooklyn, N.Y.: Kehot, 1990.

Sered, Susan Starr. *Women as Ritual Experts: The Religious Lives of Elderly Jewish Women in Jerusalem.* New York: Oxford University Press, 1992.

Shaffir, William. *Life in a Religious Community: The Lubavitcher Chassidim in Montreal.* Toronto: Holt, Rinehart and Winston of Canada, 1974.

Shmurak, Carole B. *Voices of Hope: Adolescent Girls at Single Sex and Coeducational Schools.* New York: Peter Lang, 1998.

Siegel, Chana Feiga. "A Wedding Guide." Unpublished document passed out at Siegel's wedding.

Simmons, Rachel. *Odd Girl Out: The Hidden Culture of Aggression in Girls.* New York: Harcourt, 2002.

Smith, Anna Deavere. *Fires in the Mirror: Crown Heights, Brooklyn, and Other Identities.* New York: Doubleday, 1993.

Stabiner, Karen. *All Girls: Single-Sex Education and Why It Matters.* New York: Riverhead Books, 2002.

Steinsaltz, Adin. *The Long Shorter Way: Discourses on Chassidic Thought.* Northvale, N.J.: Jason Aronson, 1992.

———. *The Thirteen Petalled Rose: A Discourse on the Essence of Jewish Existence and Belief.* New York: Basic Books, 1980.

Sulloway, Frank J. *Born to Rebel: Birth Order, Family Dynamics, and Creative Lives.* New York: Pantheon Books, 1996.

Taylor, Jill McLean, Carol Gilligan, and Amy M. Sullivan. *Between Voice and Silence: Women and Girls, Race and Relationship.* Cambridge: Harvard University Press, 1995.

Touger, Malkah. *Please Tell Me What the Rebbe Said: Torah Insights Adapted from the Works of the Lubavitcher Rebbe*. Brooklyn, N.Y.: Sichos in English, 1993.

Ward, Janie Victoria. "Raising Resisters: The Role of Truth Telling in the Psychological Development of African American Girls." In *Urban Girls: Resisting Stereotypes, Creating Identities*, edited by Bonnie J. Ross Leadbeater and Niobe Way, 85–99. New York: New York University Press, 1996.

Waskow, Arthur. *Godwrestling—Round 2: Ancient Wisdom, Future Paths*. Woodstock, Vt.: Jewish Lights Publishing, 1996.

Way, Niobe. *Everyday Courage: The Lives and Stories of Urban Teenagers*. New York: New York University Press, 1998.

Wellesley College Center for Research on Women. *How Schools Shortchange Girls—The AAUW Report: A Study of Major Findings on Girls and Education*. New York: Marlowe and Company, 1995.

Winkler, Gershon. *The Soul of the Matter: A Jewish-Kabbalistic Perspective on the Human Soul before, during, and after "Life."* New York: Judaica Press, 1992.

Wiseman, Rosalind. *Queen Bees and Wannabes: Helping Your Daughter Survive Cliques, Gossip, Boyfriends, and Other Realities of Adolescence*. New York: Crown, 2002.

Wolf, Naomi. *Promiscuities: The Secret Struggle for Womanhood*. New York: Random House, 1997.

Yankelovich, Shulman. *Girls' School Alumnae: Accomplished, Distinguished, Community Minded*. Concord, Mass.: National Coalition of Girls' Schools, 1990.

Zakutinsky, Rivka, and Yaffa Leba Gottlieb. *Around Sarah's Table: Ten Hasidic Women Share Their Stories of Life, Faith, and Tradition*. New York: Free Press, 2001

Zalman, Rabbi Shneur. *Likkutei Amarim Tanya*. Brooklyn, N.Y.: Kehot, 1996.

Index

In the book, Lubavitchers in Crown Heights who are not public or historic figures are identified using pseudonyms. A few non-Lubavitchers have pseudonyms as well. The reason is to preserve privacy; pages 69 and 122 discuss this issue. In the index, a pseudonym is followed by a parenthesized qualifier describing the person. For example: Lehrer, Rochel (a Lubavitch girl); Lehrer, Tzipi (Rochel's mother). Qualifiers also follow the real names of two historic figures—Rabbi Menachem Mendel Schneerson and Rabbi Schneur Zalman. All other real names are unqualified, as they normally would be in an index. Also note that, at times, the index offers a slightly more expansive definition of a Yiddish or Hebrew word than appears in the book. The book uses short, relevant definitions to fit the fast-paced mood of the narrative; at times the index offers a bit more information.

About the Author

STEPHANIE WELLEN LEVINE holds an A.B. from Brown University and a Ph.D. from Harvard's American studies program. She teaches at Tufts University and lives in Cambridge, Massachusetts.